# ISO
# 14000

# ISO 14000

## Issues & Implementation Guidelines for Responsible Environmental Management

### James L. Lamprecht

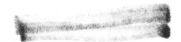

**amacom**

**American Management Association**

New York • Atlanta • Boston • Chicago • Kansas City • San Francisco • Washington, D.C.
Brussels • Mexico City • Tokyo • Toronto

This publication is designed to provide accurate and authoritative
information in regard to the subject matter covered. It is sold with the
understanding that the publisher is not engaged in rendering legal,
accounting, or other professional service. If legal advice or other expert
assistance is required, the services of a competent professional person should
be sought.

Library of Congress Cataloging-in-Publication Data

Lamprecht, James L., 1947–
    ISO 14000 : issues & implementation guidelines for responsible
environmental management / James L. Lamprecht.
        p.   cm.
    Includes bibliographical references and index.
    ISBN 0-8144-0353-0 (hc)
    1. Environmental management—United States.   2. Environmental
policy—United States.   3. Industrial management—Environmental
aspects—United States.   4. Environmental protection—United States.
5.   ISO 14000 Series Standards.   I. Title.
GE300.L36   1996
658.4'08—dc20                                              96-42575
                                                               CIP

Printing number

10   9   8   7   6   5   4   3   2   1

# Contents

# Preface

The need for environmental policies was recognized by ancient civilizations long ago. In the Western world, Greece and Rome established elementary environmental policies in the fields of agriculture, forestry, mining, and commerce. But, as J. Donald Hughes notes, no ancient autocracy remotely approached the ability of a modern industrial state to keep informed about its citizens and see that they perform their social duties."[1] Thus, although Greek city-states and Roman emperors were well aware of the economic need to manage the environment, their policies were hardly enforced and limited in geographic scope.

Today, people throughout the world have become increasingly aware of the economic and political aspects of environmental issues. In India, a $2.8-billion power project was halted, allegedly because the project's environmental impact had not been properly addressed. In Nigeria, an environmental activist and well-known playwright who objected to having the state-run oil industry pollute his tribal land was suspiciously accused of having committed murder and summarily hanged with eight other activists. In Denmark, ecologists warn that organochlorines used to make PVC plastics, solvents, and pulp and paper products are threatening human reproduction.[2]

Although people have long recognized that issues concerning the environment do not respect political boundaries, it was not until the late 1960s and early 1970s that attempts were made to deal with environmental issues at a global level. It was also during this period that the subject of environmental management began to emerge. In one of the earliest books on environmental management, Morton and Marsha Gorden wrote in their concluding chapter that the target for environmental managers (whom they saw as scientists) is the maintenance of life-support systems of the biosphere.

> [T]he manager has the task of allocating resources to maintain the health of the biosphere. . . . The environmental manager's

job is to put man's exploitation of nature on an overall sustained yield basis modified by technology. Sustained yield in
this context means using the earth's renewable resources so
that the capital goods are maintained while only the interest
is consumed.[3]

In order to manage the environment and achieve sustainability, the
Gordens also realized that the role of man had to be defined in the
larger context of nature:

[W]ithout an identity to relate us to the world of nature, we are
hard pressed to find guidelines for environmental managers.
Until we have found some perspective on ourselves, until we
are willing to listen to the advice of environmental scientists,
and until we have given politicians the capacity to regulate
relations among men so as to respect the relations of man to
nature, we cannot manage the environment.[4]

Since the early 1970s some of the concerns and questions raised by
the Gordens and others have been partly addressed, but others still
remain to be addressed. The importance of sustainable development
recognized by the Gordens, and rediscovered in the late 1980s, led most
industrialized nations to issue, during the early 1990s, national reports,
or even policies, on the environment as well as various other studies on
sustainable development. Recognizing that the environment must be
addressed at the global level, several international agencies such as the
United Nations, the World Bank, and the International Organization for
Standardization (ISO) began to address the problem head-on.[5] In 1996,
the ISO began to publish parts of its long-awaited ISO 14000 series,
which includes the ISO 14001 standard for environmental management
systems (EMS). Although favoring a different approach and emphasis
from what the Gordens perceive to be the principal responsibilities of
environmental managers, the ISO 14001 standard is probably the best
mechanism currently devised by an international organization to address some of the ethical perspectives raised by the Gordens.[6]

## Scope of the Book

The subject of the environment and environmental management can be
analyzed and considered from different points of view. Ecologists,

environmentalists, deep ecologists, environmental engineers, waste management experts, economists, lawyers, environmental auditors, governmental agencies, and the public at large are all aware, although with varying levels of conviction and perception, of a broad range of environmental issues. The ecologist and environmentalist are not likely to address the same issues as the environmental engineer or environmental manager, who must simultaneously accommodate the needs of shareholders, government regulators, and environmentalists. As far as some ecologists are concerned, to say that the environment can be managed reflects not only a contradiction but also a total misunderstanding of the role of man and industry vis-à-vis the environment. And yet, to some members of the international community who have served on the technical committee responsible for the release of the international environmental management system standard known as ISO 14001, the management of the environment is an absolute necessity and inescapable conclusion if one wants to begin to reverse the deleterious effects intrinsically linked to an ever increasing and expanding global industrialization.

To further complicate matters, the environment cannot be studied in isolation. Indeed, the environment is not only a local concern but also a national and global concern. It must be viewed across all levels. Figures 1 and 2 show the ramification of these levels.

| | |
|---|---|
| *Global level:* | ISO 14001 and other ISO 14000 standards |
| *National level:* | Green plans or national environmental policies |
| *Regional level:* | Regional, state, or provincial environmental policies including ISO 14001 |

Since the subject of environmental pollution and prevention knows no geographical boundaries, the management of pollution and of pollution prevention cannot be exclusively viewed from a local point of view. Hence the need to reflect on the many ancillary topics and global significance of environmental management. Aware of these requirements, I realized early on that I wanted to cover a broad range of issues that would allow me to look at environmental management from historical, global (that is, international), legal, and practical perspectives. Although aware of the fact that the international standard on environmental management systems (ISO 14001) had been written in an attempt to bring about, in theory at least, global environmental harmonization, I knew, as did many others, that the ISO 14001 standard raised some difficult legal as well as practical questions. On the one

**Figure 1.** The environmental hierarchy and network.

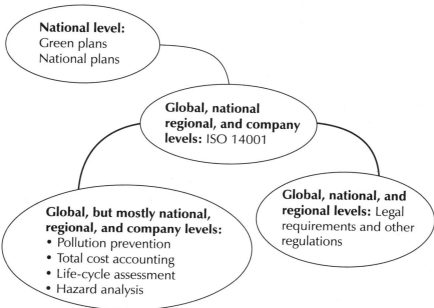

hand, people would want to know how to implement an ISO 14001 environmental system or at least how to modify or adapt their current system to the ISO 14001 model. On the other hand, many individuals—who are likely to work for small to medium-size companies and for whom environmental management must be squeezed between health and safety regulations, human resources, and a few more responsibilities—would also want to know what environmental management is all about, what it means, why it might be valuable, how it evolved, and whether or not it is the same everywhere. They might also want to know how other companies practice environmental management. What are some implementation examples? What are some examples of environmentally induced economic benefits? In an attempt to answer these and other questions, I came up with two sets of objectives. These two sets of objectives cut across all levels, from the global to the regional and down to the micro level of the corporation. My first objective is therefore to:

▸ Offer a brief historical overview of the evolution of environmentalism through the ages and up to the emergence and evolution of the U.S. Environmental Protection Agency (Chapter 1).

**Figure 2.** The sphere of influence and interest surrounding ISO 14001.

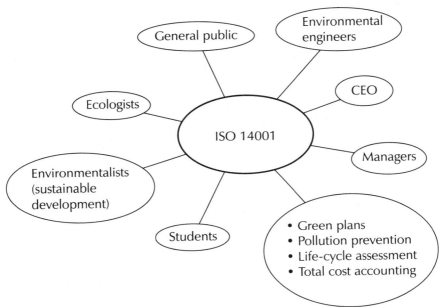

▸ Provide an overview of the evolution of European environmental policies leading to the development of national policies such as the Netherlands' green plans and the development of the ISO 14001 environmental management system (Chapter 2).
▸ Review some of the current legal problems of global environmentalism (Chapter 4 and others).

My second objective is to address the practical issues of everyday environmental management. For this purpose I focus on the following themes:

▸ The ISO 14001 standard and how to implement it. This chapter also compares ISO 14001 with other similar national or state programs (Chapters 3 and 4 and Appendixes A, E, and F).
▸ The economics of environmental management, including a detailed explanation of the benefits of environmental cost accounting (Chapters 5 and 6 and Appendixes B and C).
▸ The concepts of Design for the Environment and the life-cycle methodology (Chapter 7 and Appendix G).

▶ Some of the hazard evaluation techniques developed by the chemical industry (Chapter 8).

▶ Examples of pollution prevention techniques across several industries (Chapter 9 and Appendix H).

▶ Accounts from a broad range of industries relating to the economic benefits associated with pollution prevention (Chapter 9).

▶ An exemplary environmental management program designed to address the ISO 14001 standard (with more included in Appendix A).

▶ Samples of environmental policies, accounting tables needed to perform total cost accounting, and definitions of key terms (Appendixes A–H).

The ten chapters contained within the covers of this book are subdivided into four independent, yet interrelated, parts. Part I (Chapters 1 and 2) presents a brief historical overview of environmentalism and ecological movements and introduces the reader to the evolution of environmental management issues from a U.S. and European perspective. Part II (Chapters 3 and 4) is devoted to an analysis and review of the ISO 14001 standard. In Part III (Chapters 5 through 8) I present some of the important concepts and tools that are likely to be needed by environmental managers in years to come if they are to implement an effective environmental management system such as that suggested by the ISO 14001 standard for environmental management. Part IV (Chapters 9 and 10) includes several case studies of pollution prevention programs implemented by various industries and presents many documented examples of the economic advantages relating to pollution prevention programs. A series of eight appendixes (A–H) includes additional cases studies and examples of topics presented in Parts II through IV. The book is organized in such a way as to allow readers to start at any point they may wish.

The book brings together under one cover many topics having to do with pollution prevention and environmental management. It is intended for anyone who is interested in learning more about the important issues and difficulties relating to the responsibility of the global environmental manager, as well as for individuals such as ecologists, environmentalists, environmental auditors, students, managers, the general public, and the environmental engineers or managers who will need to implement an environmental system or enhance or upgrade their current system.

# Acknowledgments

I would like to thank the staff of Ceres for providing me with the many company reports as well as relevant articles; Greg Scheiffer of SETAC, Pensacola, Florida; Michael McCutcheon Johnson of the Toxics Reduction Unit of the Department of Ecology, Olympia, Washington; the staff of CETESB of São Paulo, Brazil; Brenda Lang of Millar Western Pulp, Whitecourt, Alberta, Canada; Tim Hagen of Linton Industries in California; Guy Zacklad of the Direction Regionale de l'Industrie de la Recherche et de l'Environnement (DRIRE) for the Ile-de-France, France; Gildas Bourdais of the French Normalization Society (AFNOR); Daniel C. Jenzen of Franklin Associates, Inc., Prairie Village, Kansas, for providing me with an example of a complete life-cycle study; Angie Dierks of the Tellus Institute, Boston, Massachusetts; Dr. Mark A. Cohen of the Graduate School of Management at Vanderbilt University; the staff at the Resource Renewal Institute, San Francisco; and many other individuals besides.

I would like to express my special appreciation to Joe Cascio, chair of the U.S. technical advisory group 207 on ISO 14000, for reviewing the chapters on ISO 14001. I would also like to thank Anthony Vlamis, Kate Pferdner, and Robert Griffin of AMACOM, without whose help this book could not have been realized.

Dr. James Lamprecht
1420 N.W. Gilman Blvd., Suite 2576
Issaquah, WA 98027
*Phone*: 206-644-9504
*Fax*: 206-644-9524
*e-mail*: jim@wolfenet.com

# Notes

1. (Albuquerque: University of New Mexico Press, 1975), p. 153.
2. Associated Press, "India orders halt to its top foreign investment," *The San Diego Union-Tribune* (August 4, 1995), p. A-23; "Nigerian minister says environmentalist is a murderer who deserves to hang," *The Seattle Times* (November 10, 1995), p. A13; Neil Winton, "Industrial chemicals distorting sexuality, ecologists warn," *The Seattle Times* (June 11, 1995), p. A27.
3. Morton Gorden and Marsha Gorden, *Environmental Management Science and Politics* (Boston: Allyn and Bacon, 1972), pp. 534–37.
4. Gorden, *Environmental Management*, p. 538.
5. Although the World Bank and the European Bank for Reconstruction and Development

(EBRD) have long claimed to favor environmental impact assessments before granting loans, recent reports suggest that despite the establishment of an environmental department, the World Bank "has financed a seemingly endless line of poorly designed, environmentally damaging development projects. . . ." See David Hunter, "The World Bank's New Inspection Panel: Will It Increase the Bank's Accountability?" in *Center for International Environmental Law*, No. 1 (April 1994), p. 2; and Donald M. Goldberg,"EBRD's Environmental Promise: A Bounced Check?" *Center for International Environmental Law*, No. 3 (December 1994), pp. 1–7.

6. The Gordens recognize that "[E]nvironmental issues, broadly conceived, cannot all be handled by the environmental manager *as scientist*" (*Environmental Management*, p. 536, emphasis added). It is clear that for the Gordens, the professionalization of the environmental manager means the need to be trained as a scientist.

# Part I

# Preliminary Considerations

In this introductory part, the long history of man's impact on the environment is briefly reviewed. Chapter 1 offers an overview of some early examples of environmental problems and of how different civilizations have attempted to deal with them. It also describes early examples of environmental policies, management, and auditing that were developed and practiced in the United States, particularly in the state of California, long before the British Standards Institution came up with its highly advertised environmental management standard known as BS 7750. The chapter concludes with an early example of environmental regulatory programs from the state of California.

Chapter 2 shifts to the global scene and describes some current attempts by innovative governments, notably the Netherlands, to develop and implement national environmental policies known as green plans. The chapter also includes a discussion relating to some of the lessons learned from the U.S. experience as to the strengths and limitations associated with environmental laws, and presents an overview of international and regional environmental issues such as the North American Free Trade Association (NAFTA). A review of European environmental developments that have led to the publication of the much heralded international environmental management standard known as ISO 14001 concludes the chapter.

# 1

# Environmental Mismanagement Through the Ages

The destructive influence of man's economic activities on the environment has been observed by Western philosophers for the last two millennia. In the third century B.C. Eratosthenes described, in a style reminiscent of today's ecologists and environmentalists, how, on the island of Cyprus, severe land erosion was brought about by the felling of trees needed for the shipbuilding industry, the smelting of copper, and the mining of silver. The destruction of forests that led to increased soil erosion, stream sedimentation, and the eventual reduction—or, in some cases, eradication—of the fish population was well known to Greek philosophers and geographers such as Plato, Strabo, and Aristotle.[1] This continued assault on the landscape and fragile ecosystem, observed long ago in ancient Greece, Mesopotamia, the Indus Valley, and the jungles of Mesoamerica, brought about by increased population pressures as well as by cultural and socioeconomic demands, often led to the environmental collapse and eventual destruction of whole cultures. In a chapter entitled "The Lessons of Easter Island," historian Clive Ponting explains that the cause of the collapse of the Easter Island culture "and the key to understanding the 'mysteries' of Easter Island was massive environmental degradation brought on by deforestation of the whole island." (Deforestation was needed for the erecting of statues.) "After 1600," Ponting explains, "Easter Island society went into decline and regressed to ever more primitive conditions. Without trees, and so without canoes, the islanders were trapped in their remote home, unable to escape the consequences of their self-inflicted, environmental collapse."[2]

3

The destruction of forests—brought about in part by local customs—which led to the eventual downfall of the Easter Island culture, may well represent a microcosm of things to come for the planet as a whole. Indeed, what the Easter Islanders (and many other cultures before and since) did not seem to realize, or at least did not comprehend soon enough, was that their continual attack on the closed system which was their island was affecting other insular ecological niches. The concept of interconnectedness, well known to ecologists, was apparently not yet fully appreciated by early civilizations. Consequently, the belief that *their* island could *serve their needs* for eternity would lead to the Easter Islanders' eventual annihilation.

The belief that nature must be subservient to man and the persistent need by many, but certainly not all, cultures to abuse or otherwise want to dominate nature can be traced back to Egyptian mythology and the Old Testament:

> Since man was the highest creature, all nature must have been created for him, an idea which must be one of the oldest of which there is a written record, for it is clearly expressed in ancient Egyptian creation myths. . . . All beings which existed before the flood were commanded by the Creator to be fruitful and to multiply, man receiving in addition the command to take possession of the earth. . . . Man by divine command assumes a powerful control over nature.[3]

Historical chronicles do certainly indicate that man acted, and continues to act, as though he had a divine right to abuse, attack, and mismanage the environment. Clive Ponting, for example, writes that as early as 312 B.C. the Tiber was so polluted that Romans had to find other sources of water. By the thirteenth century most major European cities were already suffering from severe urban pollution. In Siena, Italy, pigs were used to clean the Piazza del Campo. In 1366, Paris had to force its butchers to leave the city because "the Seine river could no longer absorb the thousands of carcasses and other rubbish."[4] Stream pollution was such a serious problem in England that various laws were passed from 1541 to 1648, but they were rarely enforced (a contemporary problem to which we shall return in a later chapter).

Environmental pollution resulting from man's industrial activities continued to be chronicled throughout the Middle Ages. The effect of mining on animals and the environment in general, already known to ancient Greek philosophers, was rediscovered by Georgius Agricola in his *De Re Metallica* (1556).

> [T]he strongest argument of the detractors is that the fields are devastated by mining operations. . . . The woods and groves are cut down, for there is need of an endless amount of wood for timber, machines and the smelting of metal. And when the woods and groves are felled, then are exterminated the beasts and birds, very many of which furnish a pleasant and agreeable food for man. Further, when the areas are washed, the water which has been used poisons the brooks and streams and either destroys the fish or drives them away.[5]

Agricola's observations, which merely confirmed earlier observations by Plato, Aristotle, Strabo, and others, clearly indicate that by the sixteenth century the deleterious impact of industrial activities on various ecosystems and biosystems was, if not scientifically explained, at least understood.

By the late sixteenth century, much of the environmental wisdom expressed by the ancient Greeks, Egyptians, Mesopotamians, and medieval chroniclers had been rediscovered by European philosophers, naturalists, and scientists. The naturalist Georges-Louis Leclerc, better known as Comte Buffon (1707–1788), wrote extensively on the profound effect man had made on nature thanks to his domestication and artificial selection of plants and animals. Despite his overall optimism, Buffon nonetheless noted that man would have destroyed nature long ago, "if by a fecundity superior to his depredations she did not repair the havoc he makes."[6]

One of the significant differences between the pre- and post-seventeenth-century periods was that the precursors to today's nation-states that began to emerge by the beginning of the seventeenth century were busy creating nascent bureaucracies that would allow them to attempt to regulate man's activities against nature. In France, for example, a concern over the severe consequences of deforestation led Colbert to issue his *Forest Ordinance* of 1669. It was also during this period that scientists began to establish and document causal relations between diseases and industrial pollution. Bernardino Ramazzini, professor of practical medicine at the Universities of Modena and Padua between 1682 and 1714, identified a potter's disease caused by lead poisoning and discovered that hatters were subject to mercury poisoning. He also associated the ulcerated lungs and sores found in the mouths of glassmakers with the use of borax and antimony.[7]

With the arrival of the nineteenth century and the age of modern industrialization, scientists began to write increasingly about the negative side effects associated with the industrial revolution. It is only natural that one of the earliest documented examples of air pollution and acid rain was observed in England in 1859 and described a few years later by Robert Smith in his book *Acid and Rain* (1872). This renewed awareness of the detrimental impact of man's activity on the environment and, even more important, on humankind itself led some governments to begin writing legislation designed ultimately to protect society from industrial pollution and polluters. In some cases, governments even attempted to police industries. Examples of such actions would include the British Parliament's enactment of a law in 1821 that made it easier for individuals to sue the owners of furnaces that were emitting large quantities of particulate. By 1863, Parliament had enacted a pollution standard known as the Alkali Act. The act

> required the manufacturer of alkali—a chemical widely used in the manufacturing of soap, glass and textiles—to remove 95 percent of the hydrochloric acid emitted by factories. To enforce this emissions standard, the British government established the world's first pollution control agency, which they named the Alkali Inspectorate.[8]

As the population surrounding the cities continued to migrate toward the growing urban centers in search of jobs, urban pollution problems magnified. By the early 1800s, most European city dwellers were well aware of the filth and foul smells that permeated their streets and neighborhoods. But it was not until the mid-1850s that the management of urban waste became a (partial) reality in some of the largest metropoles. Early examples of Western cities attempting to control their waste by designing comprehensive sewerage projects date from 1842 in Hamburg, 1855 in Chicago, and 1860 in Berlin.[9]

## Early Environmentalists

Despite the many accounts of environmental abuses chronicled throughout the ages by numerous scholars, one should not necessarily conclude that the environment with all its associated fauna was always perceived as something that had to be conquered and/or destroyed at all cost. Medieval philosophers such as the Italian monk Saint Francis of Assisi (1182?–1226), often considered the father of Western environmentalism, recognized the beauty of nature and of the animal kingdom. In some cases, the rights of animals may appear to have been carried to extremes. Indeed, in an age in which pesticides and insecticides had not yet been discovered, it was not unusual in many medieval towns throughout Europe to witness so-called animal trials. Such trials would pit farmers (the prosecution) against animals (the defendants) that were accused of having caused great devastation in the fields. In 1545 and 1587, for example, the inhabitants of the village of Saint-Julien in France pleaded their case in court against insects, which were duly represented by a lawyer. The lawyer argued, in a style that would no doubt have pleased Saint Francis of Assisi, that since animals were created by God, they had the same rights as men and therefore had a right to feed themselves! The insects won the case.[10] Although these cases of animal trials may appear ludicrous to most contemporary observers (at least to most Westerners), one should not forget that nearly four centuries later a law professor from the University of Southern California by the name of Christopher Stone would propose, in his now famous *Should Trees Have Standing: Toward Legal Rights for Natural Objects,* that trees and nature in general should be granted legal rights much like those enjoyed by humans and corporations.[11] Many American farmers would probably argue that the exuberant enforcement by some environmentalists and federal agencies of the Endangered Species Act (1973) reminded them of such medieval trials.[12]

From 1850 on, several authors began to write about the interconnectedness and holistic aspect of nature; the concepts and theoretical foundation of ecology were rapidly evolving. Although she did not use the word *ecology*—the term was probably first coined by the German Ernst Heinrich Haeckel in 1866—the British physical geographer Mary Somerville described the basic laws of ecology in the 1848 edition of her *Physical Geography.* In the United States, George Perkins Marsh, building on the work of European researchers, published in 1864 his influential *Man and Nature,* in which he describes how the features of the physical earth, particularly forests, are modified by human action.[13] And, as early as 1904, the German geographer Ernst Friedrich came very close to writing about the need to support sustainable economic development, an important theme rediscovered in the late 1970s and early 1980s. As Clarence Glacken explains, "Friedrich distinguished between the simple exploitative economy which did no permanent harm and the characteristic exploitative economy which destroyed so much of the environment that it led to impoverishment of a people."[14]

Aware that pristine areas were rapidly disappearing, the Scottish-born American naturalist John Muir (1838–1914) was to play a major role in the drafting of the 1864 Yosemite Preservation Act, which helped set aside the world's first national park in central California.[15] As this growing sense of the vulnerability of wildlife and landscapes began to spread abroad, other countries were to follow suit. In England, for example, the preservation of open land and its associated wildlife was addressed by a few societies such as the National Trust (founded in 1894) and the Council for the Preservation of Rural England (founded in 1926). It was not until 1949, however, that Parliament issued the National Parks and Access to Countryside Act.[16]

In the United States, the period from 1900 to 1950 appears to have been characterized by occasional studies of water and air pollution. The economist K. William Kapp, for example, cites several studies on air pollution and water pollution conducted in the United States and Great Britain as early as 1914 and extending through the 1930s and 1940s. Early attempts at determining the cost of air pollution, and thus quantifying what economists refer to as externalities (a concept that was probably first introduced in the 1920s by the British economist Nicolas Pigou), are also cited by Kapp.[17] On the international scene, one of the earliest international treaties that focused on environmental concerns was the 1909 Boundary Waters Treaty signed by the United States and Canada. As Thomas Goehl explains, "[T]he main premise of the treaty was that neither party may use the water on its side of the lakes to the detriment of the water, health, and property of the other side."[18]

Still, although several social scientists had already begun to use the word *ecology* and even to write extensively about human ecology as early as 1935, the subjects of ecology, environmentalism, and the impact of industrialization in general on the biosphere and geosphere were not yet formally recognized, nor were they integrated into a unified field of investigation.[19] Indeed, it was not until after the severe dust storms of the mid-1930s suffered by several American midwestern and southern states (the Dust Bowl) that the United States government decided seriously to focus on the issue of man's impact on the environment. The series of investigations following the Dust Bowl crisis led researchers to conclude that the severe soil erosion brought about by a series of intense and consecutive windstorms was partly caused by climatic factors (hot, dry weather) and poor land management that encouraged overgrazing and unsatisfactory farming techniques. The Dust Bowl, Aldo Leopold was to observe a decade later, was to some extent a case of short-sightedness on the part of farmers who had abused the land and ignored fundamental, but still not well-understood, principles of ecology. In his concluding comments on land ethics, Leopold notes that "[T]he farmers, in short, have selected those remedial practices which were profitable anyhow, and ignored those which were profitable to the community, but not clearly profitable to themselves."[20]

In Europe, similar conclusions were reached. During the period from 1929 to 1933, the Water Pollution Research Board conducted a comprehensive survey of the Tees estuary (in the northern industrial area of England known as Teeside). The research revealed that industrial pollution caused by untreated organic material discharges was responsible for the steady decline in migratory birds and salmon. Yet, it was not until 1968 that the local River Authority advised the Teeside County Borough Council of its intent to exercise the Rivers (Prevention of Pollution) Acts of 1951 and 1961.[21]

By 1952, the need to address man's deleterious activities and the impact of various cultures on the planet and biosphere in general was recognized. Under the leadership of geographer Carl Sauer, sociologist Lewis Mumford, and zoologist Marston Bates, as well as many other world-renowned climatologists, anthropologists, and social scientists, a symposium on *Man's Role in Changing the Face of the Earth* took place June 16–21, 1955, in Princeton, New Jersey.[22] Yet, despite the impressive gathering of scholars who presented what were to become classic papers, one is struck by the paucity of comments relating to pollution or industrial pollution in general. A perusal of the index shows that only sixteen references (out of 1,152 pages of text) could be found under the headings "Pollution" or "Industrial pollution." The majority of these references deal with air and water pollution, subjects already well researched by the late 1940s. The sole reference to industrial pollution is attributed to Lewis Mumford, who, in his closing summary, in which he focused on the danger of "atomic energy," observed that "[F]or all apparent concern to lower the death rate, we have scarcely yet begun to cope with the *problems of ordinary industrial pollution*."[23]

## The Emergence of Environmental Awareness in the United States

By the late 1930s and early 1940s, Americans had begun to recognize the importance of managing rather than abusing the environment. The price for mismanagement had been painfully felt during the years 1934 to 1936 by thousands of farmers and tens of millions of others who depended on their products. Researchers continued to write on the subjects of land use, ecology, and the environment in general, but it was not until 1962, when Rachel Carson published her profoundly influential *Silent Spring*, that the public at large began to comprehend the deleterious effects of chemicals such as DDT on the fauna, people, and the environment in general (see Table 1-1).[24] The interconnectedness of all species living in the closed system known as the earth was becoming evident.

With the publication of *Silent Spring*, Rachel Carson made Americans aware of the holistic nature of ecology. It was up to Barry Commoner to concisely summarize, in his famous four basic laws of ecology, the deleterious interconnectedness and impact of industrial activities on the environment.

*Barry Commoner's Four Basic Laws of Ecology*

| | |
|---|---|
| *First Law of Ecology:* | Everything is connected to everything else. (The naturalist John Muir was well aware of this law.) |
| *Second Law of Ecology:* | Everything must go somewhere. |
| *Third Law of Ecology:* | Nature knows best. |
| *Fourth Law of Ecology:* | There is no such thing as a free lunch.[25] |

**Table 1-1.** The concentration of DDT in the food chain.

| Source | Parts per Million |
|---|---|
| River water | 0.000003 |
| Estuary water | 0.00005 |
| Zooplankton | 0.04 |
| Shrimps | 0.16 |
| Insects-*Dipteria* | 0.30 |
| Minnows | 0.50 |
| *Fundulus* | 1.24 |
| Needlefish | 2.00 |
| Tern | 2.80–5.17 |
| Cormorant | 26.40 |
| Immature gull | 75.50 |

SOURCE: Andrew Goudie, *The Human Impact on the Natural Environment* (Cambridge, Mass.: The MIT Press, 1994), p. 98, quoting C. A. M. King, *Introduction to Physical and Biological Oceanography* (London: Edward Arnold, 1975), Table 8.7, p. 301.

In the mid-1960s, several authors began to expand on the themes first introduced by Carson. Titles such as *The Destruction of California, America the Raped,* and *The Greening of America* appeared and some, such as *The Greening of America,* even became best-sellers.[26] As government agencies began to try to address the many problems caused by industrial pollution, some government officials soon realized that the environment was not easily managed. Raymond Dasmann, who had witnessed the effects of poor coordination and the resulting inefficiencies of California's bureaucracies, warned in his conclusion to *The Destruction of California* that

> those building a state park system seem to operate in ignorance of the plans of other agencies that would destroy it. We cannot afford to have the various organizations and groups engaged in either preservation or development working in isolation from one another. . . . California can be a model that all other regions will try to follow. But unless we act now to stop the forces of destruction that are at work, the state that once was green and golden may become an object lesson that shows only what other areas must avoid.[27]

Dasmann's remarks were indeed prophetic and may have influenced some California politicians.

## Early Examples of Environmental Policies: The Case of California

With a population in excess of 32 million (1990), California and its economic vitality have always been the envy of the rest of the nation. California's leadership in the field of environmental management is probably a direct consequence of its economic vitality and population pressure (half of which is concentrated in the southern, semiarid portion of the state). It was during the energy crisis of the early 1970s that Californians, who rely perhaps more than any other Americans on their freeways and cars to get them to and from work, began to realize that their state desperately needed an energy policy. The California Energy Commission (CEC) was formed and charged with protecting the environment. By 1974, the Warren-Alquist Act (first passed in 1973 but vetoed by then Governor Reagan) was signed into law.[28] The Warren-Alquist Act was probably the first state legislation to recognize that a principal goal of electric and natural gas utilities' resource planning and investment shall be to minimize the cost to society of the reliable energy services that are provided by natural gas and electricity, *and to improve the environment and to encourage the diversity of energy resources through improvement in energy efficiency and development of renewable energy resources,* such as wind, solar, and geothermal energy. . . . It is further the policy of the state and the intent of the Legislature to employ a range of measures to reduce wasteful, uneconomical, and unnecessary uses of energy, thereby reducing the rate of growth of energy consumption, prudently conserve energy resources, and assure statewide environmental, public safety, and land use goals.[29]

With the establishment of agencies such as the well-known Southern California Air Quality Management District, the process of monitoring water, air, and ground pollution began. After a decade of little or no progress, improvements in water and air quality first became noticeable by the mid-1980s. Although most visitors to southern California might wonder what these improvements were, those of us who lived in California during the 1960s, 1970s, and 1980s can testify that, despite an increase in population and the resulting millions of traveled miles, air pollution on average is often less than it used to be. Of course, a clear day in Los Angeles is not the same as a clear day in Nome, Alaska; air cleanness is unfortunately a relative concept (as any conversation with most Angelenos will remind you).

By the late 1970s and early 1980s, the environmental auditing of companies was routinely practiced in California. In 1986, or some ten years before the international community would come up with its ISO 14001 standard and six to seven years before the United Kingdom was to release its BS 7750 environmental management standard, California's legislature devised in its California Quality Assessment Act (Chapter 1507, Statutes of 1986) a way to register environmental assessors (REAs). The act defines environmental assessors as individuals who, "through academic training, occupational experience, and reputation, are qualified to objectively conduct one or more aspects of an environmental assessment. . . ."[30] The success of California's many environmental and energy conservation programs came to be emulated by many other states. By the mid-1970s, California had become the leading environmentalist state in the Union; however, this could not have happened had it not been for a series of federal acts that began to be passed from 1969 on (see Table 1-2).

**Table 1-2.** Chronology of selected U.S. federal environmental legislation.

**The National Environmental Policy Act** of 1969 (NEPA), signed into law January 1, 1970, was the first act to require federal agencies to conduct environmental impact studies (EIS) to assess the environmental effects of major action. Since the 1980s, the use of environmental impact studies has been adopted by several European as well as other countries.

**The Clean Air Act** (CAA) was first enacted in 1955, rewritten in 1963, 1965, and 1967 and significantly amended in 1977. The CAA requires the Environmental Protection Agency (EPA) to establish maximum allowable concentrations for pollutants such as carbon monoxide, sulfur dioxide, particulate matter, ozone, nitrogen oxide, and lead. While the EPA sets national ambient air quality standards (NAAQS), it is up to each state to meet or exceed them.

**The Clean Water Act** (CWA) of 1972 initially focused on municipal sewage and industrial discharges. It was not until 1987 that "nonpoint sources"—that is, the nearly 50 percent of water pollution runoff coming from agricultural and mining operations, road salting, construction sites, city streets, and so on—were finally considered.

**The Federal Insecticide, Fungicide, and Rodenticide Act** of 1972 (FIFRA) regulates the registration (to be renewed every five years), marketing, and use of pesticides. Only a fraction of the more than 50,000 pesticides have been reviewed by the EPA.

**The Endangered Species Act** of 1973 recognizes that endangered species of wildlife and plants "are of aesthetic, ecological, educational, historical, recreational, and scientific value to the Nation and its people."[1]

**The Safe Drinking Water Act** (SDWA) was adopted in 1974 and substantially amended in 1986. The act requires the EPA to set standards, known as maximum contaminant levels (MCLs), for contaminants in public drinking water supplies.

**The Resource Conservation and Recovery Act** (RCRA) of 1976 addresses the disposal of solid waste. A list of hazardous waste is periodically updated by the EPA.

**The Surface Mining Control and Reclamation Act** (SMCRA), enacted in 1977, attempts to control the degradation of landscape erosion and water pollution associated with surface mining.

**The Comprehensive Environmental Response, Compensation, and Liability Act** (CERCLA or Superfund) was enacted in 1980 and amended in 1986. The CERCLA or Superfund attempts to remedy the improper disposal of hazardous waste in the past. The cost of cleanup is generally funded by private organizations that have been found to be associated, no matter how remotely, with the manufacturing, storage, or disposal of hazardous waste. If no solvent party can be found to pay the bill, billions of dollars of Superfund money are available.

**The Emergency Planning and Community Right-to-Know Act** of 1986 requires federal, state, and local governments and industry to work together in developing plans to deal with chemical emergencies and community right-to-know reporting on hazardous chemicals. Title III, Section 313 of the act requires companies to report precise data on releases to the air, water, and land, which are recorded in the Toxics Release Inventory (TRI). As we shall later see, the right-to-know act is found in one of the clauses of ISO 14001.

**The Toxic Substances Control Act** (TSCA) attempts to regulate the entry of toxic substances into the product stream. The EPA is to develop rules requiring manufacturers to test the substances they produce to determine the risk, if any, they pose to human health.

[1]Congressional text quoted in Jon Naar, *Design for a Planet* (New York: Harper & Row, 1990), p. 238.

## Creation of the Environmental Protection Agency

Prior to 1970, as many as fifteen different agencies operating across five federal jurisdictions (Department of Health, Education and Welfare, Department of the Interior, the Food and Drug Administration, the Atomic Energy Commission, and the Federal Radiation Council) attempted to coordinate and control various environmentally related programs. In an attempt to alleviate the lack of coordination already observed by Dasmann in California, the United States Environmental Protection Agency (EPA) was created on December 2, 1970. The agency is decentralized into ten regional offices, which are "responsible for implementing the national policies programs, overseeing the Federal environmental programs delegated to the States, approving grants and providing technical assistance to the States, and reviewing Environmental Impact Statements for Federal actions."[31]

In order to monitor and track its progress in cleaning up the environment, the EPA, as well as many other agencies, measures and maintains databases on environmental indicators such as the amount of lead in drinking water, the amount of pollutants in the air, the amount of toxic chemicals released into the environment by industry, and the

Table 1-3 reveals that the environmental impact on the air, water, land, underground, and public sewage varies greatly by industry. For example, in 1989 the paper industry released the highest percentage (13.46 percent) of its toxic waste to surface water, the balance escaping to the atmosphere! Most other industries transfer less than 4.00 percent. The primary metals industry transferred as much as 31.61 percent of its waste to land. The chemical and petroleum industries transferred as much as 39.75 percent and 24.35 percent, respectively, to underground. Public sewage is heavily contaminated by the food industry, which transferred as much as 55.26 percent of its waste to it. Finally, one notices that although the bulk of toxic waste ends up in the air, the furniture, tobacco, printing, plastics, and lumber industries lead all other industries in the percentage of toxic substances they released into the air. It would be interesting to compare similar statistics with other nations (see Chapter 2 for a discussion of the Netherlands Green Plan).

**Table 1-3.** Environmental distribution of toxicities release inventory and transfers by industry, 1989.

| Industry | Total Releases (lbs. million) | Environmental Distribution (% of total releases and transfers) | | | | | |
|---|---|---|---|---|---|---|---|
| | | Air | Surface Water | Land | Under- ground | Public Sewage | Off-Site |
| Food | 67.80 | 27.77 | 4.15 | 6.41 | 1.63 | **55.26** | 4.79 |
| Tobacco | 1.49 | **93.14** | 3.04 | 0.10 | 0.00 | 1.11 | 2.61 |
| Textiles | 46.08 | 65.90 | 2.16 | 0.10 | 0.00 | **23.79** | 8.04 |
| Apparel | 2.06 | 65.78 | 0.01 | 0.02 | 0.00 | 21.42 | 12.76 |
| Lumber | 37.82 | 89.42 | 1.74 | 0.30 | 0.00 | 0.19 | 8.36 |
| Furniture | 65.37 | **92.51** | 0.00 | 0.03 | 0.00 | 0.93 | 6.52 |
| Paper | 313.25 | 61.94 | **13.46** | 3.17 | 0.00 | 14.68 | 6.75 |
| Printing | 60.92 | **90.85** | 0.01 | 0.00 | 0.00 | 1.23 | 7.91 |
| Chemicals | 2,745.77 | 27.07 | 3.98 | 3.89 | **39.75** | 12.65 | 12.66 |
| Petroleum | 103.14 | 51.20 | 3.65 | 2.31 | **24.35** | 11.82 | 6.66 |
| Plastics | 194.50 | 85.04 | 0.36 | 0.12 | 0.01 | 2.74 | 11.72 |
| Leather | 24.86 | 49.83 | 0.92 | 1.03 | 0.00 | **37.15** | 11.06 |
| Stone/clay | 47.49 | 47.52 | 1.47 | 5.39 | **13.84** | 2.09 | 29.69 |
| Primary metals | 756.81 | 31.25 | 2.09 | **31.61** | 4.87 | 2.02 | 28.15 |
| Fabricated metals | 207.38 | 61.83 | 0.15 | 0.52 | 0.16 | 4.06 | 33.28 |
| Machinery | 74.92 | 72.30 | 0.53 | 0.41 | 0.00 | 3.79 | 22.96 |
| Electrical | 145.76 | 65.29 | 0.46 | 0.95 | 0.03 | 9.78 | 23.48 |
| Transportation | 245.32 | 80.50 | 0.05 | 0.07 | 0.00 | 3.18 | 16.20 |
| Photographic | 69.54 | 67.64 | 0.62 | 0.14 | 0.00 | 4.36 | 27.24 |
| Miscellaneous | 38.89 | 64.74 | 0.09 | 0.14 | 0.00 | 1.20 | 33.83 |
| Multiple codes | 437.28 | 54.80 | 2.18 | **17.30** | 4.40 | 5.91 | 15.41 |
| No codes | 19.22 | 60.27 | 0.87 | 0.23 | 0.00 | 9.32 | 29.32 |
| Total | 5,705.67 | 42.54 | 3.31 | 7.79 | 20.70 | 9.66 | 16.00 |

SOURCE: U.S. Environmental Protection Agency, *The 1989 Toxics Release Inventory National Report,* EPA 560/4-91-014 (Washington, D.C.: EPA, 1991). Reproduced in Table 92 of *Environmental Quality,* 22nd Annual Report, published by the Council on Environmental Quality.

amount of pesticides and herbicides leached into groundwater (see Tables 1-3–1-6 for examples of types of statistics maintained by the EPA and other agencies). (The concept of monitoring and measuring pollutants is one of the fundamental premises of the ISO 14001 environmental management standard; see Chapter 3.)

## Conclusion

Man's impact on the environment can be traced back to at least the last two to three millennia. Yet, until the mid-eighteenth century, the effects of man's activity on the environment were generally localized. Today, in an age in which the earth is still seen as a giant landfill of limitless storage capacity, countries do not hesitate to export their toxic wastes anywhere in the world.[32] As it becomes increasingly difficult, and thus more expensive, to export toxic wastes, some nations have begun to recognize the need to reduce or even recycle or eliminate altogether the generation of waste. Over the past twenty-five years, the efforts of international, national, and nongovernmental agencies have begun to pay off. Although much work remains to be done, the age of global environmental awareness is fast approaching.

---

*USA Today*, in its October 21, 1992 issue, p. 13A, lists 132 American cities in which the parts per million (ppm) lead count exceeds the maximum of 15 ppm. Some of the largest readings (100 or more ppms) were found in Charleston, South Carolina (211 ppm), Escambia Co., Florida (175 ppm), Newton, Massachusetts (163 ppm), Framingham, Massachusetts (100 ppm), and Utica, New York (100 ppm). Overall, as many as thirty cities (eleven of which were in Massachusetts) had lead readings greater than or equal to 45 ppm. In ten cities, more than 50 percent of the children had high levels of lead in their bloodstreams. In Cleveland, Philadelphia, and Boston, 62 to 69 percent of children had high lead levels.

---

**Table 1-4.** Farm pesticide use, 1964–1991 (in millions of pounds of active ingredients).

| Year | Herbicides | Insecticides | Fungicides | Total |
|------|-----------|-------------|-----------|-------|
| 1964 | 76 | 143 | 72 | 291 |
| 1966 | 112 | 138 | 79 | 328 |
| 1971 | 207 | 127 | 130 | 464 |
| 1976 | 374 | 130 | 146 | 650 |
| 1982 | 451 | 71 | 30 | 552 |
| 1986 | 410 | 59 | 6 | 475 |
| 1987 | 365 | 57 | 7 | 429 |
| 1988 | 372 | 60 | 8 | 440 |
| 1989 | 394 | 61 | 8 | 463 |
| 1990 | 392 | 63 | 8 | 463 |
| 1991 | 403 | 66 | 9 | 478 |

SOURCE: U.S. Department of Agriculture, Economic Research Service, Agricultural Resources as reproduced in Table 54 of *Environmental Quality*, 22nd Annual Report of the Council on Environmental Quality.

**Table 1-5.** Factory releases: top fifteen corporate offenders.

| Corporations and Their Locations | 1990 Toxics Releases (lbs.) |
|----------------------------------|-----------------------------|
| 1. American Cyanamid Co., Westwego, Louisiana | 162,030,982 |
| 2. Magnesium Corp. of America, Toole, Utah | 95,049,351 |
| 3. Monsanto Co., Alvin, Texas | 64,823,729 |
| 4. Vulcan Chemicals, Wichita, Kansas | 59,188,879 |
| 5. Freeport McMoran, Saint James, Louisiana | 56,538,815 |
| 6. Du Pont, New Johnsonville, Tennessee | 50,682,660 |
| 7. Inland Steel Co., East Chicago, Indiana | 50,003,965 |
| 8. Courtaulds North America, Inc., LeMoyne, Alabama | 45,933,030 |
| 9. Asarco, Inc., East Helena, Montana | 40,304,296 |
| 10. Tennessee Eastman Co., Kingsport, Tennessee | 39,150,570 |
| 11. Du Pont, Pass Christian, Mississippi | 38,893,130 |
| 12. Du Pont Beaumont Works, Beaumont, Texas | 37,206,498 |
| 13. Freeport McMoran, Uncle Sam, Louisiana | 36,155,967 |
| 14. Du Pont, Victoria Site, Texas | 35,097,213 |
| 15. BP Chemicals, Port Lavaca, Texas | 32,617,374 |

SOURCE: U.S. Environmental Protection Agency, *The 1990 Toxics Release Inventory National Report* (Washington, D.C.: EPA, 1993).

**Table 1-6.** Top ten worst states by industrial waste.

| Top Ten States | 1990 Releases (lbs.) |
|---|---|
| 1. Louisiana | 427,382,518 |
| 2. Texas | 418,792,435 |
| 3. Tennessee | 207,482,411 |
| 4. Ohio | 168,392,276 |
| 5. Utah | 125,433,121 |
| 6. North Carolina | 123,947,781 |
| 7. Michigan | 119,854,915 |
| 8. Illinois | 118,994,314 |
| 9. Alabama | 112,575,087 |
| 10. Florida | 106,558,514 |

SOURCE: U.S. Environmental Protection Agency, *The 1990 Toxicities Release Inventory National Report* (Washington, D.C.: EPA, 1993).

## Notes

1. Clarence J. Glacken, "Changing Ideas of the Habitable World," in William L. Thomas, Jr., ed., *Man's Role in Changing the Face of the Earth* (Chicago: Chicago University Press, 1956), pp. 70–92.
2. Clive Ponting, *A Green History of the World* (New York: Penguin Books, 1991), pp. 5, 7.
3. Clarence J. Glacken, "Changing Ideas of the Habitable World," in William L. Thomas, Jr., ed., *Man's Role in Changing the Face of the Earth*, pp. 72 and 74. The Glacken citation on page 72 is from Henri Frankfort et al., *Before Philosophy: The Intellectual Adventure of Ancient Man* (Harmondsworth, England: Penguin Books, 1951). Glacken was to further elaborate his thoughts on the philosophies of man vis-à-vis nature throughout the ages in his masterful (but little known) scholarly work *Traces on the Rhodian Shore, Nature and Culture in Western Thought from Ancient Times to the End of the Eighteenth Century* (Berkeley and Los Angeles: University of California Press, 1967).

    Islamic scholars have documented that the Quran also contains many environmental references, including to sustainability. Citing the Quran, Dr. Mawil Izzi Dien, for example, explains that "Allah created the human race for a great reason, namely that they might act as viceroy upon the earth. . . . Their mastery of the earth is for its betterment and development and not for evil or misuse." "Shari'a and Environment," Feb. 9, 1993, unpublished text found on Internet. Dr. Dien's e-mail address is izzidien-@uk.ac.lampeter. See also "Environment: An Islamic Perspective," by Sultan A. Ismail at ihasan@galileo.cs.clemson.edu. I do not know if these addresses are still active. Similar views towards the environment could no doubt be found in Eastern philosophies.
4. Clive Ponting, *A Green History of the World*, p. 352.
5. C. G. Down and J. Stocks, *Environmental Impact in Mining* (London: Applied Science Publishers, 1977), p. 7, quoted in Andrew Goudie, *The Human Impact on the Natural Environment* (Cambridge, Mass.: The MIT Press, 1994), p. 113.
6. Count Buffon quoted in Glacken, "Changing Ideas of the Habitable World," p. 77.
7. For a summary of Ramazzini's accomplishments, see Gary E. R. Hook, "Ramazzini: Father of Environmental Health?" *Environmental Health Perspectives* 103, no. 11 (November 1995): 2.

8. David Vogel, "Environmental Policy in Europe and Japan," in Norman J. Vig and Michael E. Kraft, *Environmental Policy in the 1990s: Toward a New Agenda* (Washington, D.C.: CQ Press, A division of Congressional Quarterly Inc., 1990), p. 258.

9. Abel Wolman, "Disposal of Man's Waste," in William L. Thomas, Jr., ed., *Man's Role in Changing the Face of the Earth*, p. 808. One should note that the street collection of household waste was already practiced in China by the end of the eighteenth century. See Clive Ponting, *A Green History of the World*, p. 353.

10. Luc Ferry, *Le nouvel ordre ecologique* (Paris: Bernard Grasset, 1992), pp. 9–10. Ferry cites several references. One should note that scientists recently (1995) discovered a method to biogenetically insert insecticides into plants such as potatoes, for example. The bug eating the potato is slowly killed, thus eliminating the bug. However, entomologists have warned that insects will sooner or later build up an immunity to the "killer potato" and eventually thrive. To prevent this from happening, entomologists and one chemical manufacturer who has been convinced recommend that farmers set aside 25 percent of their field for growing normal potatoes. The rationale for such a strategy is that insects must be fed in order to prevent a breed of superbugs from evolving. While I believe medieval farmers would have understood the entomologists' argument, I am not sure that today's farmers will be able to resist the temptation to earn (at least for a short while) an additional 25 percent profit. The legal rights of animals was also recognized by early Muslim lawyers. This information is provided by Dr. Mawil Izzi Dien of St. David's University College–Lampeter, University of Wales, in his unpublished "Shari'a and Environment."

11. Christopher D. Stone, *Should Trees Have Standing: Toward Legal Rights for Natural Objects* (Los Altos, Calif.: William Kaufmann, 1972): "I am quite seriously proposing, that we give legal rights to forests, oceans, rivers and other so-called 'natural objects' in the environment—indeed, to the natural environment as a whole" (p. 9). Dr. Stone's argument is not as absurd as it may sound. In fact, his argument for the guardianship of nature is well thought out and elaborated further in two additional books that we shall review later: *Where the Law Ends: The Social Control of Corporate Behavior* (New York, Harper & Row, 1975) and *The Gnat Is Older Than Man: Global Environment and Human Agenda* (Princeton, N.J.: Princeton University Press, 1993).

12. For examples of farmers fighting the Endangered Species Act and federal and state agencies, see Sonja Hillgren, "The courtroom summons," *Farm Journal*, November 1994, pp. 16–17, and Charles Johnson, "Cornered in California," *Farm Journal*, Mid-March 1995, pp. 12–13.

13. For a brief overview of the contribution of these and other nineteenth-century geographers, see Preston E. James, *All Possible Worlds: A History of Geographical Ideas* (New York, Bobbs-Merrill, 1972) and the introduction to Andrew Goudie's *The Human Impact on the Natural Environment*, pp. 1–8.

14. Glacken, "Changing Ideas of the Habitable World," p. 85.

15. John Muir, *The Yosemite* (New York: Doubleday, 1962; first published 1912). The acts of June 30, 1864, October 1, 1890, and March 3, 1905, are reproduced in Appendix A of Muir's book.

16. Goudie, *The Human Impact on the Natural Environment*, p. 380.

17. Pigou's early works on the economics of cost are found in his 1920 *The Economics of Welfare* and *A Study of Public Finance* (London, Macmillan & Co., 1928). For a brief summary of Pigou's thesis, see Paul Hawken, *The Ecology of Commerce: A Declaration of Sustainability* (New York, Haper Business, 1993), pp. 75–90, and K. William Kapp, *The Social Costs of Private Enterprise* (Cambridge, Mass.: Harvard University Press, 1950). Kapp's work is probably one of the earliest by an economist to attempt to link economics with environmental issues, thus creating the field of environmental economics often referred to as "green economics," which will be covered in a later chapter. Some of Kapp's historical references would include: "Social cost of air pollution" (University of Pittsburgh, Department of Industrial Research, Bulletin No. 3, *Psychological Aspects of the*

*Problem of Atmospheric Smoke Pollution* (Pittsburgh, 1913). The cost of air pollution was also quantified in Manchester, England, where the cost of household washing was found to be greater than in cleaner Harrogate; see the Manchester Air Pollution Advisory Board, 1918. Kapp also cites several studies conducted in the mid-1930s.

18. Thomas J. Goehl, "Nobody Said It Would Be Easy," *Environmental Health Perspectives* 103, no. 12 (December 1995): 4.

19. One early work on human ecology was J. W. Bews, *Human Ecology* (London: H. Milford, 1935).

20. Aldo Leopold, *A Sand County Almanac* (New York: Oxford University Press, 1949), p. 208.

21. Geoff Essery, "Managing Environmental Improvement Within a Major Chemical Complex," in *Business and the Environment*, ed. Denis Smith (New York: St. Martin's Press, 1993) p. 121.

22. The symposium's proceedings, totaling almost 1,200 pages, were edited by William L. Thomas, Jr., and published in 1956 as *Man's Role in Changing the Face of the Earth* (Chicago: Chicago University Press, 1956).

23. Lewis Mumford, "Prospect," in *Man's Role in Changing the Face of the Earth,* p. 1147, emphasis added.

24. Some early work would include Raymond Dasmann, *Environmental Conservation* (New York: John Wiley, 1959); E. H. Graham, *Natural Principles of Land Use* (New York: Oxford University Press, 1944); E. P. Odum, *Fundamentals of Ecology* (Philadelphia: W. B. Saunders Company, 1959); and Rachel L. Carson, *Silent Spring* (Boston: Houghton Mifflin Co., 1962).

25. Barry Commoner, *The Closing Circle* (New York: Alfred A. Knopf, 1971), p. 44.

26. Raymond F. Dasmann, *The Destruction of California* (New York: Collier Books, 1965); Gene Marine, *America the Raped: The Engineering Mentality and the Devastation of a Continent* (New York: Avon Books, 1969); Charles A. Reich, *The Greening of America* (New York: Bantam Books, 1970).

27. Raymond Dasmann, *The Destruction of California,* pp. 199 and 201.

28. One should also note that about 1971, the State of Hawaii passed a senate bill (S.B. 1132) that led to the creation of the Office of Environmental Quality Control and the Environmental Center at the University of Hawaii (see Gregory Bateson's *Steps to an Ecology of Mind* (New York: Ballantine Books, 1972), p. 488.

29. Warren-Alquist Act (January 1995), Pete Wilson Governor, §§25000.1 and 25007, pp. 1 and 4. See also Chapter 5, "California Sunshine," in Curtis Moore and Alan Miller, *Green Gold* (Boston: Beacon Press, 1994), pp. 105–24.

30. California Health and Safety Code, Section 25570.2.

31. United States Environmental Protection Agency, *Environmental Management*, EPA/600/M-91/039. The ten regions are: Boston, New York, Philadelphia, Atlanta, Chicago, Dallas, Kansas City, Denver, San Francisco, and Seattle.

32. For an excellent account of how companies export their toxic wastes to Africa, Latin America, or Asia, see the report published by the Center for Investigative Reporting and Bill Moyers, *Global Dumping Ground* (Washington, D.C.: Seven Lock Press, 1990).

# 2

# The Emergence of Global Environmental Awareness

After the 1955 international symposium held in Princeton, New Jersey, the world had to wait another seventeen years before the first United Nations-sponsored international conference on the human environment was held in Stockholm in 1972 (see Table 2-1). Yet, despite the success of this UN-sponsored conference, not much was to happen until 1980, when the Carter Administration published its *Global 2000 Report.* Although the report was well received abroad, it attracted very little attention in the United States. As more and more researchers began to talk about environmental degradation, the problems generated by man's impact on the environment could no longer be ignored by world leaders. The Montreal Protocol (1987), which addressed the production of ozone-depleting substances, led to specific quantitative objectives designed to achieve eventual elimination of certain fluorocarbons and chlorofluorocarbons.

The 1980s and 1990s were to see an increase in international symposia and other gatherings. In 1987, the World Trade Commission published its influential *Our Common Future.* The document, known as the Brundtland report, reiterated the concept of sustainable development, and quickly became the foundation for some early commitments on the part of a few governments regarding the importance of formulating national environmental plans and policies as a first step toward an international understanding of global environmental problems. In 1989, Costa Rica established by a presidential executive decree the INBio Planning Commission (Instituto Nacional de Biodiversidad), whose purpose is to conduct a national biodiversity inventory within a decade. By late 1994, several European countries had stated their intention to commit themselves to the basic principles of sustainability formulated

**Table 2-1.** Chronology of some important events relating
to the environment.

| | |
|---|---|
| **1955:** | First International Symposium on "Man's Role in Changing the Face of the Earth" is held in Princeton, New Jersey. The symposium attracts international scholars such as Lewis Mumford, Kenneth Boulding, Teilhard De Chardin, and numerous others. |
| **1972:** | First UN Conference on the Human Environment is held in Stockholm, Sweden. |
| **1972:** | The Club of Rome publishes its controversial doomsday report entitled *The Limits of Growth*. |
| **1980:** | The *Global 2000 Report* is published during the Carter Administration. The report is generally ignored in the United States but receives international attention. More than 1.5 million copies are sold and the report is translated into eight different languages. |
| **1987:** | The Montreal Ozone Protocol addresses the issue of CFCs. |
| **1987:** | The World Commission on Environment and Development, headed by Norwegian Prime Minister Gro Harlem Brundtland, publishes its *Our Common Future*, in which the term *sustainable development* is popularized. |
| **1989:** | The Netherlands publishes the first National Environmental Policy Plan (NEPP), known as a green plan. New Zealand and Canada follow suit within two years. |
| **1992:** | The UN Conference on Environment and Development, also known as the Rio Earth Summit, is held. Agenda 21 calls for sustainable development. |
| **1992:** | The Business Council for Sustainable Development and Stephan Schmidheiny publish *Changing Course: A Global Business Perspective on Development and the Environment*. |
| **1996:** | The ISO 14001 Environmental Management Standard is published. |

during the 1992 Rio Earth Summit. As for the United States, although it had been a leader in developing national environmental legislation during the late 1960s and early 1970s, its leadership and innovation, as in the field of environmental technology, for example, has been seriously eroded since the late 1980s. Despite President Clinton's establishment of the Environmental Technology Initiative (ETI) in 1993 and other proenvironment programs such as the President's Council on Sustainable Development (PCSD), one must still look to other countries for leadership and innovative approaches.[1]

Since the mid-1980s, several countries have become aware of the need to write national environmental laws and seriously to address environmental issues. Increasingly, terms such as *ecoindustry, ecoparks,* and *ecopeace* are being introduced by journalists and academicians throughout the world.[2] However, as we shall now see, lessons from the United States have demonstrated that there is a long, tortuous path separating the codification of environmental laws and the implementation and enforcement of such laws.

## Enforcing Environmental Regulations: Strengths and Limitations

By the late 1970s, the Environmental Protection Agency (EPA) was well aware of the fact that it was impossible to regulate industries without some enforcement capabilities. In an attempt to strengthen its position, the EPA began to assume responsibilities for inspections and for responding to and investigating violators operating in states without approved programs. These efforts led to new interagency partnerships designed to further solidify the EPA's enforcement capability. During the 1990s, the EPA, the Securities and Exchange Commission (SEC), the Occupational Safety and Health Administration (OSHA), and the IRS began to pool government resources "to catch and penalize companies not in compliance with any of a dozen or so key laws."[3]

One of the most serious limitations faced by the EPA is that it cannot monitor the Department of Defense (DOD), by far the greatest polluter of all time. For example, when the groundwater near Picatinny Arsenal in Pennsylvania was found to have carcinogenic chemicals up to 700 times greater than EPA drinking water standards for groundwater, the EPA could not do anything. Indeed, the Department of Justice had ruled some years earlier that a United States agency such as the DOD could not be sued by the EPA. The army, for example, relies on its own Installation and Recovery Program (IRP) to identify and control the migration of hazardous waste. In essence, the Pentagon pays for cleaning up its own mess.[4]

Other problems relate to the one-size-fits-all approach favored by most federal and states agencies. As Councilman Edward Hayes explains, every other year and usually during the same month, the city of Columbus, Ohio, finds itself having to spend a lot of money because it is in violation of the EPA's strict 3-parts-per-billion (ppb) standard for the herbicide atrazine used on Ohio's cornfields. Hayes comments that

Columbus might find, for example, that money spent on health clinics for poor neighborhoods would save more lives than the federally mandated technology for controlling atrazine. . . . Consider, too, the benefits of better local knowledge. A national data base of agricultural chemical use by watershed would let the EPA tailor regulations locally.[5]

Finally, one must also wonder if the fines assessed by the various regulatory agencies are reasonable. A client of mine was recently found in violation of a Federal Aviation Agency (FAA) regulation for having mailed two cans of a substance classified as hazardous. The selling price for the two cans, which were mailed inadvertently, was $15.00. The initial fine was set at $40,000 and eventually negotiated down to $7,500 after my client had spent over $3,500 in legal fees! Similar horror stories have been told by countless others.[6]

## The Limits of the Law

During the mid-1970s, the legal scholar Christopher Stone proposed that environmental laws could never regulate companies because laws only react to situations and obviously cannot prevent problems. However, innovative approaches could be used to better regulate corporations. As an example of innovation, Professor Stone cites the California Insurance Code, which "provides that each insurance company must designate some particular officer whose function it is to receive the report of the insurance commissioner; the law then insists that 'such officer shall . . . inform [the company's] members that a copy of such a report is available for inspection' " by them. Then, intruding even further into the corporation's information processes, it adds, "there shall be entered in the minutes of each such meeting the fact that such officer did so inform the members present." In other words, certain information critical to the company's health has to go to the board—with no room for anyone to claim later that he "never saw it."[7] Moreover, in order to ensure that a company satisfies its legal obligation, the legal system can no longer rely on the establishment of fines (which, according to Stone, are often set too low). Since corporations cannot be imprisoned, some California judges have had to rely on clever innovative techniques to ensure that companies act responsibly. Thus, when Judge James B. Parsons was faced with the decision of how to monitor the California oil giant ARCO, he suggested that a probation officer would visit (in a sense audit) ARCO to ensure that the corporation had satisfied the spillage program condition of its probation.

# The Need for Change

The nearly two decades of a "command and control" philosophy have led to some bitter reactions on the part of most industries and business-people alike. To these individuals, the words *environmental regulations* usually induce a severe allergic reaction often followed by some well-chosen curse words. The limitations of the command and control approach to pollution control have been recognized for several years. To some, such as Ralph Nader and Barry Commoner, the command and control process was doomed to fail simply because limiting pollution or monitoring it at the end of the pipe was not as good as simply banning polluting substances. As early as 1971, Commoner had suggested that the EPA adopt a set of principles similar to those favored by preventive medicine in order to eradicate diseases.[8] To many environmentalist advocates, the concept of risk analysis favored by the EPA, which proposed "acceptable levels" of pollution, was unacceptable because it froze levels of pollution in place and prevented industries from innovating in what matters most, namely, pollution reduction, prevention, and ultimately elimination.

After some careful consideration, the EPA finally recognized that the one-size-fits-all approach was no longer practical and eventually accepted that it had to change its focus to prevention. Ever since 1989, the EPA has moved away from the often expensive focus on "command and control" protection—that is, regulating pollutants as they are released into the environment, and cleaning up pollutants after they have been released—to source reduction through its pollution prevention programs. This emphasis on preventing and/or reducing pollutants before they enter the environment helps decrease the risk to human health while, at the same time, the cost of regulating and cleaning up pollution is substantially reduced.

The EPA's new "Common Sense Initiative" philosophy is designed to de-emphasize mandatory, punitive compliance in favor of a voluntary, consensual approach. The drastic shift in philosophy was already evidenced in 1995 when the EPA announced that it had eliminated some 1,400 pages of obsolete regulations and revised 9,400 more.[9] Another example of the EPA's willingness to change its ways is the XL Project (eXcellence and Leadership), which enables individual companies to develop their own ways of improving the environment (see box). As we shall see in Chapter 3, the XL Project overlaps with some of the requirements specified in the International Standard 14001.

## Selection Criteria for XL Projects

**Environmental results:** Projects will be chosen only if they are able to achieve environmental performance that is superior to what would be achieved through compliance with current and reasonably anticipated future regulation. Explicit definitions and measures of "cleaner results" should be included in the project agreement negotiated among stakeholders.

**Cost savings and paperwork reduction:** The project should produce cost savings or economic opportunity and/or result in a decrease in paperwork.

**Stakeholder support:** Stakeholders such as the local communities near the project, local or state governments, businesses, and environmental and other public interest groups should support the project.

**Innovation/multimedia pollution prevention:** Projects should find innovative processes, technologies, or management practices that prevent the generation of pollution to air, water, or soil.

**Transferability:** EPA is interested in new approaches that could be applied more broadly to other industries or other facilities in the same industry.

**Feasibility:** The project should be financially, technically, and administratively feasible.

**Monitoring, reporting, and evaluation:** Projects should have clear objectives and measurable requirements in order for the EPA and the public to evaluate the success of the project and enforce its terms. Also, the project sponsor should be clear about the time frame within which results will be achievable.

**Shifting of risk burden:** The project must protect worker safety and ensure that no one is subjected to unjust or disproportionate environmental impacts.

Unfortunately, despite the valiant efforts of the EPA, the United States, unlike Canada and several European and other countries, still does not have a national environmental policy; nor does it have a

Department of Environmental Affairs. The Council on Environmental Quality (CEQ) no longer has the resources to produce its once-valuable reports. Current (1995–1996) political debate regarding the need for environmental protection and policies is not very encouraging. Fortunately, valuable lessons have been learned by some innovative countries. In Europe, for example, few countries have gone as far as the Netherlands has in terms of implementing and enforcing its environmental laws.

## National Green Plans: The Case of the Netherlands

Inspired by the recommendations of the Brundtland report (1987), the government of the Netherlands decided to implement the world's first green plan in 1988. New Zealand, Singapore, and Canada followed the Dutch lead soon after.[10] Green plans, Huey D. Johnson explains,

> are comprehensive, ecosystem-based initiatives designed to save the forest, not just the trees. Instead of passing laws that attack each problem one by one in isolation, these countries have created approaches that cut across traditional lines in ways that make sense for their resources, population, and industry. And within government itself, they have pulled together all the major ministries and agencies into one coordinated effort to achieve environmental quality.[11]

An excellent example of a green plan is the Dutch National Environmental Policy Plan. The Dutch government recognized very early on that a national environmental policy could not be achieved without a global environmental management whose scope would include not only local regions but also the world as a whole. This is what the Dutch government said:

> The main objective of *environmental management* is to preserve the environment's carrying capacity for the sake of sustainable development. The carrying capacity of the environment is damaged if, as a consequence of *environmental quality*, irreversible effects can occur within the time lapse of one generation; effects such as death or diseases among humans, exposure to serious nuisance and harm to well-being, the extinction of plant and animal species, soil fertility or the cultural heritage,

and impediments to land use and economic development. (Second Chamber Session 1988–1989, 21 137, nos. 1–2.)

Environmental management involves preventing or abating the undesired effects of human activities or operations. Human activities or activities which can cause such effects are called sources. Sources and effects are linked together by chains of cause and effect: emissions of substances and waste streams, dispersion in the environment, changes in environmental quality and the resulting changes in the health of human beings, animals, plants and ecosystems. The effect can occur on various levels of scale: local, regional, fluvial, continental and global.[12]

The central objective of the Netherlands' environmental management policy is sustainable development, which is defined as the means of satisfying the needs of the present generation without compromising the ability of future generations to meet their own needs. One of the difficulties with the concept of sustainability is that it is relatively easy to define but much more difficult to quantify. As Drs. Edward W. Manning and Wayne K. Bond of State of the Environment Reporting, Environment Canada (Ottawa), observe,

To know when an ecosystem is being used sustainably, we must be able to *measure* sustainability. Doing so is particularly difficult, however. Our information about most ecosystems generally comes from those who manage the ecosystems for specific purposes (e.g., farmlands and fisheries). As a result, this information often overlooks other functions supported by these systems. . . . A further difficulty is that much information about use of the environment is site-specific and therefore may not reflect the state of the system as a whole.[13]

In an attempt to address these difficulties and to ensure sustainability, the Dutch government issued two National Environmental Policy Plans (NEPP 1 and NEPP 2), which were submitted for review to various industries, trade associations, and citizen groups.[14] The Dutch NEPPs identify eight major themes: climate change, acidification, eutrophication, toxic and hazardous pollutants, waste disposal, disturbance, water depletion, and resource dissipation. For each of these themes, national objectives and target reductions are set for each of the eleven groups of targeted industries: agriculture, industry, refineries, retail trade, transport, consumers, construction industry, waste disposal industry, drinking water supply industry, sewage and wastewater treatment, and research institutions (see, for example, Tables 2-2, 2-3, 2-4, and 2-5). By setting national objectives and targets, the Dutch government anticipated the international standard for environmental management (ISO

**Table 2-2.** Emission ceilings for $SO_2$ emissions in the Netherlands.

| | |
|---|---|
| In 1985 total | 276** |
| In 1994 total | 176 |
| In 2000 total | 105 |
| Of which by industry (69)* | 15 |
| By refineries (95)* | 36 |
| By electric power plants (65)* | 30 |
| By traffic and households (47)* | 24 |

*The numbers in parentheses indicate 1985 emissions.
**Unit is kilotons/year (1,000 tons/year).

**Table 2-3.** Emission ceilings for $NO_x$ emissions in the Netherlands.

| | |
|---|---|
| In 1985 total | 544** |
| In 1994 total | 435 |
| In 2000 total | 268 |
| Of which by industry and refineries (83)* | 37 |
| By electric power plants (82)* | 40 |
| By households (24)* | 11 |
| By road traffic (272)* | 112 |
| By other sources (83)* | 68 |

*The numbers in parentheses indicate 1985 emissions.
**Unit is kilotons/year (1,000 tons/year).

**Table 2-4.** Emission ceilings for $NH_3$ emissions in the Netherlands.

| | |
|---|---|
| In 1985 total | 253** |
| In 1994 total | 177 |
| In 2000 total | 82 |
| Of which by agriculture (238)* | 70 |
| By industry (6)* | 3 |
| By households (9)* | 9 |

*The numbers in parentheses indicate 1985 emissions.
**Unit is kilotons/year (1,000 tons/year).

**Table 2-5.** Emission ceilings for VOC emissions in the Netherlands.

| | |
|---|---|
| In 1985 total | 459** |
| In 1994 total | 337 |
| In 2000 total | 194 |
| Of which by industry (118)* | 45 |
| By small firms (80)* | 40 |
| By households (32)* | 15 |
| By agriculture (24)* | 6 |
| By passenger cars (138)* | 35 |
| By trucks (42)* | 30 |
| By other traffic (15)* | 15 |
| By combustion plants (10)* | 10 |

SOURCE: Tables 2.1, 2.2, 2.3, *NEPP1* and *NEPP2*.
*The numbers in parentheses indicate 1985 emissions.
**Unit is kilotons/year (1,000 tons/year).

14001), which, as we shall see in the next chapter, requires companies to set internal objectives and targets.

To ensure the success of the environmental policy, various instruments in the form of legislation and regulation, strict enforcement of the regulations (that is, penalties), and financial incentives have been devised. Naturally, such ambitious schemes could not be implemented without allocating significant financial resources. Table 2-6 outlines a sector-by-sector financial commitment of the Dutch government vis-à-vis its national environmental policy.[15]

Finally, it is important to note that the environmental commitment of the Dutch government is not limited to its national policy. Being at the receiving end of all the fluvial pollution (from the Rhine) and agricultural contamination generated by at least four other European countries, the Dutch are certainly well aware of the imperative need to manage environmental pollution on a global scale.

> The Dutch government does not see any inherent conflict between an open trading system and sound environmental policy. In fact, it is partly in the interests of the environment that the government supports a further liberalization of trade. A progressive environmental policy need not be an obstacle to trade *if all the countries involved coordinate their environmental aims and instruments. . . .* The Dutch government is therefore emphatically in favor of pursuing the difficult option of achiev-

**Table 2-6.** Net annual costs per sector of current policy and additional NEPP 2 policy, 1990–2010 (in millions of guilders).

| Sector | 1990 Cost | 1995 Cost | 2000 Cost | 2010 Cost |
|---|---|---|---|---|
| Agriculture | 260* | 1076 | 1876 | 2145 |
| Mining | 222 | 212 | 212 | 200 |
| Industry | 1965 | 3938 | 5153 | 5769 |
| Of which petroleum industry | 244 | 572 | 728 | 689 |
| Public utilities | 464 | 739 | 1066 | 1200 |
| Construction | 431 | 727 | 786 | 866 |
| Commercial and service sector | 808 | 1372 | 1844 | 1884 |
| Transport | 528 | 1038 | 1395 | 3229 |
| Households | 2570 | 4497 | 6344 | 7406 |
| Government | 2212 | 3913 | 4072 | 3811 |
| Total | 9460 | 17513 | 22748 | 26512 |
| As % of GNP | 1.9% | 2.7% | 3.1% | 2.7% |

*All amounts are expressed in constant 1994 prices, with the exception of 1990 total costs, where current prices are used.

ing internationally recognized environmental standards and ensuring the worldwide application of the 'polluter pays' principle. This approach is based on a complementarity (sic) between trade policy and environmental policy.[16]

In North America, Canada's Green Plan was released in December 1990. Canada's Green Plan contains more than 100 initiatives, which were to be implemented by 1996 at a cost of $3 billion. Despite the fact that the "whole process was a bit hurried," Huey Johnson concludes that "the final green plan provides the comprehensive framework upon which Canada will build its environmental policy in the future."[17] [Note: Canada unfortunately abandoned its Green Plan in 1995; see note 10.]

## Environmental Management in Europe

The European Community (EC) ventured into environmental programs in 1973 when the first directives, including standards for the marketing, use, and labeling of pesticides and for the disposal of toxic wastes, were written. For the most part, these rules and standards promulgated by the EC had little effect on national regulatory policies and were in effect ignored.[18] By the late 1970s, however, the fact that environmentally

---

### *Examples of NEPP 2 activities*
### *(page cited in parentheses)*

**Agro-ecolabeling for agriculture:** International agreement with Belgium and Germany regarding the emissions policy for ammonia such that foreign contribution to ammonia deposition in the concentration areas is reduced to 200 acid equivalent/hectare/year. (216)

**Industry:** International agreement covering the release of HFCs to the atmosphere. "The motivation here is to achieve environmental policy at the international level comparable to that pursued nationally." (218)

**Refineries:** A reference is made to an international $SO_2$ emissions standard for refineries in the European Community. (219)

**Transport:** A tightening of European emissions standards for hydrocarbons and $NO_x$ to 0.3 g/KWh by 1999. (221)

**Construction industry:** International certification of timber. "In consequence of the tropical timber covenant, the Netherlands will advocate an international system for the certification of sustainability produced tropical hard wood." (227)

Raise landfill charges to match those for incineration. EC leaders are the Netherlands, Germany, and Denmark.

"The great mass of the industry target group consists of small and medium-size enterprises, i.e., enterprises with fewer than 10 and 100 employees respectively. Not enough attention has yet been paid to these smaller companies in the implementation of environmental policy." (118) The NEPP 2 recognizes that this group has limited knowledge of the equipment required, of the measures to be taken.

---

friendly products could be used as a marketing and product differentiation strategy was being recognized in Europe. In Germany, the Blue Angel marking (for which there is no verification of conformity) was established in 1978.[19] Europeans discovered, however, that the marketing of so-called environmentally sound products had really nothing to do with environmental policies.

It was after the fatal 1976 chemical spill in Seveso, Italy, that the first environmental directive (directive 82/501/CEE, known as "Seveso"), aimed at controlling so-called dangerous activities, was issued in Europe in 1982. A few years later (October 31, 1986) a major fire at the chemical warehouse of the Sandoz company in Basel, Switzerland, dramatically illustrated the importance of a self-contained waterstorm system. The resulting chemical contamination of the Rhine, from Switzerland to the Netherlands, had a major impact on the fishing industry of several countries downstream from Basel and clearly demonstrated to European leaders that pollution did not recognize frontiers. The need for pan-European environmental legislation could no longer be ignored and, by 1994, as many as eighty environmental directives had been issued by the European Economic Community (EEC). Once issued by the EEC's bureaucracy in Brussels, these directives must next be adopted and, if need be, adapted to local conditions by each of the respective members of the European Community. France, for example, adopted the Seveso directive in 1984.

As European countries began to adopt various directives, certain countries, notably Denmark, but later Germany and other countries, began to link local environmental legislation to conditions of trade. Danish law (1981), for example, required that mineral water, beer, and sodas be distributed only in reusable containers. Moreover, the Danish law required that packaging had to be approved by a certified organization. Predictably, exporters viewed such acts as flagrant examples of trade restriction and promptly took their case to the European Community Court. After some lengthy deliberations, the court finally ruled (1992) that although the principle of environmental protection was *above the principles of free trade* guaranteed by the European Community, such restrictions could be imposed only under reasonable economic conditions and when there were technologically feasible solutions. So much for a clear-cut ruling!

By 1993, the value of environmental management was finally beginning to be recognized in most European countries, although for a different reason. Table 2-7 reveals that although firms surveyed in four countries in general ranked pollution prevention at the bottom of the scale, Dutch firms, when compared with those of the other three nations, gave pollution prevention the highest rating (1.46). Firms in the United Kingdom perceive environmental management from a different perspective; product image and national regulations are ranked high. Oddly enough, German firms do not seem to perceive pollution prevention as an important component of environmental management. With

**Table 2-7.** Reasons for implementing environmental management.

| Reasons | France | Germany | U.K. | Netherlands |
|---|---|---|---|---|
| National regulations | 3.26* | 3.12 | 2.86 | 3.16 |
| Product image | 2.32 | 2.29 | 2.75 | 2.35 |
| EEC regulations | 1.96 | 1.16 | 2.45 | 1.88 |
| Public opinion | 1.67 | 1.40 | 2.31 | 2.27 |
| Marketing opportunity | 1.18 | 1.93 | 1.72 | 1.50 |
| Pollution prevention | 0.93 | 0.27 | 1.19 | 1.46 |
| Competitive pressure | 0.86 | 0.76 | 1.26 | 0.82 |

SOURCE: Jean-Paul Meyronneinc, *Le management de l'environnement dans l'entreprise* (Paris: AFNOR, 1995), p. 6.
*Scale: 0 = not important, 4 = very important.

French firms, the overwhelming factor is national regulations; everything else seems a distant second. The French lack of understanding of or appreciation for marketing is evident in France's score for that category, 1.18, the lowest among the four nations surveyed.

The current difficulties surrounding the implementation and coordination of regional environmental policies experienced by members of the European Union (EU) are minuscule when compared to the more complex issues of international trade. Indeed, whatever the nature and extent of economic diversity and inequality found within the EU, it is far less than the vast schism found between the developed North and the developing South.

## International Trade Agreements and the Environment

The debate as to whether a country could or should apply its environmental laws to restrict trade with another is always hotly debated among environmentalists. Until the early 1990s, the issue of competitiveness and environmental protection was mostly academic. But when the U.S. government banned Mexican tuna because the number of dolphins killed by the Mexican fleet exceeded the limit set by the Marine Mammal Protection Act (MMPA), tension rose. Within a few months, the Mexican government brought the case to the General Agreement on Tariffs and Trade (GATT), claiming that the MMPA (established in 1972) was an example of an "inappropriate" law imposed for competitive advantage. In August 1991, a three-member panel of GATT agreed with Mexico, ruling that the U.S. embargo on Mexican tuna caught with dolphin-unsafe nets was an unfair trade barrier.[20] The rationale for the ruling was that "a country may not discriminate against a product based on the way it is produced or harvested, only on the condition of the final product itself."[21] In other words, the tuna was safe for consumers and could not be subject to restriction.

The debates regarding whether or not regional trade such as that envisaged by the North American Free Trade Agreement (NAFTA) can be associated with national environmental protection laws or regulations can often be intense and occasionally contradictory. Daniel Magraw, for example, who states that "environmental considerations played a critical role in the formulation of the North American Free Trade Agreement (NAFTA) and its related agreements and activities," concludes, somewhat optimistically, by suggesting that "NAFTA's normative and institutional innovations, if adequately funded and effectively implemented, will build a pattern of cooperation on international environmental issues and raise expectations about what is possible and appropriate."[22] Yet, within the same journal, Steve Charnovitz offers a very different point of view when he writes:

> Does NAFTA establish tight regional pollution standards? No, NAFTA does not set any environmental standards. Does NAFTA require nations to adhere to environmental treaties the same way it requires nations to adhere to intellectual property treaties? No, it does not. Does NAFTA forbid any environmentally insensitive trade? No again.[23]

Nonetheless, one could argue, as C. Ford Runge does, that without NAFTA, Mexico, Canada, and the United States would not have committed themselves to environmental improvements. In Mexico, an attempt to protect the environment had already been made with the enactment of the 1988 General Law for Ecological Equilibrium and Environmental Protection. As Runge explains, "[U]nder this law, companies seeking to begin operations or make significant changes to their factories must obtain permission from the Secretariat of Social Development (SEDESOL)."[24] Unfortunately, owing to limited financial resources, SEDESOL (founded in 1992) has not been able to enforce environmental legislation. Over the years, this inability to enforce national environmental laws has led to the notorious reputation of *maquiladoras*. In an attempt to prevent *maquiladora* factories from allowing their toxic wastes to enter sewage plants without treatment, SEDESOL began in 1991 to require factories with poor environmental records to post performance bonds.[25] Although it is uncertain whether the U.S. EPA will be able to require Mexican firms to stop polluting streams that flow northward to the United States, the creation on December 29, 1994, of a Secretariat for the Environment, National Resources and Fishing (Secretariá de Medio Ambiente, Recursos Naturales y Pesca, or SEMARNAP) is encouraging news and would indicate that Mexico is committed to its quinquennial national environmental development plan (1995–2000).[26] Finally, one should also note that on January 30, 1996, the Confederation of Industry Chambers of Mexico (CONCAMIN), the United States Council for International Business (USCIB), and the Canadian Council for International Business (CCIB) signed a trilateral memorandum of understanding (MOU) that advocates, among other things, sound management practices, information exchange across borders, and improved environmental education and training. Of particular significance to ISO 14000 advocates is the recognition by the Commission for Environmental Cooperation of the need to promote better understanding of the ISO 14000 series in North America as well as the need to address the important issue of cross-border recognition of ISO 14001 audits.[27]

## Conclusion

Obviously, if we wish to see environmental issues effectively connected with international trade, we may need to look beyond the many regional and international treaties. A partial answer to the many questions raised by a global concern for the environment may be provided by an international organization with experience in dealing with the international business community, a community that values the need to delicately balance the demands of an increasingly competitive world market against the constraints of international and national environmental policies. The International Organization for Standardization (ISO), which recently began to publish its series of standards on environmental management systems, known as ISO 14000, could become the de facto international standard for environmental management.

## Notes

1. Jonathan Lash and David Buzzelli, "The President's Council on Sustainable Development," *Environment* 37, no. 3 (April 1995): 44–45.
2. Eco-Peace was founded on December 7, 1994, by environmental nongovernmental organizations in Egypt, Israel, Jordan, and Palestine. Ecoindustrial parks are designed to

link a variety of manufacturing and service businesses into an industrial ecosystem. As of early 1995, the best-known example of an ecopark was in Kalundborg, Denmark. Information on ecoparks was provided by Ron Mader of Austin, Texas.

3. Joel Makower, *The E-Factor: The Bottom-line Approach to Environmentally Responsible Business* (New York: A Plume Book, 1994), p. 71. Even the FBI is involved with the EPA. Makower reports that the SEC will want to make sure that companies make appropriate disclosures about liability. The EPA and OSHA share information about potential environmental and health and safety problems, and the IRS wants to make sure that punitive sanctions are not deducted as business deductions.

4. Jonathan King, *Troubled Water* (Emmaus, Pa.: Rodale Press, 1985), pp. 31, 34–35, and 45.

5. Edward F. Hayes, "What's A City to Do?" *EPA Journal*, January/February/March 1993, p. 49. For a brief discussion on risk assessment, see Dorothy E. Patton, "The ABCs of Risk Assessment," *EPA Journal*, January/February/March 1993, pp. 10–13; Robert J. Scheuplein, "Uncertainty and the 'Flavors' of Risk," pp. 16–17; and Wendy Cleland-Hamnett, "The Role of Comparative Risk Analysis," pp. 18–23, in the same issue.

6. Joel Makower, for example, tells of a similar story relating to CERCLA (The Comprehensive Environmental Response, Compensation, and Liability Act). Amendments to CERCLA are known as the SARA, or Superfund Act. CERCLA refers to those who are found to have contributed hazardous waste as "potential responsible parties," or PRPs. The liability is deemed to be retroactive without limit. A small company had sold a transformer with a small amount of PCB (a well-known hazardous waste) for $10,000. Twelve years later, the company found itself dragged in by SARA as a PRP. The fine was set at $250,000. *The E-Factor*, pp. 82–83. The legal scholar Christopher Stone would probably disagree with my conclusion. Referring to the situation in the 1970s, Stone suggests that federal agencies such as the EPA

> all show evidence (the more so as they age) of protecting the industries they are supposed to regulate, rather than the public. . . . The agencies do not as a whole seem capable of developing consistent policies; they are often ineffective, and, if rarely corrupt, more than occasionally subject to influence peddling.

Christopher D. Stone, *Where the Law Ends: The Social Control of Corporate Behavior* (New York: Harper & Row, 1975), p. 107. In 1995, a television investigative report found that OSHA only rarely cited companies.

7. Stone, citing California Insurance Code §735.5 in *Where the Law Ends*, p. 151. Stone's suggestions, made in the mid-1970s, were perhaps too innovative for the time. For example, he suggested that the punishment system should be not only product-oriented but also task-oriented. In order to achieve that objective, Stone suggested that since "the law establishes job definitions for critical offices, then liabilities should be attached for the inadequate performance of those functions." Stone, p. 190. Similar (but very few) scenarios were advanced during the mid-1990s.

8. Ralph Nader's views are expressed in his "The Management of Environmental Violence," in Anthony B. Wolbarst, ed., *Environment in Peril* (Washington, D.C.: Smithsonian Institution Press, 1991), pp. 1–15. Barry Commoner's philosophy can be found in his "The Failure of the Environmental Effort," also in *Environmental Peril*, p. 41, as well as in his books. See *The Closing Circle* (New York: Alfred P. Knopf, 1971) and *Making Peace with Nature* (New York: Pantheon Books, 1990).

9. Al Gore, *Common Sense Government Works Better and Costs Less* (New York: Random House, 1995), p. 58.

10. The *Global 2000 Report* (to the Carter Administration), issued in 1980, could be considered the first national environmental policy; however, the plan was ignored in the United States soon after President Carter's electoral defeat. Although Canada officially abandoned its green plan in 1995, many of the plan's principles, such as the Environmental Effects Monitoring (EEM) program, have survived. New Zealand's Resource Management Act of 1991, which helped New Zealand consolidate its national environmental policy, is

the core legislation designed to achieve the sustainable management of New Zealand's natural and physical resources. Singapore's green plan was issued in 1992, and its implementation began in 1993.

11. Huey D. Johnson, *Green Plans: Greenprints for Sustainability* (Lincoln: University of Nebraska Press, 1995), pp. 14–15.
12. Ministry of Housing, Physical Planning and Environment, Department for Information and International Relations, *National Environmental Plan: To Choose or to Lose* (The Hague: SDU Publishers, August 1991), pp. 15 and 17.
13. Quoted from *The State of Canada's Environment* (Ottawa: Government of Canada, 1991), pp. 27–13. See, however, Tables 6-11 and 6-12 for examples of financial indicators of sustainability. Recognizing the need to monitor and assess ecosystems, Environment Canada established in April 1994 the Ecological Monitoring and Assessment Network (EMAN), a national network that connects the Ecological Science Cooperatives (ESCs) operating across Canada. One of EMAN's primary activities is to set up a national network of ecologically representative sites for monitoring ecological functions over long periods of time. EMAN does not set environmental indicators.
14. Four documents totaling over 500 pages were issued. They are entitled *National Environmental Plan: To Choose or to Lose, The Netherlands' Environmental Policy Plan 2, Report, Recommendations on and Responses to the NEPP,* and *National Environmental Policy Plan Plus.*
15. *The Netherlands' Environmental Policy Plan 2.*
16. *The Netherlands' Environmental Policy Plan 2,* p. 68.
17. Huey D. Johnson. *Green Plans: Greenprints for Sustainability,* p. 93. Canada'a green plan is reviewed by Johnson in his Chapter 6, pp. 88–102. See also *The State of Canada's Environment* (Ottawa: Government of Canada, 1991), pp. 4–24, and others. One would like to see how Canada integrates its environmental policy for sustainability with the current clear-cut practices found in provinces such as British Columbia. For numerous examples of clear-cutting in North America, see Bill Duvall, ed., *Clearcut: The Tragedy of Industrial Forestry* (Sierra Club Books/Earth Island Press, 1993).
18. Daniel Vogel, "Environmental Policy in Europe and Japan," in Norman J. Vig and Michael E. Kraft, *Environmental Policies in the 1990s* (Washington D.C.: CQ Press, 1990), p. 272.
19. Other countries were to follow: Canada, Japan, Norway, Finland, and Sweden adopted similar programs during the 1980s. France introduced its NF (Normes Françaises) environment marking in early 1992. However, contrary to the practices of other countries, the NF environment marking can be issued only by the French Association for Normalization (AFNOR), which requires that an audit of each facility be conducted. The company must also submit a sample to AFNOR for testing and possible eventual certification. See Jean-Paul Meyronneinc, *Le management de l'environnement dans l'entreprise* (1995), pp. 114–15. Japan's ecolabeling is probably the least stringent of all, which may explain how Japan was able to label over 3,500 products in less than two years.
20. Andrea C. Durbin, "The North-South Divide," *Environment,* September 1995, pp. 17–20, 37–41.
21. Ibid., p. 19. Durbin lists many other examples of North-South distrust.
22. Daniel Magraw, "NAFTA's Repercussions: Is Green Trade Possible?" *Environment,* March 1994, pp. 14 and 43.
23. Steve Charnovitz, "NAFTA's Environmental Significance," *Environment,* March 1994, p. 42. See also Charnovitz's informative "Regional Trade Agreements," *Environment,* July/August 1995, pp. 16–20, 40–45.
24. C. Ford Runge, *Freer Trade, Protected Environment: Balancing Trade Liberalization and Environmental Interests* (New York: Council on Foreign Relations Press, 1994), pp. 61–63.
25. One should also note that several nongovernmental organizations (NGO) with interests in preserving the environment are beginning to emerge throughout the world. In Mexico, for example, the Centro Mexicano de Derecho Ambiental (CEMDA) was formally launched in October 1993. Similar NGOs are operating in Brazil, Argentina, Pakistan,

the Czech Republic, and Slovakia. Information obtained from the Center for International Environmental Law (CIEL) at the American University, Washington College of Law.
26. Moreover, the current efforts of the Commission for Environmental Cooperation (CEC) suggest that a common concern for the environment will be addressed. Unfortunately, the State of the North American Environment Report will not be released until 1997.
27. Information extracted from the Commission for Environmental Cooperation (CEC) Internet Web site. CEC headquarters are located in Montreal, Quebec.

# Part II

# The ISO 14001 Standard for Environmental Management

Defending the need for environmental management, Christopher Stone some years ago, in his typical visionary style, made an interesting argument. Stone observed that since the actions of corporations "are highly charged with a public interest, they should be scrutinized the way commercial lenders scrutinize a borrower before granting a loan." Why not link loans, proposed Stone, to environmental requirements or at least to environmental responsibility?[1] Stone's suggestion has since been proposed numerous times. Indeed, many commercial lenders (here and abroad) routinely investigate potential borrowers for possible environmental liabilities before granting a loan. As environmental responsibilities become increasingly linked to financial responsibilities and liabilities, it is reasonable to expect that, within a few years, organizations wishing to apply for commercial loans may be required to show their ISO 14001 certificate. This section presents the ISO 14001 standard for environmental management and explores some of the likely scenarios that may unfold and in some cases are already happening in certain countries.

Chapter 3 defines environmental management and explains in some detail the ISO 14001 standard. The international standard is also compared to two environmental programs. Chapter 4 offers some suggestions on how to implement ISO 14001 and concludes by asking some unresolved questions relating to ISO 14001 certification.

## Note

1. Christopher Stone, *Where the Law Ends: The Social Control of Corporate Behavior* (New York: Harper & Row, 1975), p. 197. The late Dr. Alberto Kattan of Argentina, in the early 1980s, promoted ideas very similar to Stone's when he proposed that citizens had the right to act as legal owners of the public domain.

# 3

# Environmental Management and the ISO 14001 Standard

## What Is Environmental Management?

Over the years, countless definitions of the terms *environmental management* and *environmental management system* have been proposed. Comparing these definitions, one notices some similarities but also significant differences in tone and/or emphasis. For example, the international standard on environmental management, ISO 14001, offers the following definition:

*environmental management system* That part of the overall management system which includes organizational structure, planning activities, responsibilities, practices, procedures, processes and resources for developing, implementing, achieving, reviewing and maintaining the environmental policy.

If we contrast the above definition with those included in the French standard, NF X 30-200, *Système de management environnemental* (1994), one notices some significant differences. The NF X 30-200 offers the following definitions:

*environmental management* The set of managerial activities which defines the environmental policy, objectives and responsibilities and which implements these activities by means of planning for environmental objectives, measurement of results and the control of environmental effects.

43

*Note 1:* Environmental management is the responsibility of all levels of management but must be driven by executive management. The implementation implicates everyone throughout the organization.

*Note 2:* Environmental management must particularly account for economic and social aspects.

*environmental management system*   The set of organizational responsibilities, procedures, processes and necessary means to implement the environmental policy.[1]

The similarities between the two definitions are apparent and yet one certainly notices the difference in tone and emphasis. The French definition includes measurement as an integral part of the definition. It also refers (in Note 1) to the need for executive management to drive the process. Notice also that the words *environmental policy* are repeated in the French definition of environmental management system. These subtle and perhaps important distinctions also extend to the definition of environmental policy. As far as the ISO 14001 standard is concerned, an environmental policy is a "statement by the organization of its *intentions* and principles in relation to its overall environmental performance which provides a framework for action and for the setting of its environmental objectives and targets." The French standard goes beyond this, and, in fact, carefully avoids the use of the word *intentions*.

*environmental policy (NF X 30-200)*   Goals and general objectives of an entity concerning the environment as formally expressed by executive management. The environmental policy is an element of the general policy. It is understood that the environmental policy will *respect* relevant environmental legislation and regulations.[2]

The reader will note the important difference between the two definitions. ISO 14001 speaks of *intentions;* NF X 30-200 goes beyond by insisting that the environmental policy will *respect* relevant legislation and regulations. We will explore later the significance of such distinctions.

Yet, despite their respective strengths, the above definitions still feel somewhat incomplete. Indeed, one must go back to the early 1980s, in an age when few dared challenge the rationality of regulatory enforcement, to find perhaps one of the most complete definitions of an environmental management system:

An *environmental management system* is the framework for or method of guiding an organization to achieve and sustain performance in accordance with established goals and in response to constantly changing regulations, social, financial, economic, and competitive pressures, and environmental risks. When operating effectively, a corporate environmental management system provides management and the board of directors with the knowledge that

> The corporation is in compliance with federal, state, and local environmental laws and regulations.
>
> Policies and procedures are clearly defined and promulgated throughout the organization.
>
> Corporate risks resulting from environmental risks are being acknowledged and brought under control.
>
> The company has the right resources and staff for environmental work, is applying those resources and is in control of its future.[3]

The definition concludes by stating that the environmental management system provides a basis for guiding, measuring, and evaluating performance to ensure that "a company's operations are carried out in a manner consistent with a support of applicable regulations and corporate policy." Although it is true that the above definition is longer than the definitions offered by ISO 14001 or the French standard (NF X 30-200), it nevertheless encompasses all the key elements of an environmental management system.

Yet, despite the apparent completeness of this definition, one senses that something is still missing. The missing element is wonderfully captured in the definition found within the pages of the Dutch green plan given in Chapter 2 and well worth repeating here.

> The main objective of environmental management is to preserve the environment's carrying capacity for the sake of sustainable development. The carrying capacity of the environment is damaged if, as a consequence of environmental quality, irreversible effects can occur within the time lapse of one generation; effects such as death or diseases among humans, exposure to serious nuisance and harm to well-being, the extinction of plant and animal species, soil fertility or the cultural heritage, and impediments to land use and economic development.
>
> Environmental management involves preventing or abating the undesired effects of human activities or operations. Human

activities or activities which can cause such effects are called sources. Sources and effects are linked together by chains of cause and effect: emissions of substances and waste streams, dispersion in the environment, changes in environmental quality and the resulting changes in the health of human beings, animals, plants and ecosystems. The effect can occur on various levels of scale: local, regional, fluvial, continental and global.[4]

Before comparing the Dutch definition of environmental management to the others cited, it is important to note that the Dutch definition is a national policy statement within which Dutch firms must align their own corporate environmental policy statements. Having noted that distinction, there are nonetheless several aspects of the Dutch (national) definition that distinguish it from the others. First of all, the Dutch definition extends to a sustainable development of the ecosphere, which includes far more activities than those suggested within the somewhat reductionist perspective of an environmental management philosophy construed from the point of view of a private or public organization operating within a limited geographical environment. The environmental scope envisioned by the Dutch is broader. As far as the Dutch are concerned, we should consider not only human beings but also plants and animals and the ecosystem in general. Consequently, environmental management goes beyond the limited, though valuable, perspective of pollution prevention and includes issues of soil conservation, sustainable exploitation of forests, stream sedimentation control, and many other environmentalist goals not usually considered by a company's environmental engineer. An example of a global environmental management issue of importance to the Dutch government is the international certification of timber. The Dutch National Environmental Policy Plan specifies that, "In consequence of the tropical timber covenant, the Netherlands will advocate an international system for the certification of sustainability produced tropical hard wood" (227).

To the Dutch, environmental management is more than the *intention* of an organization to satisfy its environmental objectives and targets (ISO 14001). The Dutch speak of sustainable development and of environmental quality that may affect the well-being of the cultural heritage and the ecosystem. To the Dutch, the responsibility of environmental management goes beyond merely local needs; it is intrinsically linked to environmental effects on "various levels of scale," from the local to the global. These objectives and responsibilities are clearly stated throughout the Dutch national green plan, and it may well be several decades before the same sense of global commitment toward the ecosphere is recognized and practiced by other nations.

## The ISO 14001 Standard

Most individuals familiar with the ISO 9000 series of standards will recognize that although not perfect, the ISO 14001 standard and its associated appendix is less ambiguous and more concise than the ISO 9001 standard. Certainly, improvements will no doubt be made over the next few years. Still, one of the unfortunate aspects of the ISO 14000 series of standards is that it will eventually consist of one standard, 14001, with some twenty or more (as of 1996) guidelines (see Table 3-1). This rather unappealing inclination to proliferate documents, probably inherited from the ISO 9000 series, which began with five documents and now consists of nearly two dozen guidelines, has been the focus of some criticism on the part of many observers and may in the long run turn out to be the Achilles' heel of the ISO 9000/14000/(others to come) series of standards. Aware of this problem, some members of the technical committees are currently attempting to redirect the emphasis away from document/guidelines proliferation. Let us hope they are successful.

Of the twenty or so documents that will eventually comprise the ISO 14000 series over the next two to three years, the ISO 14001 standard, *Environmental Management Systems—Specification with Guidance for Use,* is the most important because it is the reference standard to be used by organizations wishing to have their environmental management systems officially certified/registered by a third-party registration body. Issued in 1996 and derived from the British Standards Institution's 7750 document entitled *Environmental Management System* (1992), the ISO 14001 standard traces its heritage to earlier environmental management systems developed in the United States during the late 1970s and early 1980s (see Chapter 1).[5]

The standard is based on the fundamental concepts of quality assurance and total quality management (TQM) developed over the past several decades and summarized in the successful ISO series of quality assurance and management standards known as the ISO 9000 series (issued in 1987 and revised in 1994).[6]

One can approach the ISO 14001 standard from two distinct, but not necessarily opposing, vantage points: the engineering approach and the environmentalist/ecologist approach. The engineering approach

**Table 3-1.** The ISO 14000 series.

**ISO 14001:** Environmental Management Systems—Specification with Guidance for Use

**ISO 14004:** Environmental Management Systems—General Guidelines on Principles, and Supporting Techniques

**ISO 14010:** Guidelines for Environmental Auditing—General Principles of Environmental Auditing

**ISO 14011/1:** Guidelines for Environmental Auditing—Auditing Procedures

**ISO 14012:** Guidelines for Environmental Auditing—Qualification Criteria for Environmental Auditors

**ISO 14013:** Management of Environmental Audit Programs

**ISO 14014:** Initial Reviews

**ISO 14015:** Environmental Site Assessments

**ISO 14020:** Environmental Labeling—General Principles

**ISO 14021:** Terms and Definitions for Self-Declaration Environmental Claims

**ISO 14022:** Environmental Labeling—Symbols

**ISO 14023:** Environmental Labeling—Testing and Verification Methodologies

**ISO 14024:** Environmental Labeling—Guiding Principles, Practices and Criteria for Multiple Criteria-Based Practitioner Programs—Guide for Certification Procedures

**ISO 14031:** Evaluation of the Environmental Performance

**ISO 14040:** Environmental Management—Life-Cycle Assessment—Principles and Guidelines

**ISO 14041:** Environmental Management—Life-Cycle Assessment—Goal and Definitions/Scope and Inventory Analysis

**ISO 14042:** Environmental Management—Life-Cycle Assessment—Life-Cycle Impact Assessment

**ISO 14043:** Environmental Management—Life-Cycle Assessment—Interpretation

**ISO 14050:** Terms and Definitions—Guide on the Principles for ISO/TC207/SC6 Terminology Work

**ISO 14060:** Guide for the Inclusion of Environmental Aspects in Product Standard

may tend to favor a mechanical implementation methodology, which is likely to emphasize the regulatory aspect of environmental management. The engineering approach is also likely to "throw best available technology" at every environmental problem and/or regulatory requirement. This approach has its merits but is not well suited to addressing the need for pollution prevention. The environmentalist/ecologist approach is more likely to focus on the need to develop and implement an environmental policy that would not only acknowledge the value of "best technology" but also emphasize the importance of material substitution (whenever possible), process improvement/optimization, and waste and pollution reduction and eventual elimination. I favor this second approach.

To better understand the fundamental premise of the ISO 14001 standard, one must read the standard from the perspective of total quality environmental management (TQEM). In the world of TQEM, one does not view CEOs within the usual but limited meaning of chief executive officers but, rather, within the broader context of chief *environmental* officers. Viewed from a TQEM perspective, environmental management takes on a different meaning. As Joel Makower so aptly observes: "Considering that waste and pollution are defects (in that they result from inefficiencies in the system), it follows that an ultimate goal of environmental quality is to achieve zero waste and pollution."[7] These objectives are certainly in line with the fundamental premise of the ISO 14001 standard.

## Scope of ISO 14001

In an attempt to classify the different types of pollution, I. Mieck identified several stages and causes of pollution: *pollution microbienne,* caused by bacteria living and developing in decaying materials; *pollution artisanale,* associated with small handicraft industries such as tanneries, potteries, and workshops; *pollution industrielle,* involving large-scale regional pollution; *pollution fondamentale,* which affects large regions; *pollution foncière,* typically created by agrobusinesses as they apply fertilizers, pesticides, herbicides, and biocides; and, finally, *pollution accidentale,* or unforeseen pollution caused by oil supertankers or nuclear accidents such as the Chernobyl disaster. When viewed within the context of Mieck's typology, one could propose that the ISO 14001 standard applies to the broad range of pollution and environmental management stretching from *artisanale* through agricultural *(foncière)* pollution.[8] In other words, ISO 14001 applies to all companies large and small, and its geographical scope could, in the case of multinationals (or so-called transnational corporations), extend to several regions.

## ISO 14001: What It Is and Is Not

One valuable feature of the ISO 14001 standard is that it includes a good, informative annex. In an attempt perhaps to avoid earlier misinterpretations regarding the purpose of guidelines, so prevalent with the ISO 9000 series, the opening paragraph of the annex (Annex A: Guidance on the Use of the Specification) is careful to point out that the annex "does not add to or subtract from the content of" the standard. In other words, the annex is nothing more than a supporting document written for the purpose of clarifying the standard.

As for the purpose and scope of the ISO 14001 standard, it is stated within the first two opening sections: "Introduction" and "Scope." Not surprisingly, the scope of 14001 is very broad and is intended for "all types and sizes of organizations." In the event that the reader may have missed the point, the following sentence is repeated:

The standard is applicable to *any* organization that wishes to:

a) implement, maintain and improve an environmental management system;

b) assure itself of its conformance with its stated environmental policy;

c) demonstrate such conformance to others;

d) seek certification/registration of its environmental management system by an external organization;

e) make a self-determination and declaration of conformance with this international standard.

Having defined ISO 14001's all-encompassing scope, the opening paragraphs emphasize the following general objectives:

▶ The overall aim of the standard is to support environmental protection in balance with socio-economic needs.
▶ The environmental management system can be integrated with other management requirements as found in the ISO 9000 series, for example.

▶ The standard contains only those system elements that may be objectively audited for certification/registration purposes *and/or self-declaration purposes.*[9]

▶ The standard requires an organization to formulate an environmental policy, and set objectives taking into account legislative requirements and information about significant environmental impacts. Besides complying with applicable legislation and regulations, the organization must also demonstrate its commitment to continuous improvement (as it relates to environmental issues and policies).

▶ In order to achieve environmental objectives, the environmental management system should encourage organizations to consider implementation of *best available technology* where appropriate and where economically viable. The cost-effectiveness of such technology should be fully taken into account.

*What the Standard Is* Not

▶ The standard is not intended to address, and does not include requirements for, aspects of occupational health and safety management; however, it does not seek to discourage an organization from developing integration of such management system elements.

▶ The standard does not state specific environmental performance criteria.

One should also note that a vague reference to sustainable development (which is not defined) is made in the first paragraph of the standard.[10]

## A Quick Look at the Standard Through Some Key Sentences

The most frequently used verbs in the standard are *establish* and *maintain*. These verbs are invariably associated with the word *procedure*, as in "establish and maintain procedure." However, the ISO 14001 standard is significantly different from the ISO 9001, ISO 9002, or ISO 9003 standards *in that the term* documented procedure *is excluded from most paragraphs.* Although one could argue that it would be difficult to establish and maintain procedures without documenting them (thus relying on verbal means of communication, favored by most small to medium-size organizations), the obsession with documenting everything, typical of the ISO 9000 series, is, so far, nonetheless tactfully and intelligently bypassed in ISO 14001.

Exceptions to the above rule include the following:

‣ The organization shall establish and maintain *documented* environmental objectives and targets, at each relevant function and level within the organization (4.2.3, *Objectives and targets*).
‣ Roles, responsibility and authorities shall be defined, *documented* and communicated in order to facilitate effective environmental management (4.3.1, *Structure and responsibility*).
‣ The organization shall establish and maintain documented procedures to monitor and measure on a regular basis the key characteristics of its operations and activities that can have a significant impact on the environment (4.4.1, *Monitoring and measurement*).[11]

Besides the above requirements, the following "shall sentences" define the overall purpose of the standard. In the majority of cases, all "shall sentences" must be addressed, unless of course particular conditions make one or more either irrelevant or not applicable to your company. However, even in such cases, it is recommended that you briefly explain why the sentence(s) or clause(s) is/are not applicable. Before describing the requirements of each clause, let us look at what any organization *shall* have to do if it wants to implement an environmental system that will comply with the ISO 14001 standard.

An organization:

‣ *Shall define* its environmental policy.
‣ *Shall identify* the environmental aspects of its activities, products or services that it can control, . . . the training needs (of personnel), . . . those operations and activities that are associated with the identified significant environmental impacts (and plan these activities) to ensure that they are carried out under specified conditions, . . . [shall establish and maintain procedure to identify] potential for and respond to accidents and emergency situations.
‣ *Shall determine* (those activities) which can have significant impact on the environment . . . whether or not the environmental system *conforms* to planned arrangements.
‣ *Shall ensure* that these impacts are considered in setting the organization's objectives.
‣ *Shall keep* information up-to-date.
‣ *Shall consider* legal and other requirements when reviewing objectives.
‣ *Shall provide* resources essential to the implementation and control of the environmental management system.

‣ *Shall appoint* management representatives who *shall have the authority to ensure* that the environmental management system is established, implemented and maintained and who *shall report* on the performance of said system.

‣ *Shall require* that all personnel (who have an impact on the environment) shall be competent on the basis of education, appropriate training and/or experience and have received appropriate training (as required).

‣ *Shall consider* processes for external communication on its significant environmental aspects and record its decision.

‣ *Shall review and revise* emergency preparedness and response procedures.

‣ *Shall monitor and measure* the key characteristics of its operations and activities that can have a significant impact on the environment.

‣ *Shall calibrate and maintain* monitoring equipment (and maintain records).

‣ *Shall evaluate* compliance with relevant environmental legislation and regulations.

‣ *Shall take action to mitigate* any (environmental) impacts caused by nonconformances.

‣ *Shall implement and record* changes in procedures.

‣ *Shall store and disposition* records to demonstrate conformance to the requirements of this standard.

‣ (Management) *shall review* the environmental system to ensure that it is effective and address possible need for changes to policy, objectives or other elements.

## ISO 14001: Environmental Management System

The surprisingly short standard consists of only five major paragraphs, which are generally broken down into several subparagraphs. A description of each of the paragraphs follows. The association with the ISO 9001 standard is demonstrated by referring (in parentheses) to the closest ISO 9001 paragraph.

### 4.2. Environmental Policy (ISO 9001 §4.1)

This paragraph requires the organization to *define* its environmental policy. To prevent organizations from either copying someone else's environmental policy or writing flowery policies with little substance, the standard also requires that the organization *ensure* that its environmental policy satisfies several important conditions:

1. The policy must be appropriate to the nature, scale, and environmental impacts of its activities, products, or services. In other words, the environmental policy of a chemical plant that may produce several tons a day of a variety of potentially hazardous chemicals should be different in scope from the policy of a small manufacturing assembly plant that may use 50 to 100 pounds of chemicals a day.

2. In addition, a *commitment* must be stated with regard to *continuous improvement, pollution prevention, compliance with relevant environmental legislation and regulations,* or other requirements to which the organization subscribes. These requirements are rather clear: Any organization that wishes to be compliant with the ISO 14001 standard must not only ensure that it satisfies all local (national) laws and regulations; it must also apply fundamental principles of total quality management to demonstrate its commitment and/or intent to continuously improve the quality of the environment by preventing pollution. It is important to understand that an ISO 14001 audit will not be a compliance audit whose purpose is to ensure that all relevant laws are complied with. Rather, the primary task of ISO 14001 auditors will be to verify that the organization has an effective management system that conforms to ISO 14001 and is designed to ensure that all relevant local and/or national laws are adequately addressed.

3. The commitments specified in 2 must be set within well-defined *objectives and targets.* This requirement is important because it prevents organizations from making vague statements such as "we will improve our waste management program by focusing on waste reduction." The standard wants to know what your objectives are and how you will quantify these objectives so as to measure your effectiveness in achieving the goals stated in your policy (see other paragraphs below).

4. Finally, the organization's environmental policy must be *documented, implemented, maintained, and communicated* to all employees and made available to the public.

For examples of environmental policies from U.S. and foreign firms, see Appendix E.

## 4.3. Planning

### 4.3.1, Environmental Aspects (Nearly Equivalent to ISO 9001 §4.2.3)

The choice of the word *aspects* is most unfortunate because it does not convey a clear meaning. Unfortunately, by merely repeating the word *aspects,* the usually informative appendix does not, in this instance, offer much assistance. The ISO 14001 standard defines environmental aspects as the "[E]lement of an organization's activities, products or services which can interact with the environment." Unfortunately, such a broad definition may not be very helpful. Indeed, if an organization is to operate *within* a well-defined geographical boundary known as "the environment," it must, by the very nature of its existence, *interact* with that environment (air, soil, water). In turn, such (organizational-environmental) interactions are likely to lead to some form of *impact* on the environment. Nevertheless, one can deduce the probable intended meaning. The organization must *establish, document,* and *keep up-to-date* a procedure that will *identify* its activities, products, or services that can have a significant impact on the environment (e.g., air, soil, and water pollution or even noise pollution, which is generally regulated by urban zoning regulations). For countries that have environmental laws, most of these activities, products, and services have already been defined and continue to be reviewed and updated by way of a multitude of national or provincial laws, congressional acts, city or county ordinances, and myriad regulations (e.g., health and safety regulations, transportation regulations for hazardous chemicals, hazardous waste disposal, storage, etc.).

The standard contains, in my opinion, an unfortunate convoluted sentence that is likely to lead to some confusion and abuse (though the appendix tries to clarify the meaning): "The organization shall establish and maintain (a) procedures to identify the environmental aspects of its activities, products or services *that it can control and over which it can be expected to have an influence. . . .*" Who shall determine whether the organization adequately controls activities over which it is "expected to have an influence" remains to be seen.

### 4.3.2, Legal and Other Requirements (No ISO 9001 Equivalent)

This paragraph requires the organization to have a procedure that will identify or otherwise give access to legal and other requirements applicable to the environmental aspects of its activities, products, or services. This requirement simply states that it is the responsibility of an organization to ensure that it is informed as to all legal and other requirements, such as regulatory guidelines.

### 4.3.3, Objectives and Targets (No ISO 9001 Equivalent Yet)

This is one of the very few places where the word *documented* is used. The organization is required to establish and maintain *documented* environmental objectives and targets that are consistent with the environmental policy and the commitment to pollution prevention. Obviously, one effective way to satisfy this clause is to set quantifiable objectives that will be monitored and hence *measured* periodically. With regard to the setting of environmental objectives, the standard seems oddly timid in its approach, for it requires only that the organization *shall consider* legal requirements, technological options as well as financial, operational, and business requirements, "and the views of interested parties." In fact, the explanatory notes associated with this paragraph (found in the appendix) emphasize, oddly enough, that organizations are not obliged to use environmental cost-accounting methodologies, the very tool that can be most helpful in cases of financial cost assessment! (See Chapter 6 for a discussion on environmental cost accounting.)

The use of metrics or indices (also known as *performance goals*) is not new to companies. Some years ago, the Polaroid Corporation developed a toxic use and waste reduction (TUWR) index to measure its "green performance." The TUWR index takes into account not only toxic use and waste reduction but also the consumption of energy and water, pollution from electricity use, and lower impacts gained from greener product design. Thorn EMI, a music and electronics giant based in London, also establishes green targets and monitors progress toward those targets for each of its business groups. In its 1993 environmental report, "the company promised a 15 percent to 20 percent cutback in energy consumption for its Canadian music unit."[12] The multinational Du Pont has set a dozen environmental performance goals to be achieved by certain target dates.[13] The use of so-called green metrics, such as cardboard recycling, food composting, reduced electrical consumption (energy conservation), and collecting and monitoring of surface water, to monitor environmental objectives has also been successfully applied by grocery stores such as Larry's Market in Seattle, Washington.[14]

### 4.3.4, Environmental Management Programs (Similar to ISO 9001 §4.2.3)

Once objectives and targets have been set, a process of implementation must follow. The standard wants to know how the policy and its objectives will be implemented, what the time frame is, what individuals and/or functions will have the responsibility for managing, reviewing, and planning the whole environmental program from design activities to materials acquisitions, storage and disposal, and production and/or servicing. This would include new activities such as the construction of a new plant and the eventual decommission of activities.

## 4.4 Implementation and Operation

### 4.4.1, Structure and Responsibility (ISO 9001 §4.1.2)

This paragraph is very similar to the resource and management responsibilities paragraphs found in the ISO 9000 series. The organization must define, document, and communicate to all necessary parties who has the responsibility and authority to implement and control all aspects of the environmental management system. In addition, a manager must be appointed to ensure that the *performance* of the environmental management system, as defined per ISO 14001, is maintained and duly reported to upper management for review.[15]

### 4.4.2, Training, Awareness, and Competence (ISO 9001 §4.18)

All personnel whose work may potentially affect the environment must receive appropriate training to ensure that they are competent. Competency may be determined on the basis of education, appropriate training (in-house or public seminars, for example), and/or job experience. The training must be proceduralized to ensure that everyone is made aware of the importance of conforming to the environmental policy and procedures. In addition, all staff concerned with environmental matters must also be made aware of three things:

1. The actual or potential impact of their work activities
2. Their role and responsibility in abiding by procedures defined in the environmental management system, including emergency preparedness and response requirements
3. The potential consequences of departing from specified operating procedures

Records of all training activity will have to be maintained. In the United States, the above requirements should be relatively easy to satisfy. OSHA's requirements specified in 29 CFR 1910.119 (see Table 3-2) mandate that companies have programs in place to manage process hazards. Over the past two to three years, hundreds of chemical companies have trained thousands of their employees in health and safety measures, hazardous chemical management procedures, and hazard evaluation procedures/operations, etc. (see Chapter 8).

**Table 3-2.** A sample of record keeping for U.S. environmental compliance.

**Clean Water Act** permit records: 3 years from date of sampling, measurement, report, or application (40 CFR 122.41 (j)(2)).*

**Clean Air Act** continuous emissions monitoring records: 2 years from the date of reporting for all measurements, source testing, performance evaluations, calibration checks, adjustments, and maintenance (40 CFR 60.7 and 60.13).

**Resource Conservation and Recovery Act** (RCRA) waste manifest: 3 years from date waste was accepted by the transporter (40 CFR 262.40(a)).

**Comprehensive Environmental Response, Compensation and Liability Act** (CERCLA) emergency notification: Good practice to maintain records indefinitely.

**Emergency Planning and Community Right-to-Know Act** (EPCRA)—section 313 Toxic Release Form R reports: 3 years from date the report was due (40 CFR 372.10(a)), which is 4 years from when the releases occurred. Good practice to maintain records for additional years to document reductions or defend release increases due to production increases or changes in reporting instructions.

**Toxic Substances Control Act** (TSCA) Comprehensive Assessment Information Rule (CAIR) for importation, manufacture, or process of any of 19 substances: at least 3 years from date report is submitted (40 CFR 704.11).

**Occupational Safety and Health Administration** (OSHA)—200 recordable occupational injuries and illnesses and 101 supplementary information forms: at least 5 years from the date they cover (29 CFR 1904.5). Recommend retention to equal the life of the facility.

**OSHA employee exposure and medical records:** 30 years from date they cover (29 CFR 1919.20(d)).

SOURCE: June C. Bolstride, "Recordkeeping for Environmental Compliance," *Occupational Hazards* (May 1995), pp. 77–79.
*Numbers in parentheses refer to the U.S. Code of Federal Regulations (CFR). 40 CFR means Title 40 of the Code of Federal Regulations, which is the codification of the general and permanent rules published in the *Federal Register* by the executive departments and agencies of the federal government.

## 4.4.3, Communications (No ISO 9001 Equivalent)

With regard to the environmental system and so-called environmental aspects (that is, organizational activities "which can interact with the environment"), a procedure will have to be established to define how the organization communicates information internally among various functions. In addition, the procedure must define how the organization receives, documents, and responds to relevant (environmentally related) requests from external interested parties such as public authorities or citizen groups. An example of issues that could be addressed in this paragraph is how the organization communicates with public authorities on matters regarding emergency planning. Records of decisions will have to be kept (perhaps in the form of minutes or formal interdepartmental communications).

### 4.4.4, Environmental Management Systems Documentation

This paragraph merely states that the environmental management system that describes how various documents are interrelated must be documented either on paper or in electronic form.

### 4.4.5, Document Control (ISO 9001 §4.5)

This paragraph mimics clause 4.5, *Document and data control,* of the ISO 9001 standard (for further clarification, reference to the ISO 9001 standard might be helpful). Organizations that are already registered to one of the ISO 9000 standards will have no difficulty implementing this clause. A procedure must be established to define how documents relating to the environmental system are controlled. This means that the procedure must ensure the following:

- ‣ Documents are periodically reviewed and revised as necessary and approved by authorized personnel (one will also need to identify who has the authority to create and modify documents).
- ‣ The allocation of relevant and up-to-date documents is identified.
- ‣ Obsolete documents are reviewed for all points of issue.
- ‣ Any obsolete documents retained for legal and/or knowledge preservation purposes are suitably identified.

### 4.4.6, Operational Control (ISO 9001 §4.9)

The correspondence table found at the end of the 14001 document associates this paragraph with the following ISO 9001 paragraphs: 4.2, *Quality system procedure;* 4.3, *Contract review;* 4.4, *Design control;* 4.6, *Purchasing;* 4.7, *Control of customer-supplied product;* 4.8, *Product identifica-*

## *Example of an External Communication From Monsanto*

Monsanto recognized some time ago that people in general are not interested in parts per million of chemicals per cubic centimeters of air but, rather, want to know if and how an emission or discharge to the environment will affect their families. Therefore, in an attempt to effectively communicate with the public at large, the Monsanto Company established community advisory councils (CACs), which include, as some of their panel members, a cross section of the public (teachers, housewives, businessmen, and local politicians). In addition, Monsanto employees and plant managers receive communication training that allows them to discuss with and explain to the community what Monsanto is achieving locally and globally in terms of environmental management. Over the years, Monsanto has learned some valuable lessons on how to interact with community members. Here are some of its do's and don'ts:

- ▸ Don't preach to your audience.
- ▸ Be willing to listen to unpleasant accusations and to discuss uncomfortable issues truthfully. Avoid becoming defensive.
- ▸ Recruit participants who can be objective. In other words, do not enlist only the help of individuals who will be predisposed to a favorable view of the company.
- ▸ Encourage discussion of all subjects.
- ▸ Act on legitimate community objections. Do not seek opinions only to ignore them.

Since small to medium-size companies are not likely to have the same resources as larger corporations, they will need to adjust their efforts accordingly. The periodic publication of brochures, newsletters, or pamphlets may be an effective way to communicate with the public. In some cases, an environmental quality manual, or an abridged version of the manual, may also be used as a means to communicate with the public at large.

*tion and traceability; 4.9, Process control; 4.15, Handling, storage, packaging, preservation, and delivery;* and, *4.19, Servicing!* Although I have worked with the ISO 9001 standard for over six years, I find it difficult to agree with the correspondences given. Paragraph 4.4.6 is a very short paragraph of approximately ten lines. It is difficult to imagine that ten lines could be matched with as many as nine relatively long ISO 9001 paragraphs.

In my opinion, paragraph 4.4.6 attempts to capture the intent of paragraph 4.9, *Process control,* of ISO 9001 without duplicating the text. The result is a somewhat vague and short list of "requirements." Three major objectives must be satisfied:

1. Operational procedures must be established to prevent deviations from the environmental policy and its associated objectives and targets. In other words, one cannot have operational procedures that contradict the essence of the environmental policy and objective.

2. To satisfy 1, it is likely that "operating criteria" will have to be specified for certain procedures. In other words, operating parameters will have to be defined. This is already automatically achieved in most chemical plants, paper mills, steel plants, aluminum plants, and some foundries. These industries often rely on sophisticated and very expensive software to "run" their plants. A different scenario will have to be planned for in other industries, particularly in small manufacturing concerns that are not fully automated.

3. The standard attempts to include suppliers and contractors in the requirements stated in 1 and 2 above. The standard appears to be saying that an organization should also ensure that the procedures and/ or products provided by its suppliers and contractors do not violate its environmental policy. (See Chapter 8, particularly the HAZOP discussion, for some examples of how to address this paragraph.)

### 4.4.7, Emergency Preparedness and Response (No ISO 9001 Equivalent)

The title of this paragraph is self-explanatory. The organization must periodically test, review, and revise, as necessary, its emergency preparedness and response procedures. The purpose of these reviews is to ensure that all potential emergency situations and preventive responses have been considered (see Chapter 8 for some suggestions).

## 4.5. Checking and Corrective Action

### 4.5.1, Monitoring and Measurement (ISO 9001 §§4.10.5 and 4.11)

In order to track the performance of objectives and targets set in the environmental policy, the organization must establish and maintain a procedure to monitor, measure, and record, on a regular basis, the key characteristics of its operations and activities that have a significant impact on the environment (as defined in 4.4.6, *Operational control*). This requirement is quite logical; how else can one monitor the effective implementation of continuous environmental improvement measures?

In addition, procedural means to evaluate compliance with relevant environmental legislation and regulations must also be established (see 4.5.4, *Environmental management system audit*, for suggestions).

### 4.5.2, Nonconformance and Corrective and Preventive Action (ISO 9001 §§4.13 and 4.14)

As with all previous paragraphs, a procedure must be established defining who has responsibility and authority for investigating environmental nonconformances or, more precisely, nonconformances relating to the environmental management system (which could include, for example, accidental spills or releases, unplanned increases in waste production, etc.).

If the corrective or preventive action(s) suggest additional (or more specific) training or changes to procedures or processes (and associated training), such changes shall be implemented and recorded. Naturally, appropriate document control will follow as required. For example, obsolete procedures will have to be updated and all old documents must be either retrieved from all points of issue or updated.

### 4.5.3, Records (ISO 9011 §4.16)

Legible records of all activities relating to this international standard (i.e., ISO 14001) must be maintained to *demonstrate* conformance. A procedure will have to be written stating how records are stored, traced, disposed of, and protected against deterioration or loss. Such a procedure may already exist for companies registered to one of the ISO 9000 standards. The retention time for all records needs to be established. In the United States, the guidelines seen in Table 3-2 have been suggested.

### 4.5.4, Environment Management System Audit (ISO 9001 §4.1.3)

The International Chamber of Commerce defines an audit as

> a management tool comprising a systematic, documented, periodic and objective evaluation of how well environmental organization, management and equipment are performing with the aim of helping to safeguard the environment by: (i) facilitating management control of environmental practices; (ii) assessing compliance with company policies, which would include meeting regulatory requirements.[16]

The audit procedure must ensure that the environmental management system is periodically audited. An important difference between the 9000 series and 14001 is that, unlike the 9000 series, 14001 does *not* require that audits be "carried out by personnel independent of those having direct responsibility for the activity being audited." The purpose of environmental audits, which must be documented, is to ensure that the environmental management system addresses the requirements of the ISO 14001 standard and that it is effective. Results of these audits must be reported to management for review (see 4.5, *Management review*).

The concept of internal environmental audits has made many U.S. firms very uneasy. The general feeling is that governmental agencies such as the EPA will use the results of internal audits to assess additional fines. This is unlikely to happen, however, because under the new audit policy announced by the EPA in 1995, the EPA would offer "reduced penalties and a safe harbor from criminal referrals for companies that voluntarily disclose and fix identified violations found through auditing."[17]

### 4.6, Management Review (ISO 9001 §4.1.3)

This last paragraph is an extension of the previous one in that it requires top management to periodically review the suitability, adequacy, and effectiveness of the environmental management system. The purpose of these management reviews, which must be documented, is to assess whether or not changes need to be made to the policy, objectives, or other elements of the environmental system. The continuous improvement loop is now closed.

As one reviews the five major headings of the ISO 14001 standard, one discovers that the Plan, Do, Check, Act cycle developed by Dr. Walter Shewhart during the 1930s (and reintroduced by Dr. W. Edwards Deming during the 1950s) was adopted by contributors to the ISO 14001 standard:

| | |
|---|---|
| *4.1, general requirements.* | |
| *4.2, Policy.* | |
| *4.3, Planning:* | PLAN(P) |
| *4.4, Implementation and operation:* | DO(D) |
| *4.5, Checking and corrective action:* | CHECK(C) |
| *4.6, Management review:* | ACT(A) |

## ISO 14001: Similarity to Other Programs (Responsible Care®, CERES, and Others)

The principles stated within the ISO 14001 environmental management system are certainly not new. Most of what is contained within the standard has already been stated by others, often with greater clarity and more rigor. One could cite, for example, the ten guiding principles of the Process Safety Code of Management Practices specified by the Chemical Manufacturers Association's (CMA) Responsible Care® initiatives. The concept of formulating a set of principles designed to improve the management of chemicals was first conceived by the Canadian chemical industry in 1984. The U.S. chemical industry (as well as that of countries such as the United Kingdom and France, for example) adopted the principles in 1988, and in October 1990 the Responsible Care® initiatives were formally released. Responsible Care® was made an obligation of CMA membership, and all CMA members have pledged their support.

In reviewing the twenty-two management practices defining the Process Safety Code summarized in Table 3-3, it is easy to see the relationships with the ISO 14001 standard. And yet, despite the overlap (management's commitment, accountability, performance measurement, emergency management, employee training, incident investigation, communication), the two documents are certainly not identical. One striking difference between the two sets of documents is that the Process Safety Code does devote its Management Practice 18 to safe work practices (the reader will recall that ISO 14001 specifically states that it does not address such issues; however, it "does not seek to

**Table 3-3.** Summary of the Process Safety Code of Management Practices (corresponding ISO 14001 paragraphs listed in parentheses).

| *Management Leadership* | *Technology* |
|---|---|
| Commitment (4.2) | Design Documentation (4.4.6 — )* |
| Accountability (4.6) | Process Hazards Information |
| Performance Measurement (4.5.1) | (4.4.7 — )* |
| Incident Investigation (4.4.7 — )* | Process Hazard Analysis (4.4.7 — )* |
| Information Sharing | Management of Change |
| CAER** Integration (4.4.3 — )* | |

| *Facilities* | *Personnel* |
|---|---|
| Siting | Job Skills (4.4.2 — )* |
| Codes and Standards | Safe Work Practices (4.4.2 — )* |
| Safety Reviews | Initial Training (4.4.2 — )* |
| Maintenance and Inspection (4.5.1 | Employee Proficiencies (4.4.2 — )* |
| and 4.4.6 a) | Fitness for Duty |
| Multiple Safeguards | Contractors (4.4.6 c — )* |
| Emergency Management (4.4.7) | |

SOURCE: *Responsible Care: A Resource Guide for the Process Safety Code of Management Practices* (Chemical Manufacturers Association, Inc., 1990), pp. 2–8.
*A minus sign following the ISO 14001 paragraph number indicates that the 14001 requirement is not as demanding as the Process Safety Code. In many cases, one could infer that a requirement could be linked to a particular process safety code. Naturally, as is the case with the ISO 9000 series, interpretations will vary.
**CAER, which stands for Community Awareness and Emergency Response, involves building communication channels between industry and the public. Similar programs exist in a few other countries.

discourage an organization from developing integration of such management system elements").

Written for the chemical industry, the Process Safety Code (PSC) is much more detailed and specific. The code obviously focuses on process safety. The emphasis on training, also addressed in paragraph 4.4.2, *Training, awareness, and competence* of ISO 14001, is quite obvious when one realizes that six of the management practices (17–22) address job-related skills. For example, whereas ISO 14001 makes only a vague reference to suppliers and contractors (4.4.6, *Operational control*, subparagraph c), Management Practice 22: Contractors of the Code includes as many as twenty points that must be addressed by an organization.

Comparing Responsible Care® with ISO 14001, one must conclude that ISO 14001 is, by necessity, more generic. In other words, by being more industry-specific, the twenty-two management practices listed in Responsible Care® complement and in all cases go beyond the requirements listed in 14001, but they *do not* duplicate all requirements of the international standard. Specifically, one notes the absence of any reference to records or record retention (4.5.3 of 14001) or to the need for environmental management system audits (4.5.4). Still, if a chemical plant is ISO 9001- or 9002-registered, these activities are already performed for the maintenance of the quality assurance system and can very easily be expanded to include environmental records and auditing (which is already conducted in many plants).

## ISO 14001 and the CERES Principles

Founded in 1989, the Coalition for Environmentally Responsible Economies (CERES)[18] is a nonprofit membership organization comprised of leading social investment professionals, environmental groups, religious organizations, public pension trustees, and public interest groups. The CERES Principles, released in 1989 as the Valdez Principles, "represent a comprehensive ten-point environmental ethic devised to encourage the development of positive programs to prevent environmental degradation, assist corporations in setting policy, and enable investors to make informed decisions regarding environmental issues" (see Table 3-4).

The CERES Principles have been adopted by approximately two dozen companies. In reviewing approximately thirty CERES reports submitted by a broad range of companies ranging from Ben & Jerry's to General Motors, Sunoco, and The Body Shop (manufacturer and retailer of skin and health-care products, United Kingdom), one notices that the length and degree of completeness of these environmental reports vary greatly. Thus, although many companies attempt to answer the ninety-one questions that make up the CERES Report, some companies simply submit a brief truncated report, while others seem to rush through the report. This lack of consistency is partly owing to the fact that the CERES Report (as with ISO 14001 and other international standards) seems, inadvertently, to focus on large companies, particularly chemical or petrochemical corporations, which are very familiar with the many EPA and OSHA regulations. Not surprisingly, smaller businesses are more likely to struggle with many of the questions.

Still, when one compares the ISO 14001 standard with the CERES Principles, obvious differences in emphasis quickly become apparent. A perusal of Table 3-4 reveals that ISO 14001 emphasizes the need to

**Table 3-4.** Comparison of the CERES Principles with ISO 14001.

| CERES Principles | ISO 14001 |
|---|---|
| **Protection of the biosphere**<br>We will reduce and make continual progress toward eliminating the release of any substance that may cause environmental damage to the air, water, or the earth or its inhabitants. We will safeguard all habitats affected by our operations and will protect open spaces and wilderness, while preserving biodiversity. | Commitment to improve and even reduce pollution, but only a vague reference to sustainable development. Does not come close to the first CERES principle. |
| **Sustainable use of natural resources**<br>We will make sustainable use of renewable natural resources, such as water, soils and forests. We will conserve nonrenewable natural resources through efficient use and careful planning. | Sustainable development is mentioned in the opening paragraph (*Introduction*) only as "environmental matters including sustainable development." The term is not defined. |
| **Reduction and disposal of wastes**<br>We will reduce and where possible eliminate waste through source reduction and recycling. All waste will be handled and disposed of through safe and responsible methods. | No specific reference to wastes and their disposal, but requires that a company must specify in its policy a commitment to set objectives and targets and to reduce pollution (see 4.2 and 4.3.3). |
| **Energy conservation**<br>We will conserve energy and improve the energy efficiency of our internal operations and of the goods and services we sell. We will make every effort to use environmentally safe and sustainable energy sources. | Although a company could certainly include such requirements in its environmental policy, no specific references to energy conservation are found in the standard. |
| **Risk reduction**<br>We will strive to minimize the environment, health and safety risks to our employees and the communities in which we operate through safe technologies, facilities and operating procedures, and by being prepared for emergencies. | The standard mentions (*Introduction*) that companies should consider the use of best available technology if such technologies are cost-effective. The introduction does specify that "This standard is **not** intended to address, and does not include requirements for, aspects of occupational health and safety management." Still, paragraph 4.4.7, *Emergency preparedness and response*, addresses the issues of safety. Paragraph 4.4.3, *Communications*, addresses the need for "external communication" on "significant environmental aspects." |

*(continues)*

**Table 3-4.** *(Continued)*

| CERES Principles | ISO 14001 |
|---|---|
| **Safe products and services**<br><br>We will reduce and where possible eliminate the use, manufacture or sale of products and services that cause environmental damage or health or safety hazards. We will inform our customers of the environmental impacts of our products or services and try to correct unsafe use. | Nothing equivalent in ISO 14001; however, local or national laws generally require a manufacturer to issue or print warnings on labels. Since ISO 14001 requires companies to "comply with relevant environmental legislation and regulations," one could infer that the standard partly matches this CERES principle. Still, nothing in 14001 specifically addresses the opening sentence. |
| **Environmental restoration**<br><br>We will promptly and responsibly correct conditions we have caused that endanger health, safety or the environment. To the extent feasible, we will redress injuries we have caused to persons or damage we have caused to the environment and will restore the environment. | Nothing equivalent in ISO 14001. |
| **Informing the public**<br><br>We will inform in a timely manner everyone who may be affected by conditions caused by our company that might endanger health, safety or the environment. We will regularly seek advice and counsel through dialogue with persons in communities near our facilities. We will not take any action against employees for reporting dangerous incidents or conditions to management or to appropriate authorities. | ISO 14001 does cover some of the issues relating to this CERES principle, although not with the same emphasis. The need to communicate or inform the public is briefly referenced in 4.2, *Environmental policy*, which states that the company's environmental policy must be made available to the public. Paragraph 4.4.3, *Communications*, simply states that "The organization shall consider processes for external communication on its significant environmental aspects and record its decision." |
| **Management commitment**<br><br>We will implement these Principles and sustain a process that ensures that the Board of Directors and Chief Executive Officer are fully informed about pertinent environmental issues and are fully responsible for environmental policy. In selecting our Board of Directors, we will consider demonstrated environmental commitment as a factor. | Several paragraphs (4.2, 4.3.4, 4.4.1, 4.4.4, 4.4.4, and 4.5) cover the intent of this principle. One could say that one of the basic principles of ISO 14001 is to have a management structure/system organized to satisfy this CERES principle: management commitment and management review of the environmental system. |
| **Audits and reports**<br><br>We will conduct an annual self-evaluation of our progress in implementing these Principles. We will support the timely creation of generally accepted environmental audit procedures. We will annually complete the CERES Report, which will be made available to the public. | Paragraph 4.5.4, *Environmental management system audit*, specifically addresses this principle. However, audit results need not be made available to the public. |

satisfy legal requirements, develop procedures, and manage the environmental system—three of the ISO 14001 paragraphs have the word *management* in the heading, and reference to management is made in two more paragraphs. There is little doubt that ISO 14001 is an environmental *management* system. The CERES Principles, by contrast, recognize the importance of management, but the emphasis on "principles" makes it different from ISO 14001. Thus, whereas the CERES Principles emphasize the need for corporations to protect the earth and act responsibly toward the environment in order to allow "future generations to sustain themselves" (the Dutch would concur), the ISO 14001 standard is more business-friendly and specifies only that the "organization shall consider" the implementation of a particular point. It is evident that ISO 14001 is a compromise document written so as not to alienate the business community. There is little doubt that ISO 14001 will not satisfy most environmentalists; still, it is a good first step toward helping companies throughout the world to begin considering environmental issues. Indeed, when Anita Roddick, founder of the very successful, but in recent years much maligned, British firm The Body Shop, wrote her *Body and Soul*, she lamented that

> [T]oday's corporations have global responsibilities because their decisions affect world problems concerning economics, poverty, security and the environment. Yet while global business binds the planet in a common fate, there is no international code of practice, no agreement on mutual responsibilities. And so much *could* be done.[19]

The ISO 14001 standard *could*, if implemented responsibly, become the needed international code of practice.

## Notes

1. Definitions quoted from Jean-Paul Meyronneinc, *Le management de l'environnement dans l'entreprise* (Paris: AFNOR, 1994), pp. 210–11.
2. NF X 30-200, quoted in Meyronneinc, p. 211.
3. J. Ladd Greeno et al., *Environmental Auditing: Fundamentals and Techniques* (New York: Arthur D. Little, Inc., 1985), p. 6.
4. Second Chamber Session 1988–1989, 21 137, nos. 1–2. Reproduced in *National Environmental Plan: To Choose or to Lose* (The Hague: SDU Publishers, 1991), pp. 8–91.
5. In their eagerness to be recognized as environmental leaders, a few companies throughout the world were, as early as 1994, already achieving registration to the near equivalent, but more demanding, British Standard's Institution's 7750: *Environmental Management System* (issued in 1992). The rationale for such a strategy was that when the ISO 14001

standard was published in 1996, these "leaders" could rapidly switch, or upgrade (actually downgrade since 7750 is a bit more demanding than 14001), their BS 7750 certificate to an ISO 14001 certificate.

6. Numerous books have been written about the ISO 9000 series. My own contributions include the following titles: *ISO 9000: Preparing for Registration* (New York: Marcel Dekker ASQC Press, 1992); *Implementing the ISO 9000 Series* (New York: Marcel Dekker, 1993); *ISO 9000 and the Service Sector* (Milwaukee: ASQC Quality Press, 1994); and *ISO 9000 for Small Business* (Milwaukee: ASQC Quality Press, 1995).

7. Joel Makower, *The E-Factor: The Bottom-Line Approach to Environmentally Responsible Business* (New York: A Plume Book, 1994), pp. 6–7.

8. I. Mieck, "Reflections on a typology of historical pollution: complementary conceptions," in P. Brimblecombe and C. Pfister, eds., *The Silent Countdown* (Berlin: Springer-Verlag, 1990), pp. 73–80.

9. The value of self-declaration is questionable and it is likely that the market will request third-party certification.

10. The opening paragraph of ISO 14001 reads as follows:

    Organizations of all kinds are increasingly concerned to achieve and demonstrate sound environmental performance by controlling the impact of their activities, product or services on the environment, taking into account their environmental policy and objectives. They do so in the context of increasingly stringent legislation, the development of economic policies and other measures to foster environmental protection, and a general growth of concern from interested parties about environmental matters including *sustainable development*.

    Introduction of ISO 14001, p. 4 of ISO/DIS 14001, emphasis added.

11. The requirement for documentation was not included in the February version of the draft document, perhaps an oversight.

12. Bill Birchard, "By the Numbers," *Tomorrow*, 1995, pp. 52–53.

13. Some examples would include reducing hazardous waste by 35 percent compared to 1990 levels; reducing toxic air emissions by 60 percent compared to 1987 levels by 1993; phasing out chlorofluorocarbons (CFCs) by 2000 at the latest, etc. Bruce Smart, *Beyond Compliance: A New Industry View of the Environment* (World Resources Institute, 1992), p. 189.

14. Bryant Rogers, "Green Management Equals Profit," *Energy & Environmental Management*, 1995, no pagination.

15. Environmental performance is defined as: "Measurable results of the environmental management system, related to an organization's control of its environmental aspects, based on its environmental policy, objectives and targets." ISO 14001 definition 3.8.

16. International Chamber of Commerce, *Environmental Auditing* (Paris, 1989), quoted in David Owen, "Emerging Green Agenda: A Role for Accounting," in Denis Smith, ed., *Business and the Environment: Implications of the New Environmentalism* (New York: St. Martin's Press, 1993), p. 60.

17. "Audit Privilege Is Incentive for Enviromental Compliance," *Occupational Hazards*, May 1995, p. 98.

18. Not to be confused with the California Environmental Resources Evaluation System, also known as CERES.

19. Anita Roddick. *Body and Soul: Profits with Principles—The Amazing Success Story of Anita Roddick and The Body Shop* (New York: Crown, 1991), p. 17.

# 4

# Implementing ISO 14001 and Other Issues

One should not confuse the ISO 14001 environmental *management* system with other considerations such as technological, regulatory, and/or administrative requirements that may be associated with the management system. In other words, ISO 14001 is not about *how* a company disposes or reduces its hazardous waste or about *how* it reengineers its processes to become more environmentally efficient, and so on. Yet there are many, including environmental consulting firms, who would want to convince you otherwise. Indeed, the following quotation, found on one of the many electronic web sites available on the Internet, illustrates how dangerous misinformation can be. One section of the advertisement proclaimed the following: "We are providing input on waste minimization, waste reduction and recycling in accordance with "ISO 14000 guidance." A review of Table 3-1 will demonstrate that there is in fact no such "ISO 14000 guidance."

The ISO 14001 standard is about how an organization will implement a management structure that will ensure, among other things, that hazardous waste or chemical reduction programs will be implemented, that processes will be documented, environmental targets established and achieved, appropriate training conducted, and so on. I emphasize this fact because one can already witness a marketing process—oddly similar to what happened with the ISO 9000 series— whereby the ISO 14001 standard is becoming many things to many experts. Environmental engineers, for example, see 14001 from their perspective. Waste management engineers see it through their waste management point of view. Government officials seem to think that it will somehow help them to reduce their enforcement efforts or will assist them in their enforcement efforts. Quality assurance consultants see it as yet another means to introduce their multifaceted methodologies. Of course, all these individuals are partly correct in their interpretation(s), but the fact remains that ISO 14001 is not only about waste management or environmental auditing; it is not only about satisfying local or national environmental laws or about monitoring effluents; it is about the *management* of all these things and more.

One significant and welcome difference between ISO 9000 models and ISO 14001 is the 14001 requirement to state objectives and targets and to monitor and measure said objectives. In other words, if your environmental policy states your commitment to a reduction of 15 percent per year in volatile organic compounds emission, you had better keep records and be prepared to prove you claims quantitatively.

Organizations that are considering implementing ISO 14001 will likely discover that the amount of effort required to achieve readiness will depend on one or more of the following interrelated factors:

1. Whether the organization is already registered to one of the ISO 9000 models for quality assurance
2. Whether the organization already has a system designed to manage its chemical and toxic wastes
3. Whether the organization is a large corporation of 1,000 or more employees or a small to medium-size firm with less than 200 employees

In addition, although the overall structures of ISO 14001 management systems should be similar throughout the world, the contents and amount of detail contained within these systems will necessarily vary from country to country.

## Implementation Strategy

Organizations embarking on an ISO 14001 implementation project should not assume that much new development will be required. For some organizations, such as chemical companies belonging to the Chemical Manufacturing Association, ISO 14001 will probably be a relatively easy system to implement. Most of the management structure should already be in place. However, for many other companies, such as print shops, photo processing shops, metal treatment shops, paint shops, electronic firms, or any of the thousands of small to medium-size companies that process many chemicals but do not necessarily have an environmental management plan, ISO 14001 will naturally be more demanding, though not necessarily overwhelming.

The first task is to read the standard and, for each paragraph, determine whether or not the requirements are currently addressed. Correctly assessing the requirements is not always a simple task. People tend either to overestimate what is said in the standard or to fail to address all the requirements. For example, many companies currently have environmental policies, but few are phrased in such a way as to completely address all the requirements of paragraph 4.2 of ISO 14001 (see Appendix E for examples).

If, as is likely to be the case, a requirement is not satisfied, or is only partly satisfied, it will have to be addressed. Experience from ISO 9000 implementation would suggest that when addressing a paragraph, the user should avoid the following classic mistake:

*Do not develop an intricate procedure that reads well but is impossible or nearly impossible to maintain.* This is a typical mistake. My advice would be to develop a simple process that will help you address the intent of the standard. When writing or developing a procedure, always remember that *you will need to test the process/procedure for a few weeks.* If you follow these simple steps, you should be able to have a working process within that time frame:

1. *Make sure all responsible parties are involved.* Management must encourage operators as well as all administrative staff likely to be affected by the process/procedure.

2. *Accept all pertinent information.* At first, people will want to include all sorts of detailed information, but this will invariably lead you to develop a very complex process. Once you have what is perceived by the group to be all the pertinent information, ask the group to cut the process description in half. Repeat as needed. As you start simplifying your process you will be forced to distinguish between training issues and operational issues. One of the reasons why procedures tend to be too long and too detailed is that people do not recognize that there is no need to include information that should already be covered by training or experience. In other words, avoid writing procedures that include sentences such as, "Turn switch on. Wait one minute. Press green button. . . ." Such detailed information should either be part of the training process or a minimum requirement for operating the process.

3. *Release the procedure or process as a provisional procedure;* then wait a few weeks to see how effective it is. Do not hesitate to reduce or add text as required. Formally release the new procedure and revise periodically to ensure continuous improvement.

## Structure of the Environmental System

The structure of the environmental system will vary and depend on a few external factors. For example, the nature and extent of national environmental requirements will necessarily affect the complexity of the environmental management system. Organizations operating in countries that have already implemented green plans (the Netherlands, New Zealand, Canada, and others, but not the United States) will have to adapt and adjust their environmental system to comply with national, provincial, and state requirements. Yet, irrespective of the nature and extent of the laws and regulations, it is likely that most environmental systems will mimic the hierarchical structure found in most quality assurance systems. Depending on the size and complexity of an organization, the fundamental structure will consist of a hierarchical pyramid consisting of from three to four levels (see Figure 4-1).

There are at least three implementation scenarios to consider. One can (1) develop, in parallel, an environmental management system (EMS) totally independent of the quality assurance management system (QMS), (2) integrate the EMS within the QMS or vice versa, or (3) cross-reference the two systems as needed. Let us explore each of these scenarios.

### Parallel EMS and QMS

This scenario assumes that an organization already has an ISO 9000-type quality assurance system or something similar. One approach would be to develop an independent EMS that would parallel (and possibly duplicate) the quality assurance system. The structure of such a system is illustrated in Figure 4-2. As can be seen, this approach results in two manuals and associated substructures. The advantage of this scenario is that the QMS does not have to be modified. The possible disadvantage is that some redundancy is likely to be introduced.

### Integrated EMS and QMS

This second approach also assumes that the organization is already certified to one of the ISO 9000 standards or has a similar system. This

**Figure 4-1.** Environmental management system pyramid.

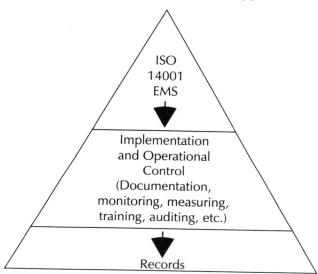

scenario takes advantage of the fact that ISO 14001 borrows extensively from the ISO 9001 standard. Rather than develop a new system, one simply integrates the EMS *within* the QMS. Naturally, in order to incorporate the ISO 14001 requirements, one would have to significantly modify the QMS. However, the two systems would be fully integrated and considered as one quality assurance (product and environment) system (see Figure 4-3).

## Cross-Referenced System

This approach is a hybrid version of the previous two scenarios in that it adopts some of the features of the parallel model and includes some features of the integrated model (see Figure 4-4). Rather than develop a completely separate system, one would cross-reference to the quality assurance system as needed. Of course, as was true for the integrated system, the QMS will have to be modified to include EMS procedures.

Although it is unlikely (as of early 1996) that an international health and occupational safety international standard will be released soon, one could nonetheless consider addressing and integrating (or developing in parallel) occupational health and work safety requirements within the EMS/QMS structure. For example, although Figures 4.1–4.4 do not

**Figure 4-2.** Parallel EMS and QMS.

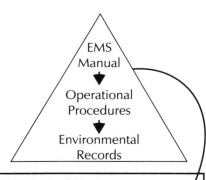

| EMS Manual / System | |
|---|---|
| 4.2 | Environmental policy |
| 4.3 | Planning |
| 4.3.1 | Environmental aspects |
| 4.3.2 | Legal and other requirements |
| 4.3.3 | Objectives and targets |
| 4.3.4 | Environmental managing programs |
| 4.4 | Implementation and operation |
| 4.4.1 | Structure and responsibility |
| 4.4.2 | Training, awareness, and competence |
| 4.4.3 | Communications |
| 4.4.4 | Environmental management system documentation |
| 4.4.5 | Document control |
| 4.4.6 | Operational control |
| 4.4.7 | Emergency preparedness and response |
| 4.5 | Checking and corrective action |
| 4.5.1 | Monitoring and measurement |
| 4.5.2 | Nonconformance and corrective and preventive action |
| 4.5.3 | Records |
| 4.5.4 | Environmental management audit |
| 4.6 | Management review |

| QMS System / ISO9001 | |
|---|---|
| 4.1 | Management responsibility |
| 4.1.1 | Quality policy |
| 4.1.2 | Organization |
| 4.1.2.1 | Responsibility and authority |
| 4.1.2.2 | Resources |
| 4.1.2.3 | Management representative |
| 4.1.3 | Management review |
| 4.2 | Quality system |
| 4.3 | Contract review |
| 4.4 | Design control |
| 4.5 | Document and data control |
| 4.6 | Purchasing |
| 4.7 | Control of customer-supplied product |
| 4.8 | Product identification and traceability |
| 4.9 | Process control |
| 4.10 | Inspection and testing |
| 4.11 | Control of inspection, measuring, and test equipment |
| 4.12 | Inspection and test status |
| 4.13 | Control of nonconforming product |
| 4.14 | Corrective and preventive action |
| 4.15 | Handling, storage, packaging, preservation, delivery |
| 4.16 | Control of quality records |
| 4.17 | Internal quality audits |
| 4.18 | Training |
| 4.19 | Servicing |
| 4.20 | Statistical techniques |

**Figure 4-3.** Integrated system blending EMS and QMS.

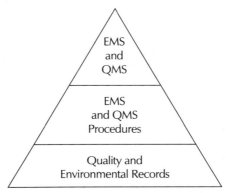

Environmental and quality policy
Responsibility and authority (4.1.2 and 4.4.1)
Management representatives (4.1.2.2 and 4.3.4)
Management review (4.1.3 and 4.6)
EMS and QMS (4.2 and 4.3)
Planning
Legal requirements
Environmental and quality objectives and targets
Contract review (4.3, –)
Design control (4.4 and 4.4.6)
Document and data control (4.5 and 4.4.5)
Purchasing (4.6, –)
Control of customer-supplied product (4.7)
Product identification and traceability (4.8;
could also be used for chemical traceability)
Process control (4.9 and 4.4.6)

*Note:* Numbers in parentheses indicate ISO 9001 and ISO 14001 paragraph references;
a dash means no equivalent paragraph in ISO 14001.

refer to health and safety issues, it would be easy to envision, using one
of the above scenarios, yet another pyramid that produced a fully
integrated environmental, safety, and product management system.

## Controlling Documents

Document control is ordinarily one of the most difficult tasks to achieve.
Fortunately, the ISO 14001 standard does not place as much emphasis

**Figure 4-4.**  Hybrid system. ·

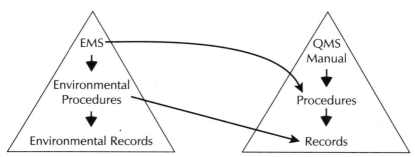

EMS in Figure 4-4 would be similar to EMS in Figure 4-2 except that
the EMS manual and lower-tier documents could cross-reference to
the quality system. For example, records for calibration of equipment
used to monitor product and environmental parameters could be
under one record system. Similarly, process parameters relating to
safety or environmental issues could also be included in procedures.
The EMS would cross-reference to the QMS as required. This system
could be perceived as an addendum to the QMS.

on the need to document procedures; however, the need to control
documents (but not data, as in ISO 9001 or ISO 9002) is clearly specified
in paragraph 4.4.5 of ISO 14001. Thanks to the use of computers,
the control of documents can be a relatively easy task to achieve.
Unfortunately, most everyone has had a very hard time controlling
printed copies. One does not need to develop elaborate systems. Fur-
thermore, one does not need to purchase overpriced and overpowered
software packages to control documents. All word processing packages
do provide adequate document control options for most companies.
The software on which this book was written allows me to insert
information such as title of the document, author's name, version,
keywords, and a couple of other items. I can also search (find) or save
documents using any one of these keywords. Moreover, documents can
be easily controlled using these basic features. There is no need to
complicate the obvious. Companies that have their computers connected via a local area network or a wide area network can provide
"read only" access to anyone who needs to read pertinent information.
"Write" privileges, that is, permission to alter documents, would be
given to a select group of individuals who have the authority and
responsibility to change documents. (See Appendix F for an example of
an environmental management manual.)

## ISO 14001: Other Issues to Consider

Before analyzing some of the strengths of ISO 14001, let us first examine some of its potential and current limitations. When I first read the standard, one of the items that attracted my attention was the requirement for an organization to "comply to relevant environmental legislation and regulations" (repeated in paragraph 4.3.2, *Legal and other requirements*). This requirement certainly makes sense for countries that have environmental legislation, but what about the majority of countries that either do not have such laws or, even when they do have environmental laws, cannot or do not enforce them because of lack of resources or political authority? The situation is even more complicated when developing countries have written unenforceable laws. Some of the difficulties surrounding the subject of environmental legislation in developing countries have been addressed by Eugene Gibson and Faith Halter, who explain that in many developing countries "deficiencies in the design and implementation of environmental laws constitute a major hurdle to environmental protection and sound natural management."[1] Part of the problem, which is complex, is that when developing countries adopt, via the mechanism of international conventions, international environmental laws such as the Convention for the Prevention of the Pollution of the Sea or the Convention on International Trade in Endangered Species, they do not enact the necessary corresponding domestic legislation. If domestic legislation does exist, it is usually not enforced. The problem is further exacerbated when developing countries adopt environmental laws developed in the industrialized world. Gibson and Halter argue that the adoption of so-called goal-oriented, or umbrella, laws that cover every imaginable issue should be avoided because such laws fail to set workable near-term goals and priorities usually addressed by "implementation-oriented" laws. As Gibson and Halter explain, implementation-oriented laws "should provide explicit direction to the implementation agencies in regard to such matters as assigning institutional responsibilities and clarifying the role of customary law, if any."[2] A specific example of the difficulties mentioned by Gibson and Halter is Mexico's experience with hazardous waste disposal. Despite great advances in developing environmental laws over the past decade, significant difficulties still exist because, as the director of the hazardous waste division of the National Institute of Ecology explains, "We've had laws no one could comply with. . . . [W]e need to promote the market for environmental services and strengthen our infrastructure."[3]

The concerns raised by Gibson and Halter are very pertinent to the ISO 14001 standard and are already unfolding in various Asian countries, such as Thailand and Indonesia, for example. In Thailand the perception that certification to the ISO 14001 standard will help improve the country's international competitiveness has led many Thai companies to take Thai environmental laws more seriously. However, even though the Thai Ministry of Industry has, since 1992, required companies to submit wastewater monitoring reports to the Department of Industry Works, "strong political and business connections and inadequate inspection and monitoring have amounted to poor quality assurance and control at numerous sites."[4] Indonesia, for its part, plans to adopt a modified version of the ISO 14000 series. Bapedal, the Indonesian environmental impact management agency, is defining the criteria necessary to meet the ISO 14001 standard. Indonesia will also have its own environmental accreditation and certification agency.[5]

The problem is certainly not limited to Asia. In the United States, for example, an estimated 2,000 jobs were lost in 1994 because a few American firms, looking for lower-cost labor, less stringent environmental regulations, and other economic advantages, elected to move their plants to Mexico or other offshore sites rather than comply with local regulations.[6] One should not, however, automatically assume that all U.S. firms move south of the border strictly in search of lower labor costs or less demanding environmental regulations. Some firms may well be forced to move to Mexico or other foreign sites simply because other foreign firms have already built plants overseas. The northern states of Sonora and Baja California along the U.S.-Mexico border, for example, have attracted numerous Asian companies over the past two to five years. Electronics, textile, automotive subassembly, and toy manufacturers from Korea, Taiwan, Japan, and Hong Kong, together with joint U.S.-Japanese ventures, have all invested hundreds of millions of dollars in several cities in the states of Sonora and Baja California.[7] Yet, although it is true that Mexico's environmental policies for hazardous wastes have yet to be strictly enforced, it is also true that the government is attempting to move forward as rapidly as possible, and it is likely that within the next few years, thanks to the continued efforts of Mexican environmental groups, so-called environmental advantages for foreign investors will eventually be considerably reduced.[8]

Although regulatory compliance is an important aspect of ISO 14001, it cannot prevent the occasional environmental disaster. Aware of this limitation, influential observers, such as Joe Cascio (chairman of the U.S. Technical Advisory Group (TAG) to Technical Committee 207), have suggested that ISO 14001 is more than mere compliance with the law, and, therefore, "if we fall into the trap of over emphasizing this legal compliance commitment, we will depreciate the value of ISO 14001 and, worse, we will miss the real point and advantage of this standard."[9]

---

## The Case of Brazil

As the leading industrial nation in Latin America, Brazil has an economy that is far more advanced than those of most other developing countries. Environmental legislation relating to pollution control dates back to 1975. Since the mid-1980s, Brazil's CONAMA (or National Council for the Environment) has issued several resolutions relating to pollution control. In addition, eleven Brazilian technical standards relating to the transport of hazardous waste, waste management, and so on have been issued. Yet, despite an emphasis on "command and control" environmental policies, there appears to be plenty of command but little control. For instance, in 1985, the valley of Mogi in the city of Cubatão (near São Paulo) experienced the worse environmental air pollution disaster in the history of the country. Indeed, during an interview conducted by the author in July 1995, officials at São Paulo's CETESB headquarters lamented that with only some 300 inspectors to monitor the more than 40,000 firms operating within the state of São Paulo, officials could only rely on public tips and phone calls to uncover violators. The Brazilian journalist Werner E. Zulauf documents numerous cases of both environmental pollution and environmental improvements in his *A Ideologica Verde: E Outros Ensais Sobre Meio Ambiente* (São Paulo: Geração Editorial, 1995).

---

## ISO 14001 and Environmental Technology

A side effect of the ISO 14001 standard (no doubt unforeseen by the technical committee) has been the push by companies specializing in environmental high-tech equipment to try to link ISO 14001 requirements with the need to purchase the latest and best environmental technology (which is *not* a requirement of ISO 14001). The belief that ISO 14001 will eventually require companies of the developing world to invest heavily in environmental technology to reduce or eliminate pollution and industrial wastes was already a concern of some of the Brazilian officials I interviewed in July 1995. Believing that ISO 14001 certification would eventually entail significant investments in environmental technology, officials at CETESB (Companhia de Tecnologica de Saneamento Ambiental, São Paulo) explained that Brazilian industries were not likely to be able to afford such investments. Moreover, they feared that Brazilian firms would eventually rely on the age-old argument that environmental control will cost jobs. Since Brazil, like most other countries, does not have an indigenous environmental technology industry (only one firm deals with environment-related monitoring equipment in São Paulo), the only alternative, so Brazilian officials seemed to believe, is to purchase foreign technology.[10] This is precisely what U.S., Japanese, and European firms might hope for. In Europe, the biannual international trade fair for waste disposal, recycling, and environmental technology and management (held most recently in December 1995 in Utrecht, the Netherlands) attracts numerous companies in search of an anticipated lucrative European environmental market.

The competition for potential environmental business is already heating up in Asia as European and American firms begin to compete for "green gold." Motivated by the news that Southeast Asian countries are expected to invest as much as $1 billion in green technologies over the next ten years, a thirteen-member environmental business mission from California visited Thailand, Indonesia, and India in September 1995.[11] In Singapore, where a joint venture between the European Union and the Singapore government (known as the Regional Institute of Environmental Technology, or RIET) was formed in July 1993, European environmental technology is already well established to help the Singapore government establish itself as a regional center in environmental technology.

## Unresolved Dilemma

A potential contradiction in the ISO 14001 certification process (not necessarily the 14001 standard itself) involves chemical plants that manufacture nationally banned chemicals. Indeed, some U.S. manufacturers continue to produce, *for export purposes only*, pesticides that were banned years ago in the United States. The irony of this scenario is that dangerous pesticides such as DDT, the soil fumigant dibromochloropropane (DBCP), and 2,4,5-T (used in the infamous defoliant known as

Agent Orange) are exported to other countries and used by them to protect their luxury crops of coffee, cocoa, pineapples, and strawberries. The circle of poison is completed when these crops are exported back to the United States! Such activities may lead to odd situations in which a U.S.-certified ISO 14001 plant is found to be exporting banned chemicals that are eventually ingested as chemical residues by unsuspecting American consumers.[12] Ironically, the EPA issued a final report in the *Federal Register* of December 16, 1980 (45 FR 82844 and 40 CFR 707) requiring exporters of chemical substances or mixtures for which submission of data is required under section 4 or 5(b) of the Toxic Substances Control Act to complete a notice of the first export. Yet, even though the EPA attempts to control the export of dangerous chemicals, no measures currently exist to control the import of agricultural products on which these dangerous chemicals have been used! Obviously, if the Department of Agriculture or other agencies were to prevent agricultural goods from entering the United States because they had been sprayed with dangerous, or even illegal, chemicals, a serious political crisis would likely follow. That is precisely one of the many problems countries will be faced with for a long time to come in the control and management of chemicals and pesticides at an international level.

The above scenario, however, cannot be blamed on any deficiencies in ISO 14001. The standard merely states that the organization in question must obey the environmental laws of the land. Obviously, in this case, the problem is with legislation that allows illegal pesticides to be manufactured for export purposes. One would hope that ISO 14001 firms that subscribe to the CERES Principles would not export pesticides banned in their own countries (see CERES Principle 6: *Safe products and services*, in Table 3-4).

Other related issues will need to be considered. One fundamental question that still remains unanswered is whether companies will choose to export their manufacturing sites to less demanding nations once the loopholes are taken out of current legislation. If the market "demands" it, American companies could, for example, export their pesticide plants to Mexico. If, or rather when, this migration occurs, citizens of any nation could be exposed to imported pesticides (or other products and chemicals) that are banned by the legislation of their respective countries.[13]

Many of the difficulties inherent in international environmental laws may well have originated in 1972, during the first international environmental conference in Stockholm, when the following principle was adopted: "[A] state is obligated to take said measures as may be necessary, to the extent practicable under the circumstances." In other words, as Christopher Stone observes, the principle contained within Stockholm Principle 21 basically states that "if it's too expensive don't fix it."[14] Stone does recognize that Principle 21 is to some extent rational in that it encourages companies not to "pay a pound of cure for an ounce of prevention."[15] In fact, a similar concept of financial limitation is strongly implied in paragraph 4.3.3 *(Objectives and targets)* of ISO 14001, which states that "when establishing and reviewing its objectives, an organization shall consider the legal and other requirements, its significant environmental aspects, its technological options and its *financial, operational and business requirements,* and the views of interested parties." Obviously, the need to develop national environmental policies and to coordinate these policies at the global level is an important issue not addressed by the ISO 14001 standard or even by United Nations rulings.

## Unresolved Dilemmas of Particular Significance to the United States

In the United States, a nation well known for its tort legal system, some people, notably lawyers with Superfund experience, have suggested that ISO 14001 certification may increase a company's liability. Proponents of this argument suggest that since an organization must now conduct internal environmental audits and maintain records of such audits, a government agency could subpoena internal audit records and use the evidence to prosecute any organization. Moreover, since under the new Sentencing Guidelines, it is no longer enough to have an effective program to ensure environmental compliance, the concern would appear to be legitimate. However, preliminary evidence suggests otherwise. At least in the United States, the Environmental Protection Agency is not likely to prosecute an organization that implements an ISO 14001 environmental management system *unless the organization in question fails to report a violation to the EPA.* Therefore, if during an internal environmental audit the company's auditors uncover an environmental nonconformance, and if the nonconformance is directly related to an environmental regulation, the local regulatory authorities (such as the EPA, for example) must be notified and a corrective action must be implemented. If this is done, the EPA will not fine the organization. In fact, that is the very reason why the EPA and other state environmental regulatory agencies are favorably impressed with the ISO 14001 standard. It requires companies to conduct internal environmental audits of their system and to act upon the nonconformances accordingly. Indeed, paragraph 4.5.4, *Nonconformance and corrective and preventive action*, reads in part as follows:

> The organization shall establish and maintain procedures for defining responsibility and authority for handling and investigating nonconformance, taking action to mitigate any impacts caused and for initiating and completing and preventing action. . . . The organization shall implement and record any changes in the documented procedures resulting from corrective and preventive action.[16]

Although it is too early to predict how other state or federal regulatory agencies will react to the ISO 14001 standard, preliminary reports indicate that state and federal agencies see the ISO 14001 standard as a friend rather than a foe. It therefore seems unlikely that these agencies would willfully want to discredit the ISO 14001 standard.

## Is ISO 14001 Registration Required?

With the possible exception of American firms, which view the ISO 14000 standard as a document likely to increase their liability, most other nations and multinational as well as national corporations perceive the ISO 14001 standard favorably. Many American companies that have gone through the ISO 9000 process seem to approach 14001 with some guarded interest. That is understandable. In a marketing process that is similar to the ISO 9000 marketing strategy of the early 1990s, the 14000 series was already being marketed as early as 1994 as a conditional requirement for anyone wishing to conduct business in Europe. The truth of such sensationalistic claims is questionable. Indeed, it is unlikely, and in fact against GATT conventions, that any country would require ISO 14001 certification as a condition of doing business in Europe. However, an identical scenario played out during the late 1980s and early 1990s and it did not prevent more and more companies from eventually requiring some form of ISO 9000 certification from their suppliers. It is therefore quite likely that a similar scenario will emerge for ISO 14001 during the next three to five years.

There are in fact several mechanisms through which ISO 14001 registration could be required. As was explained in Chapter 2, numerous European environmental directives have been written and will continue to be written over the next few years. Although most of these directives will affect only European firms, some may have an indirect impact on non-European firms. One example might be a European Union directive for lead-free packaging. Suppose Italy decides, as of January 1997, to adopt the European directive for lead-free packages. What might be the impact on American (or other) exporters to Italy whose products are wrapped in nonlead-free paper? This realistic scenario is very similar to the current requirement for CE marking for certain so-called regulated products (toys, electronic equipment, medical devices, lifting equipment, pressure vessels, etc.). At a minimum, and to avoid possible delays at the European port of entry, the American exporter would probably have to ensure that for products sent to Italy the packaging medium did not contain lead. This means that American suppliers of lead-free paper would have to be found.

This simple example illustrates how European environmental directives can affect American manufacturers and the processes they use. But would this change in process operations, required to adapt to the Italian market demand for heavy metal-free paper, automatically require American suppliers to achieve ISO 14001 certification/registration? Drawing on the ISO 9000 experience, I believe that the reasonable answer would be yes. Why? Suppose that the Italian government now adopts a national directive stating that all suppliers to the Italian government must be ISO 14001-certified.[17] Would that affect non-European suppliers? Probably yes. Indeed, since Italian suppliers will now have to become registered to ISO 14001 or an equivalent, the legal requirement is very likely to move down the supplier chain until foreign suppliers eventually become affected by the directive. Indeed, if an Italian supplier obtains some of his products, subassemblies, or even raw materials from overseas, he will have little choice but to require his (overseas) suppliers to become ISO 14001-certified/registered. The global process will begin. Within a couple of years, U.S. suppliers will begin requiring ISO 14001 certification from their own (national) suppliers.

The above scenario is not far-fetched.[18] In fact, some countries are already incorporating ISO 14001 requirements into their own legal requirements. In Brazil, for example, companies have been financially motivated to achieve ISO 9000 certification. Brazilian firms registered to one of the ISO 9000 standards can apply for low-interest loans, which in Brazil can be as low as 4 percent per month, an excellent rate when compared to the 45 percent a month experienced in July 1994! Encouraged by the program (Brazil has the highest number of ISO 9000-

registered firms in Latin America), the Brazilian government decided, in 1995, to implement a similar program with ISO 14001. No doubt, other countries will follow. It remains to be seen, however, if Brazilian firms that import goods from the United States will require their U.S. suppliers to be ISO 14001-registered/certified.

## ISO 14001: Self-Certification or Third-Party Certification?

Although the 14001 standard allows companies to self-certify their environmental management systems, it is doubtful that either customers or governmental agencies will recognize self-certification. The need for independently verified compliance, although challenged by some industries, has nonetheless its obvious advantages. One of the advantages of third-party certification is that it *could* potentially force companies to take corrective actions that were advised during environmental audits. I have emphasized the word *could* because it remains to be seen whether environmental registrars will dare withdraw an ISO 14001 certification once it has been issued to an organization. I do not know of any organization that has lost its ISO 9000 certification after having received it. Of course, this could mean one of two things: either that once registered to one of the ISO 9000 standards, companies work hard at maintaining their certification, or that no registrar wants to be the first to withdraw a certification once it has been issued. It is likely that a similar scenario will apply to the ISO 14001 certification process. One thing is certain, when certification is not issued, auditors may have a very difficult time being listened to. Eric Nelson has documented how the Alyeska Pipeline Service Co., a consortium of several oil companies operating in Prudhoe Bay, Alaska, has consistently either ignored auditor reports or pressured auditors not to report their findings.[19] As Mike Riley explains,

> [T]here are strong political and economic incentives for weak regulatory oversight: nearly 25 percent of the U.S. domestic crude oil supply flows through the pipeline, and 85 percent of the State of Alaska's revenues are generated by oil royalties. The result is that regulators often lack the political will, as well as some enforcement tools, to bring the pipeline into compliance.[20]

Let us hope that a global ISO 14001 registration would help prevent such situations from happening.

## The Value of 14001

Except for the real possibility of the certifiers becoming yet another bureaucracy, I cannot think of any negative aspects associated with ISO 14001 certification. Certainly, some unresolved issues remain, particularly with regard to the question of equivalency. Will an ISO 14001 certificate issued in some developing country be equivalent to a 14001 certificate issued in the Netherlands, Germany, the United Kingdom, or Canada? Probably not, unless the developing country has environmental laws *and enforcement capabilities* similar to those of the developed countries. As already stated in Chapter 2, this is unlikely to happen even though, in some developing countries, the ratio of environmental inspectors to industries is higher than in the United States or European countries.[21]

Still, as with any new process, a certain amount of time will have to elapse before any significant and definite conclusions can be reached. There is no doubt that within the next five years the ISO 14001 standard will evolve and improve. Differences will be resolved and some of the issues raised in this and other chapters will either be eliminated or, more likely, attenuated. The ISO 14001 standard is certainly an excellent system to bring about global environmental management awareness. It is flexible and easily adaptable to a multitude of situations. Most important, it is not, nor should it be, threatening. The standard will provide a common global reference for environmental management that can be adapted to the respective needs of each country. One of its most important virtues is that ISO 14001 allows each country to adopt the standard according to its *current economic needs and limitations*. One final appealing feature of 14001 is that within these national constraints, certification is achievable by all large or small companies.

As Joe Cascio notes:

> ISO 14001 . . . challenges each organization to take stock of its environmental aspects, establish its own objectives and targets, commit itself to effective and reliable processes and continual improvement, and brings all . . . into a system of shared and enlightened awareness and personal responsibility for the environmental performance of the organization.[22]

## Conclusion

When I attended an ISO 14001 convention in November 1995, it soon became evident that many of the questions and issues surrounding the

ISO 14001 standard were identical to what had unfolded five years before with the ISO 9000 series. People wanted to know who would have to register, who would do the registration, what it would cost, how difficult it would be to implement, and so on. As has often been true with the ISO 9000 series, the audience seemed to fear ISO 14001. ISO 14001 meant many things to many people. Environmental consultants reminded the audience that the principles of environmental management specified in 14001 were not new, and were quick to point out that their expertise was certainly available to assist companies. Similarly, environmental engineers interpreted ISO 14001 from their own prejudiced perspective. Government officials, some of whom appeared not to have read the standard, claimed that ISO 14001 would just about eliminate the need for local environmental agencies. Representatives from the EPA refused to endorse ISO 14001 and simply suggested, as any good politician would, that they would neither condone nor condemn ISO 14001. Despite repeated comments from several of the presenters, many people seemed to ignore or forget that ISO 14001 is a managerial tool. This became clearly evident to me when I interviewed representatives from a European registrar. When I asked what type of individuals would most likely audit for compliance with ISO 14001, I was told that it could not possibly be individuals with experience in the field of quality; it had to be professionals with work experience in environmental issues. The conversation very quickly drifted to the technical aspects of environmental control. When I suggested that it sounded to me as though only environmental engineers would be allowed to do environmental audits, my interlocutor admitted that perhaps others could also enter this select brotherhood of auditors. Finally, I suggested that environmental engineers were probably not the best candidates to conduct environmental *management* audits. I emphasized that ISO 14001 was not about knowing how to satisfy a particular set of environmental codes or regulations or knowing how to substitute an alternative chemical for a toxic one. Rather, ISO 14001 was about *environmental management;* therefore, people with experience auditing *managerial systems* were required. Apparently that point had not been considered.[23] Fortunately, not all registrars have the same point of view; some will consider retraining their ISO 9000 auditors to conduct ISO 14001 audits.

As was true for the ISO 9000 series, the ISO 14001 standard will mean very different things to different companies. Large chemical plants, particularly those that already satisfy Responsible Care®, should have little difficulty understanding the intent of the standard; they may nonetheless experience some difficulties implementing ISO 14001. Small to medium-size companies will most likely experience the most difficulty with the standard. The obvious challenge for small to medium-size businesses will be the lack of available human resources needed to implement and maintain ISO 14001. For companies that are already ISO 9000-registered, the task should be much easier because, in essence, ISO 14001 is nothing more than the principles of quality assurance extended to the quality of the environment in general. Thus, whereas ISO 9000 focuses on product characteristics and customer satisfaction, ISO 14001 emphasizes environmental characteristics and the demands of the community surrounding an organization. When considering who the customer is, an organization should not adopt the myopic point of view. Certainly, the customer can be viewed as the individual or group of individuals who purchase your products. The customer can also be viewed as the various regulatory agencies, such as the EPA, for example, which you must certainly keep satisfied. All these customers are unquestionably important customers. However, I would propose that as you begin implementing ISO 14001, you consider the *only* ultimate customer: earth. Earth is both our sole supplier and our most valued customer. Such concepts, no doubt incomprehensible to some business executives, are nonetheless practiced by some visionaries. Anita Roddick certainly appears to be one such visionary when she writes:

> I would love if every shareholder of every company wrote a letter every time they received a company's annual report and accounts. I would like them to say something like, "Ok, that's fine, very good. But where are the details of your *environmental* audits? Where are the details of your accounting to the community? Where is your *social* audit? How can I measure the worth of your company without knowing what you are contributing to the community or doing to help protect the planet?"[24]

An ISO 14001 environmental management system designed to have a minimum impact on the earth and, ultimately, the world's societies could certainly provide companies throughout the world with a baseline environmental system to achieve Ms. Roddick's vision.

## Notes

1. J. Eugene Gibson and Faith Halter, "Strengthening Environmental Law in Developing Countries," *Environment*, January/February 1994, p. 40.

2. Ibid., p. 42. Among the many problems faced by developing countries the authors cite: laws without clearly assigned implementation authority; limited technical capability and limited political power to monitor compliance and correct violations; corruption that leads the public to lose confidence in the legal system; and failure, on the part of the government, to encourage the participation of all affected parties.

3. Quoted in Sam Quinones, "Hazardous waste handlers see Mexico as the promised land. But environmental groups are derailing their efforts," *Mexico Business Reporter*, July/August 1995 (no pagination). As of 1995, Mexico had only two "official" landfills accepting hazardous waste (Monterrey and Hermosillo, Sonora). Both sites are isolated for most companies in Mexico. Another site may be opened in 1996 at San Luis Potosí in central Mexico.

4. "Environmental Busines Opportunities in Thailand," *Asia Pacific Economic Review* 3, no. 4 (1995): 12. The article notes that the department has only 400 inspectors for 10,000 factories. This in fact is a very good ratio of 25 factories per inspector, or two factories per month, not a very demanding schedule.

5. Xinhua News Agency, September 7, 1995, item number 0907096.

6. Another reason for developing countries to express a strong interest in the ISO 14001 standard is that international lending agencies such as the World Bank have begun to link (very unsuccessfully, one might add) environmental risk analyses to their lending requirements. In an effort to lower their liabilities, companies in the developing and developed world may also achieve ISO 14001 certification.

7. Marlene Piturro, "The Asian Tigers are setting up shop in Mexico as a low-wage backdoor to the U.S. and Canada," *Mexico Business Reporter*, July/August 1995 (no pagination).

8. Sam Quinones, "Hazardous waste handlers see Mexico as the promised land," *Mexico Business Reporter*, July/August 1995 (no pagination).

9. Joe Cascio, "The Carrot is Sweeter Than the Stick," *International Environmental Systems Update* 2, no. 11 (November 1995): 24.

10. Interest in ISO 14001 and BS 7750 was already strong in Brazil as early as June 1994. By midsummer 1995, at least four books had been published in Portuguese. A couple of popular books were a translation of Michael J. Gilbert's *Achieving Environmental Management Standards (A Step-by-Step Guide to Meeting BS 7750)* (Pitman Publishing, 1994)—*BS 7750: Sistema de Gerenciamento Ambiental* (São Paulo: IMAM, 1995) and Cyro Eyer Do Valle, *Qualidade Ambiental* (São Paulo: Pionera, 1995), which is cleverly subtitled *How to prepare for the ISO 14000 standards.*

11. See Curtis Moore and Alan Miller, *Green Gold* (Boston: Beacon Press, 1994). Moore and Miller write, p. 32, that Singapore's Ministry of Environment in 1992 allocated $609.3 million "not only to improve Singapore's own environmental health, sewage treatment, and solid waste disposal, but also to develop the nation as the regional center and transit point for environmental products and services."

12. John Harte, Cheryl Holdren, Richard Schneider, and Christine Shirley, *Toxics A to Z* (Los Angeles: University of California Press, 1990). See Chapter 14, "Pesticides," particularly pp. 125–26.

13. The migration of U.S. firms in search of cheaper labor costs has been well documented by journalists and scholars alike. Recent examples include CERES member the Timberland Co., the New Hampshire shoe company. Critics say that the company is moving for the wrong reasons. Recent difficulties are more likely to be associated with a failure to match customer needs and guessing wrong. See *Business Ethic* (July–August 1995), p. 39.

14. Christopher D. Stone, *The Gnat Is Older Than Man: Global Environment and Human Agenda* (Princeton, N.J.: Princeton University Press, 1993), p. 15, and Christopher D. Stone, *Where the Law Ends: The Social Control of Corporate Behavior* (New York: Harper & Row, 1975).

15. Stone, *The Gnat Is Older Than Man,* p. xv.

16. ISO 14001, *Environmental Management Systems—Specification with Guidance for Use,* Paragraph 4.4.2.

17. In fact, the Italian, or any other European government, is likely to require that European firms conform to the Eco-Management and Audit Scheme (known as EMAS). Although similar to ISO 14001, EMAS is in fact more demanding than 14001. As of 1995, EMAS was purely voluntary, but, given that many European auditors are already becoming registered as EMAS auditors, it is very likely EMAS will become compulsory for at least certain key industries such as chemicals and paper processing. For a description of EMAS, see Tom Tibor and Ira Feldman, *ISO 14000: A Guide to the New Environmental Management Standards* (Chicago: Irwin Publishing, 1995), pp. 77–91.
18. In February 1987 a mayor of a town in Lombardy, Italy, issued a directive prohibiting merchants from providing customers with any nonbiodegradable bags or from selling or otherwise distributing plastic bags, except for the disposal of rubbish. When challenged by Italian and foreign manufacturers, the European Court of Justice found that Waste Directive 75/442 gave the mayor the authority.
19. Eric Nelson, "Crude Behavior: Big Oil to Alaska Inspectors: Don't Squawk or Else," *Washington Free Press*, August–September 1995, pp. 10–12.
20. Mike Riley, "Despite A Serious Quality Control Crisis, Big Oil Seeks to Expand Drilling," *Washington Free Press*, August–September 1995, p. 13.
21. In the state of São Paulo, Brazil, officials at the state environmental agency cited as many as 300 inspectors for approximatley 40,000 industries, or three inspectors per forty factories—not a bad ratio. I have read similar ratios for Thailand. Of course, ratios mean nothing if there is no enforcement.
22. Joe Cascio, "The Carrot is Sweeter Than the Stick," in *International Environmental Systems Update* 2, no. 11 (November 1995): 24.
23. Part of the confusion and contradiction between the intent of ISO 14001 and the requirements for auditors is probably due to the fact that the ISO 14012 Guidelines specify that auditors should have industry expertise.
24. Anita Roddick, *Body and Soul* (New York: Crown, 1991), p. 252. The Body Shop is a member of CERES. The Body Shop has been the subject of numerous electronic debates on the Internet. Well over two dozen messages have been written about the "greenwashing" of The Body Shop.

# Part III

# Tools for Environmental Managers

Part III covers micro level implementation and application issues. The four chapters comprising Part III offer a detailed account of some important tools to be used by environmental managers. Chapter 5 reviews why economic considerations are often ignored by economists and managers alike when dealing with the financial feasibility of environmental implementation programs. Chapter 6 offers a detailed case study of total cost accounting, a useful technique developed a few years ago but unfortunately still unknown to many. Chapter 7 focuses on the difficult and time-consuming technique known as life-cycle assessment. This important managerial tool, practiced by a few environmental leaders in the United States, is very popular in some European countries. The technique is likely to become more important in the next two to three years when the Environmental Management Life-Cycle Assessment set of international requirements, such as the ISO 14040-14043 series of standards, is finally published. Chapter 7 concludes with a discussion of ecolabeling and its relationship to life-cycle analysis. Chapter 8 offers a summary of some well-known hazard evaluation techniques that can be used in conjunction with the ISO 14001 standard or other environmental programs.

# 5

# The Economics of Environmental Management

Despite the increasing volume of information published by professional journals, newspapers, television programs, and the media in general, business and industry in general have traditionally been slow or otherwise reluctant to respond to the many challenges posed by industrial pollution. This should not be surprising when one considers the clash of opinions surrounding the important issues of economics, regional development, and environmentalism.

## Economics, Economists, Entrepreneurship, and the Environment: Can They Coexist?

The economic impact of pollution and the ensuing complex ramifications for the ecosystem caused by inadequate environmental policies at the macro (governmental) and micro (business) level have been amply documented ever since the turn of the century and especially over the past forty to fifty years. In his excellent *The Human Impact on the Natural Environment*, British geographer Andrew Goudie cites numerous studies conducted during the 1960s, 1970s, and 1980s in which researchers demonstrated the destructive, and hence costly economic, impact of the pollution of various habitats. Heavy metals and methyl mercury, which builds up in tremendous quantities in marine organisms, have been shown to affect the shellfish and fishing industry. Thallium sulfate, which used to be (and may still be) spread on wheat to control rodent infestation, also afflicts birds of prey that live on the rodent. The attempt to poison and exterminate jackals led to an unexpected increase in the number of hares. In Biscayne Bay, Florida, industrial and municipal wastes from Miami were found to be linked to the high incidence of dermal tumors in several species of fish; similar observations were made in the case of whales. In Bellingham Bay, north of Seattle, Washington, sulfite wastes from paper mills were found to lead to abnormal growth in oyster larvae. Arsenic emissions from silver foundries in Germany killed deer.[1] Countless cases of acid rain (in Europe and North America), of ocean pollution caused by shipwrecked tankers, of river pollution, of pollution of the Arctic tundra (Alaska pipeline), of nuclear accidents (e.g., Chernobyl, Three Mile Island), and so on could be cited.

Sadly enough, and contrary to what was optimistically predicted by some, regional economic alliances such as the North American Free Trade Association (NAFTA) may accentuate rather than alleviate the human and health-related costs associated with environmental pollution. Along the California-Mexico border, where hundreds of *maquiladoras* (foreign, mostly U.S.-owned companies operating in Mexico) have conducted business for several years, lead and other heavy metal deposits have been measured in the soil at concentrations 40,000 times higher than the safe level. Reporting on these serious environmental problems, David Bacon writes that, "[I]n this unincorporated settlement, or *colonia*, six babies were reported born without brains in 1993, and 13 in 1994, just one of several clusters of this rare birth defect, called anencephaly, on the border."[2] Numerous other incidents of lung diseases (from air pollution), lupus, infectious diseases caused by a lack of sewer facilities, and nervous disorders suffered by farmworkers handling pesticides have been documented over the years.

In the United States, repeated incidents of "environmental violence" were mostly ignored by industries from the 1950s to the early 1970s.[3] As the United States government began to draft new environmental legislation and the EPA slowly began to enforce the laws, businesses threatened to lay off tens of thousands of workers in retaliation for what they claimed were the exorbitant costs of environmental compliance. As is often the case with highly emotional issues, claims tend to be exaggerated and often irrational. In the United States, for example, an estimated 1,300 jobs may have been lost during the late 1980s as the result of environmental protection. During the same period, GM alone is estimated to have laid off 18,000 employees for efficiency, not environmental, reasons. In Whiting, Indiana, Amoco, which has been known to discharge high levels of chlorides into Lake Michigan as well as toxic metals such as selenium, arsenic, and lead, threatened to close its oil refinery because "the state forced it to abide by a new environmental protection law designed to protect the lake."[4]

Yet, as researchers have demonstrated over the past several years, environmental regulation may in fact boost competition and business opportunities.[5] Far from causing layoffs, environmental protection expenditures totaling almost $170 billion in 1992 created in the United States more than 3.9 million jobs that same year. Ten states accounted for 56 percent of these jobs (see Table 5-1). As Roger H. Bezdek aptly notes in a very informative article, "environmental regulations do not necessarily diminish the wealth of a nation, rather, they largely transfer wealth from polluter to pollution controllers and abaters and to less polluting firms."[6]

In some cases, environmentally proactive companies can reap significant economic gains (see Chapter 9 for several case studies). Such was the case when, in September 1989, ARCO, a California-based oil company with an interest in Alaska's Prudhoe Bay oil fields, introduced to the California market its "environmental gasoline," EC-1.[7] EC-1 helped reduce carcinogenic benzene emission by 50 percent and smog-

**Table 5-1.** Jobs and sales created in the ten leading states in 1992 by environmental protection expenditures.

| State | Jobs | Sales ($ billions) |
|-------|------|--------------------|
| 1. California | 484,000 | $2.9 |
| 2. New York | 306,000 | 13.7 |
| 3. Texas | 270,000 | 10.5 |
| 4. Michigan | 188,000 | 7.9 |
| 5. Florida | 163,000 | 7.0 |
| 6. Ohio | 148,000 | 9.0 |
| 7. Illinois | 141,000 | 7.6 |
| 8. New Jersey | 140,000 | 6.2 |
| 9. Pennsylvania | 137,000 | 9.5 |
| 10. Massachusetts | 123,000 | 5.1 |
| and Virginia | 123,000 | 5.3 |
| | 2,223,000 | $84.7 |
| Total number of jobs for all 50 states = 3,958,000 | (or 56% of total US jobs) | (or 49.88% of total $169.8 expenditure) |

SOURCE: Data extracted from Table 7.3 in Roger H. Bezdek, "The Net Impact of Environmental Protection on Jobs and the Economy," in Bunyan Bryant, ed., *Environmental Justice* (Washington, D.C.: Island Press, 1995), p. 100.

generating sulfur by 80 percent. Aware that its marketing advantage would be short-lived unless other refineries were also required to match EC-1's performance, ARCO lobbied the California Air Resources Board (CARB). Its efforts were rewarded when the board approved a plan to develop strict pollution standards and improve air quality in southern California.

The failure of economists to address, or in some cases even to acknowledge, environmental issues and their connection with the economy is ably demonstrated by the Italian author Carla Ravaioli. To find out why economists were generally uninterested (in the research sense of the word) in environmental issues, Ms. Ravaioli interviewed nearly thirty world-renowned economists around the world. With the exception of a few ecologically minded economists such as Nicholas Georgescu-Roegen of the United States, Christian Leipert of Germany, Mercedes Bresso[8] of Italy, René Passet of France, Paul Ekins of England, and a handful of others, Ravaioli was forced to conclude that economists continue

> to avoid the knottiest environmental problems and are still extremely far away from the interpretation of ecologists. So much so that at times one seems to glimpse between the lines two completely different visions of the world; in the first, economics is the universal science to which all other disciplines are subordinate; in the second, economics is only one form of knowledge among many, and the interrelation between the various subjects is the essential epistemological key.[9]

## The Emergence of Green Economists

The majority of economists have expressed little or no interest in environmental issues. To many economists, the important issues to consider are those of monetary policies, international trade, economic productivity, economic modeling, employment theory, and so on. With the notable exception of a few such as Kenneth Boulding, most economists consider environmental issues to be outside the scope of their narrowly defined specialties. However, as Ralph Nader once advocated,

> [T]he issue should not be confused with competitiveness or productivity, as defined by the mercantilists. You can define productivity in the steel industry purely in terms of outputs,

sales, and profits. But you can also define it in terms of the decrease in the levels of injury and disease afflicting workers and people in the community.[10]

Most economists would argue that the issues raised by Nader are mere *externalities*. The concept of externalities was first introduced in the early 1920s by Pigou, who used it in a context other than the environment. One of the first definitions of externalities to be used in the economico-environmentalist sense of the word was introduced by William Kapp in 1950. In the introduction to his *The Social Costs of Private Enterprise*, Kapp defined the term as follows:

> The main purpose of this book is to present a detailed study of the manner in which private enterprise under conditions of unregulated competition tends to give rise to social costs which are not accounted for in entrepreneurial outlays *but instead are shifted to and borne by third persons and the community as a whole.*[11]

Recognizing that "the impairment *and* the quality of the environment (and of society) must be understood as aggregates," Kapp had already recognized that "in their present form, national income indices not only fail to subtract these social costs, but include money spent to repair the damages caused by productive activities of the past and present." This failure to look at environmental issues from a system point of view led Kapp to anticipate the limitation of the command and control approach already being attempted by the U.S. government during the late 1930s and 1940s (and rediscovered by the EPA during the 1970s and 1980s).

> In other words, instead of a search for *remedies*, an effective approach to the solution of the environmental crisis calls for prior assessment and control of the "input mix" and output pattern with a view to preventing social costs and the impairment of the environment before they occur. . . . Man must be placed at the center of the debate and more importantly human needs.[12]

Kapp's influence on Barry Commoner is clearly evident in the latter's books. In the early 1970s, Commoner, a biologist by training, became known as one of the first radical environmentalists. Avoiding the complex jargon of economists and econometricians, he wrote in a clear style punctuated with vivid metaphors. "The *hidden costs* of power production, such as air pollution," Commoner wrote, "are *social* costs; they are met, not by a single producer, but by the *public*." Commoner goes on to argue that because "the productive system 'borrows' from the ecosystem and incurs a 'debt to nature' in the form of pollution and a savings for producers, . . . environmental degradation represents a crucial, potentially fatal, *hidden* factor in the operation of the economic system."[13]

Challenging the protechnology argument, which believes that all environmental problems can be solved with the appropriate technology, Commoner suggests that environmental degradation is actually "built into the technical design of modern instruments of production."[14] Moreover, Commoner also suggests that the interconnectedness among the myriad of complex environmental systems does not lend itself to the pseudoscientific reductionist position favored by some. This philosophy proposes that since science is divided into disciplines, complex systems can be understood only if they are first broken down into separate component parts. In other words, environmental problems cannot be solved by assembling large teams of engineers. A cross-disciplinary approach is necessary.[15] One such example of cross-disciplinary activities is provided by the newly created field of environmental accounting.

## Notes

1. Andrew Goudie, *Human Impact* (Cambridge, Mass.: The MIT Press, 1994), Chapter 3, pp. 99–106 and passim.
2. David Bacon, "After NAFTA," *Environmental Action*, Fall 1995, p. 33. Other sites include the Eagle Pass/Del Rio area and the Brownsville/Matamoros area, where similar cases of anencephaly were reported in December 1994 and March 1995.
3. See Ralph Nader, "The Management of Environmental Violence," in Anthony B. Wolbarst, ed., *Environmental Peril* (Washington, D.C.: Smithsonian Institution Press, 1991), pp. 1–15.
4. See Beth Baker, "Bringing Labor and Environmentalists to the Table," *Environmental Action*, Summer 1995, p. 18 and p. 12.
5. This is the main thesis of Curtis and Alan Miller expounded in their *Green Gold: Japan, Germany, the United States and the Race for Environmental Technology* (Boston: Beacon Press, 1994).
6. Roger H. Bezdek cites several examples of exorbitant claims relating to job layoffs and hyperinflated regulation costs in "The Net Impact of Environmental Protection on Jobs and the Economy," in Bunyan Bryant, ed., *Environmental Justice: Issues, Policies, and Solutions* (Covelo, Calif.: Island Press, 1995), pp. 86–106 (quotation on p. 94). See also "Are Regs Bleeding the Economy? *Business Week*, July 17, 1995, pp. 75–76; Michael Porter, "America's Green Strategy," *Scientific American*, April 1991, p. 191, and his *Competitive Advantage of Nations* (New York: The Free Press, 1990), particularly p. 648.
7. Bruce W. Piasecki, *Corporate Environmental Strategy: The Avalanche of Change Since Bhopal*

(New York: John Wiley & Sons, 1995), p. 40. EC-1 is a lead-free gasoline for vehicles not equipped with catalytic converters.

8. Mercedes Bresso, *Ambiente e attività produttive* (Milan: Franco Angeli, 1992).
9. Carla Ravaioli, *Economists and the Environment* (London: Zed Books, 1995), p. 7. Ms. Ravaioli, who is obviously very well read on the subject, shows on several occasions her socialist sympathies. This is certainly not a reprimand, but it may account for the occasional difficulties she has trying to understand the often, but not always, lucid arguments proposed by conservative market economists such as Nobel Prize-winner Milton Friedman. The interviews are certainly entertaining to read.
10. Ralph Nader, "The Management of Environmental Violence," in Anthony B. Wolbarst, ed., *Environmental Peril* (Washington, D.C.: Smithsonian Institution Press, 1991), p. 5.
11. K. William Kapp, *The Social Costs of Private Enterprise* (Cambridge, Mass.: Harvard University Press, 1950), p. vii, emphasis added. Kapp also cites the work of F. Odum, *Our Plundered Planet* (Boston: Little Brown and Company, 1948).
12. Kapp, *Social Costs*, pp. vi, vii, xx, xxi, and xxiv.
13. Barry Commoner, *The Closing Circle* (New York: Alfred A. Knopf, 1971), pp. 195, 271, and 273. The EPA distinguishes between *private costs*, "which are the costs a business incurs or for which a business can be held accountable" (i.e., legally responsible), and *societal costs*, or externalities, "for which business is not legally accountable." See EPA, *An Introduction to Environmental Accounting as a Business Management Tool: Key Concepts and Terms.* EPA 742-R-95-001 (June 1995), p. 16. Although the distinction is valid, it seems odd, and I would suggest irresponsible, for the EPA to consider an environmental cost a societal cost only if it can be accounted for in the legal sense of the word.
14. Barry Commoner, "The Failure of the Environmental Effort," in Anthony B. Wolbarst, ed., *Environmental Peril* (Washington, D.C.: Smithsonian Institution Press, 1991), p. 41.
15. This is precisely what Huey D. Johnson emphasizes. In a tone that reminds us of Dasmann's earlier (1964–65) warnings, in *The Destruction of California*, Johnson condemns the increasing specialization in science and the universities: "There needs to be some synthesis between the school of business management and resource management in the future. The emphasis should be on management rather than science; what we need is managers who know how to use scientific information." Johnson, *Green Plans*, p. 175.

# 6

# Environmental Accounting

Following the leads established by Kapp and Commoner, green economists, environmentalists, and businesspeople alike have acknowledged,
ever since the mid-1980s, that markets do not efficiently reflect the cost
of environmental degradation. In his often quoted book, *Changing
Course*, Swiss businessman Stephan Schmidheiney writes that since
environmental costs are still treated as externalities and are therefore
not integrated into economic decisions, a "full-cost pricing," which is
the cost "of production plus the cost of any environmental damage
associated with it," must be developed.[1]

Within the context of ISO 14001, environmental accounting and the
technique of total cost accounting are invaluable tools. Indeed, references
to financial and business requirements are often alluded to or even
explicitly stated in several paragraphs of ISO 14001. For example, one of
the opening paragraphs of ISO 14001 (introduction) states that "[I]nterna-
tional environmental standards are intended . . . to assist organizations to
achieve environmental and *economic* goals." Moreover, paragraph 4.3.3,
*Objectives and targets*, specifically states that "[W]hen establishing and
reviewing its objectives, an organization shall consider the legal and
other requirements, its significant environmental aspects, its technological
options *and its financial, operational and business requirements*, and the views
of interested parties." One can also read in paragraph 4.4.1, *Structure and
responsibility*, that "[R]esources include human resources and specialized
skills, technology *and financial resources*." Clearly, contributors to the ISO
14001 standard were well aware of the need to balance environmental
management issues with financial and business issues. Yet, despite this
awareness, one reads in paragraph A.3.3, of Annex A that "[T]he reference
to the financial requirements of the organization is not intended to
imply that organizations are obliged to use environmental cost accounting
methodologies." Thus, after having repeatedly referred to the need for
financial considerations, contributors to ISO 14001 seem to go out of their

way to make sure that they do not endorse environmental cost accounting techniques. This is unfortunate but understandable. It is unfortunate because, as we shall now see, environmental cost accounting, and particularly the technique known as total cost accounting, is a very valuable tool to financially account for a host of environmentally related costs. Total cost accounting is actually becoming a requirement in some states. The state of Washington, for example, requires the use of a simplified version of total cost accounting (see Appendix A). Nonetheless, one can understand why the ISO 14001 technical committee did not want to be perceived as endorsing or favoring, and thus requiring, the use of one environmental cost accounting technique over another.

## Properly Costing Pollution Prevention

The call for full-cost pricing and its associated full-cost accounting has not been ignored. In the United States, one of the motivations for better accounting for environmental costs comes from the Securities and Exchange Commission (SEC), which requires "publicly held companies to report fully and accurately any information that is 'material' with respect to the company's business and financial position. This applies to all information, including environmental claims and contingent liabilities."[2] As senior executives begin slowly to recognize the financial rewards associated with running a "green business," efforts to improve pollution prevention are renewed. Indeed, a 1995 study conducted by Vanderbilt University and the Washington-based Investor Responsibility Research Center, Inc. (IRRC) found that in more than 80 percent of comparisons, "low polluters" performed better financially (with an approximately 1 percent higher return on assets) than "high polluters."[3]

Since the early 1990s, U.S. and Canadian firms have been trying to estimate their costs of pollution prevention. Yet, despite the many success stories associated with pollution prevention practices, a recent EPA report correctly points out that

> [T]he vast majority of American manufacturers have been slow to move away from traditional end-of-the-pipe strategies. If prevention investments are, in fact, in the self-interest of the firm, what accounts for the continuing reluctance to aggressively move toward a more preventive practice in implementing pollution management choices?[4]

The EPA's report attributes this lack of response on the part of industry to: (1) the organizational structure and behavior of firms, which inhibit pollution prevention projects from entering their decision-making proc-

**Table 6-1.** Estimated environmental costs by industry for France (in millions of French francs, 1992, 5FF = $1.00).

| Sector | Specific Investments* | Process Change | Risk Prevention* | Total | Percentage of Total Investments |
|---|---|---|---|---|---|
| Refinery | 114 | 285 | 31 | 430 | 5.8% |
| Nonrefinery energy | 426 | 33 | 50 | 509 | 1.1 |
| Steel | 331 | 119 | 17 | 467 | 12.7 |
| Nonferrous metal extraction | 69 | 278 | 23 | 371 | 3.7 |
| Minerals, glass, construction materials | 147 | 79 | 21 | 247 | 3.1 |
| Chemical industry | 631 | 261 | 314 | 1206 | 9.1 |
| Other chemical industries | 151 | 61 | 57 | 269 | 2.8 |
| Foundries | 198 | 68 | 28 | 294 | 3.3 |
| Mechanical | 52 | 48 | 10 | 110 | 1.2 |
| Electrical and electronics | 114 | 44 | 63 | 221 | 1.1 |
| Automotive and transport | 132 | 92 | 45 | 269 | 0.9 |
| Agriculture and food industries | 438 | 165 | 22 | 625 | 2.8 |
| Textile and leather | 78 | 22 | 3 | 103 | 2.8 |
| Paper | 432 | 185 | 36 | 653 | 8.2 |
| Other Sectors | 91 | 58 | 16 | 165 | 1.3 |
| Total | 3403 | 1798 | 736 | 5939 | 2.8% |

SOURCE: Jean-Paul Meyronneinc, *Le management de l'environnement dans l'entreprise* (Paris: AFNOR), p. 101. Meyronneinc's source is the statistical unit of the French Ministry of Industry (SESSI).
*Specific investments include end-of-cycle investments, recycling equipment, and filters. Risk-prevention costs would include spill retention areas and storage tanks for chlorine.

ess, and (2) economic and financial hurdles that are linked to methods of capital allocation and budgeting, which, in turn, force pollution prevention projects to compete with other projects for limited capital resources. Since environmental projects defy conventional cost analysis procedures, they tend invariably to lose out when these limited capital resources are allocated. But why are environmental costs so difficult to ascertain and so often underestimated?

When asked to estimate environmental costs as a percentage of total operational costs, most environmental managers in the United States and other countries estimate the cost to range anywhere from 1 to 3 percent, notable exceptions being the steel, chemical, and paper industries (see Table 6-1). However, when a total cost accounting analysis is conducted, companies have discovered that the actual costs can jump to as much as 22 percent of total operational costs.[5] Why the difference? One of the primary reasons for such underestimation is that standard accounting principles (as governed by the Generally Accepted Accounting Principles, or GAAP) are too coarse and inadequate to properly identify and/or allocate the many environmental costs that tend to be scattered throughout a facility (see Table 6-2).

Traditional cost accounting methodology misallocates cost because it lumps all environmental costs into one general "overhead" category, which is then spread evenly among each product, process, and department. This method unfairly assigns environmental costs to environmentally safe products, processes, or departments. A more logical approach would be to assign costs only to products, processes, and/or departments that handle and/or generate waste or pollution in general. Figure 6-1 illustrates how the cost associated with toxic waste B is correctly reassigned after having first been misallocated to the general category of overhead. Figure 6-2 demonstrates how typical variable and fixed costs often inadvertently "hide" environmental costs.

## Total Cost Assessment

Writing on the principles of "total cost assessment," Allen White has observed that "if accounting practices misrepresent the true profitability of prevention options, both business and the environment lose out. Correcting such bias requires an approach we call 'Total Cost Assessment' (TCA)."[6] TCA encompasses four elements: cost inventory, cost allocation, a time horizon, and financial indicators (see box on page 106).

### TCA Methodologies

Three approaches to TCA have been developed over the past eight to ten years.[7] They are:

## *Total Cost Assessment*

*Total Cost Assessment (TCA) integrates environmental costs into a capital budgeting analysis. The following costs are considered by TCA:*

**Cost inventory:** This includes (a) **direct costs** such as capital expenditures and operational and maintenance costs; (b) **hidden costs** such as compliance costs, insurance, on-site waste management, and on-site pollution control equipment; (c) **liability costs** such as penalties and fines, personal injury, or property damage; and (d) **less tangible benefits** such as increased revenues from enhanced product quality, enhanced company and product image, reduced health costs, and increased productivity.

**Expanded time horizon:** TCA evaluates costs and benefits over five or more years.

**Cost allocation:** In order to properly allocate for cost, Allen White explains, a precise mass balance and costing of how materials flow into, through, and out of the manufacturing process is required. This is more difficult than it seems and will likely require more precision in data collection to avoid confounding cost allocation. Yet one must be careful not to seek too much precision, because sooner or later greater precision outweighs the cost of collecting the data.

**Financial indicators:** Some of the most popular financial indicators are net present value (NPV), internal rate of return (IRR), return on investment (ROI), and payback (see Appendix B for further definitions and examples of calculations).

1. *Financial Analysis of Waste Management Alternatives* (1987), developed by the General Electric Corporation ("GE method"). The GE method is used to identify and rank waste minimization investment options.

2. *PRECOSIS* (1989), developed by the George Beetle Company and designed to support the financial analysis of waste reduction.

3. *Pollution Prevention Benefits Manual,* or "EPA method" (1990), developed for the U.S. Environmental Protection Agency. The EPA method is designed to assist in the cost comparison of one or more pollution-prevention (PP or $P^2$) alternatives to current industrial prac-

**Table 6-2.** Types of hidden environmental costs.

| *Regulatory* | *Up-Front* | *Voluntary* |
|---|---|---|
| • Notification | • Site studies | • Community relations |
| • Reporting | • Site preparation | • Monitoring |
| • Monitoring/Testing | • Permitting | • Training |
| • Studies/Modeling | • R&D | • Environmental audits |
| • Remediation | • Engineering/ | • Qualifying suppliers |
| • Record keeping | Procurement | • Reports |
| • Plans | • Installation | • Insurance |
| • Training | | • Planning |
| • Inspections | *Conventional Costs* | • Feasibility studies |
| • Manifesting | Capital equipment | • Remediation |
| • Labeling | Materials | • Recycling |
| • Preparedness | Labor | • Environmental studies |
| • Protective equipment | Supplies | • R&D |
| • Medical surveillance | Utilities | • Habitat protection |
| • Environmental | Structures | • Landscaping |
| insurance | Salvage value | • Financial support to |
| • Financial insurance | | environmental groups |
| • Pollution control | *Back-End** | • Other projects |
| • Spill response | • Decommissioning | |
| • Stormwater | • Disposal of inventory | |
| management | • Postclosure care | |
| • Waste management | • Site survey | |
| • Taxes/Fees | | |
| • Audits (for 14001) | | |

| | *Contingent Costs** | |
|---|---|---|
| • Future compliance costs | • Remediation | • Legal expenses |
| • Penalties/Fines | • Property damage | • Natural resource |
| • Response to future | • Personal injury damage | damages |
| releases | | • Economic loss damages |

| | *Image and Relationship Costs** | |
|---|---|---|
| • Corporate image | • Relationship with | • Relationship with |
| • Relationship with | professional staff | lenders |
| customers | • Relationship with | • Relationship with host |
| • Relationship with | workers | communities |
| investors | • Relationship with | • Relationship with |
| • Relationship with | suppliers | regulators |
| insurers | | |

SOURCE: EPA, *An Introduction to Environmental Accounting as a Business Management Tool: Key Concepts and Terms* (EPA 742-R-95-001, June 1995), p. 9.
*Back-end costs, or exit costs, are costs such as decommissioning and cleanup that arise following the useful life of processes, products, systems, or facilities. Contingent costs, or contingent liabilities, may or may not occur in the future (fines and penalties for future regulatory infractions). Image and relationship costs may result in intangible benefits. These costs may include annual environmental reports, voluntary environmental activities, and community actions.

**Figure 6-1.** Environmental accounting: traditional vs. revised cost allocation.

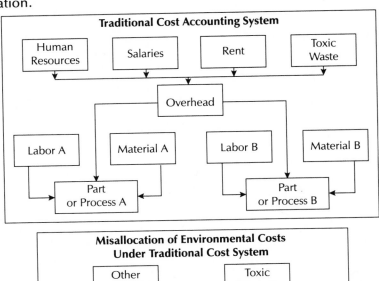

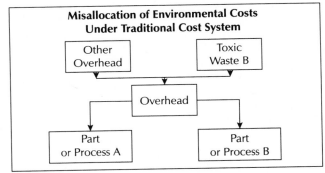

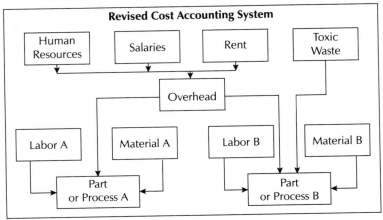

**Figure 6-2.** Examples of hidden environmental costs.

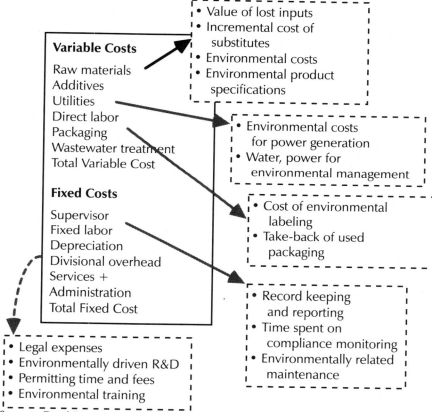

Source: Daryl Ditz et al., "Environmental Accounting: An Overview," in Daryl Ditz et al., *Green Ledgers: Case Studies in Corporate Environmental Accounting* (A World Resource Institute Book, 1995), p. 12.

tices.[8] Only the EPA P[2] method will be described here; a simple case study of raw material reduction and its associated economic benefits is presented in Appendix C.

### EPA's Pollution Prevention (P²)

One of the appealing aspects of the EPA's P[2] method is that it allows for the differentiation of four types of costs, which are set up in a hierarchy as follows:

*Tier 0:* Usual costs:          Equipment, labor, and materials
*Tier 1:* Hidden costs:         Compliance and permits
*Tier 2:* Liability costs:      Penalties/fines and future liabilities
*Tier 3:* Less tangible costs:  Consumer responses and employee rela-
                                tions

The hierarchy progresses from the least difficult costs (Tier 0) to the most difficult, and therefore least accurate, costs (Tier 3). Fortunately, one does not need to evaluate all costs in order for the technique to be valuable (see Case Study). Table 6-3 lists examples of typical costs by tier.

---

### *Case Study*

The following case study of the EPA's method is a slightly simpli-fied version of the one found in Appendix A-1 of the EPA's *Total Cost Assessment (see note 2).*

#### Background

This specialty paper mill produces approximately 190 tons per year of a variety of uncoated and on-machine and off-machine coated papers, carbonizing, book, and release base paper. Wastewater from the mill is pumped to a neighborhood mill for treatment. Because total suspended solids and biochemical oxygen demand (BOD) are reportedly higher than industry average, the neighbor-hood mill has asked the specialty mill to reduce wastewater flow. A study was commissioned to review the design and operation of the mill and to recommend changes that would help reduce peak effluent flows, reduce BOD in the effluent, and reduce total fresh water intake. Two process modifications were recommended.

To assess the economic feasibility of the project, the company conducted its own financial analysis (Tables 6-4–6-6). To verify the accuracy of its analysis, the company hired a consulting firm to conduct a TCA analysis (Tables 6-7–6-10). A comparison of the two studies is summarized in Table 6-4 (for a definition of net present value, internal rate of return and other terms that relate to this section, see Appendix B). A more detailed analysis follows (Tables 6-5–6-10). (*Note:* Calculations are reproduced for the first ten years. Enough information is provided in the following tables for the reader to complete Table 6-9 for years 11–15, which is included in Appendix B.)

**Table 6-3.** Typical costs associated with each tier.

## Tier 0:  Usual Costs

*Depreciable Costs*
  Equipment
  Materials
  Utility connections
  Site preparation
  Installation
  Engineering and procurement

*Expenses*
  Start-up costs
  Permitting costs
  Salvage value
  Training costs
  Initial chemicals
  Working capital
  Disposal costs
  Raw material costs
  Utilities costs
  Catalysts and chemicals
  Operating and materials supplies
  Insurance costs

*Operating Revenues*
  From sale of primary products
  From sale of marketable by-products

## Tier 1:  Hidden Costs

*Facility's regulatory status* under RCRA, CERCLA, SARA Title III, Clean Air Act, OSHA, and relevant state regulatory programs (see Chapter 1 for definition of terms).

*Technology-forcing regulatory requirements* and the costs associated with them.

*Cost Components for Regulatory Activities*
  Notification
  Reporting
  Monitoring/Testing
  Record keeping

**Table 6-3.** (continued)

Planning/Studies/Modeling
Training
Inspection
Manifesting
Labeling
Preparedness/Protective equipment (maintenance)
Closure/Postclosure assurance
Medical surveillance
Insurance and special taxes

**Tier 2:  Liability Costs (estimated via equations provided in the EPA manual)**

Soil and waste removal treatment
Groundwater removal and treatment
Surface sealing
Personal injury
Economic loss
Real property damage
Natural resource damage

**Tier 3:  Less Tangible Costs**

These costs are estimated by using equations included in the EPA manual.

The financial calculation for the net present value of the project is shown in Table 6-10. The reader is referred to Appendix B for a definition and explanation of some key terms as well as a listing of additional tables required for the appropriate coefficients. The net present value (NPV) of $1,348,753 indicates that, given the cash flow (shown in column 2 of Table 6-10), the project will be repaid within approximately two years and nine months. This result is much more optimistic than the original company's study, which concluded that the payback period would be more than eleven years (see Table 6-4).

# Advantages of TCA

Although total cost accounting has been practiced by a few companies for the past five to ten years, it is still ignored by too many companies. It is likely that within the next two to five years this practice will change. Indeed, some states have begun to require companies to prepare some

**Table 6-4.** Summary and comparison of cost items in company and TCA cost analyses.

| | Company Analysis | TCA Analysis |
|---|---|---|
| Capital Costs | | |
| Purchased equipment | X* | X |
| Materials (e.g., piping, electrical) | X | X |
| Utility system | X | X |
| Site preparation | X | X |
| Installation (labor) | X | X |
| Engineering contractor | X | X |
| Contingency | X | X |
| Operational Costs | | |
| Direct Costs | | |
| Raw Materials/Supplies | P** | X |
| Labor | X | X |
| Indirect Costs | | |
| Energy | P | X |
| Water | — | X |
| Sewerage | X | X |
| Total Capital Costs | $809,700 | $1,743,820 |
| Annual Savings (before interest and taxes) | $116,245 | $658,415 |
| Financial Indicators | | |
| Net present value: years 1–10 | ($702,855) | $1,242,536 |
| Net present value: years 1–15 | ($587,346) | $1,808,384 |
| Internal rate of return: years 1–10 | 0% | 36% |
| Internal rate of return: years 1–15 | 6% | 38% |
| Simple payback (years) | 11.4 | 2.8 |

*X = cost(s) included
**P = cost(s) partially included

form of environmental financial statements. The state of Washington, for example, initiated the concept in the early 1990s (see Appendix A).

But, besides statutory requirements, there is at least one other reason why companies should seriously begin to consider the use of TCA. Investors and the financial market in general may soon begin to look for environmental indicators before investing in companies. One organization, the Investor Responsibility Research Center, Inc. (IRRC), in Washington D.C., produces an annual *Corporate Environmental Profiles Directory* (CEPD) in which organizations are rated using several environmental efficiency indices, or EEIs. The indices are based on concepts similar to those used

**Table 6-5.** Company estimates of capital costs.

| | Cost | Totals |
|---|---|---|
| Capital costs | | |
| Purchased equipment | | |
| Equipment—phase I | $330,853 | |
| Equipment—phase II | $15,132 | |
| | | $345,985 |
| Materials | | |
| Piping | $183,690 | |
| Electrical | $67,721 | |
| Instruments | $68,455 | |
| Structural | $54,946 | |
| | | $374,812 |
| Utility connections | | 0 |
| Site preparation | | 0 |
| Installation | | |
| Contractor | $397,148 | |
| | | $397,148 |
| Engineering/contractor | | |
| Engineering | $166,946 | |
| Consultants | $44,100 | |
| | | $211,046 |
| Start-up training | | 0 |
| Contingency | | 0 |
| Permitting | | 0 |
| Initial catalysts/chemicals | | 0 |
| Depreciable capital | | $1,328,991 |
| Working capital | | 0 |
| Subtotal | | $1,328,991 |
| Interest on debt | | 0 |
| Total capital requirement | | $1,328,991 |
| Salvage value | | 0 |
| Equity | | 100% |
| Debt | | 0 |
| Interest rate on debt (%) | | 12.0% |
| Debt repayment (years) | | 5 years |
| *Equity investment* | | $1,328,991 |
| *Debt principal* | | 0 |
| *Interest on debt* | | 0 |
| *Total financing* | | $1,328,991 |
| *Depreciation period (years)* | | 15 |
| *Income tax rate (%)* | | 40 |
| *Escalation rate (CVIF)* | | 5% |
| *Cost of capital for net present value (%)* | | 15% |

*Note:* The EPA's example has a value of 16%.

**Table 6-6.** Company estimates of operating costs.

| Operating Costs | Current Process | Alternative | Difference (Current − Alternative) |
|---|---|---|---|
| Raw materials/supplies | $536,700 | $382,700 | $154,000 |
| Waste management | 0 | 0 | 0 |
| Utilities | 273,000 | 307,635 | (34,635) |
| Labor | 0 | 3,120 | (3,120) |
| Other | 0 | 0 | 0 |
| Regulatory compliance | 0 | 0 | 0 |
| Insurance | 0 | 0 | 0 |
| Maintenance % of capital | | | |
| Labor | 0% | 0% | 0% |
| Materials | 0% | 0% | 0% |
| Overhead % of Labor | 0% | 0% | 0% |
| Revenues | 0 | 0 | 0 |
| Marketable by-products | | | |
| Total | $809,700 | $693,455 | $116,245 |

in the Standard & Poor's financial indices to rate the financial performance of companies. Some of the indices computed by the IRRC include an emissions efficiency index, a spill index, a penalty index, and a compliance index evaluated on ten U.S. statutes (RCRA, CWA, TSCA, OSHA, AEA, and so on; see Table 1-2 for definitions). In addition, the report includes information on the company's environmental management and policy, environmental auditing and reporting, sustainability indicators, and environmental achievements and projects (see Table 6-11). Some of the information contained within the report is either directly related to requirements listed in the ISO 14001 standard or is a logical extension of the international standard. For example, one notes that the name of the corporate environmental officer is recorded as well as the person he reports to. The report also indicates whether or not the company has an environmental policy (4.2 of ISO 14001) and whether or not suppliers are evaluated and selected on the basis of environmental risk factors (4.4.6 d), ISO 14001). The names of those on the board of directors responsible for overseeing environmental matters are listed (4.4.1, ISO 14001). Information is also collected on environmental audits (4.5.4, ISO 14001) and emission reductions (4.3.3, ISO 14001). Under the compliance data section (see Table 6-12), one can verify the company's management commitment to comply with relevant environmental legislation and regulations as well as other requirements (4.2 c), 4.3.2, ISO 14001). Other linkages to ISO 14001 could be found.

**Table 6-7.** TCA capital cost estimates (same as company estimates).

| Capital Costs | Totals |
|---|---|
| Equipment | $345,985 |
| Materials | $374,812 |
| Utility connections | 0 |
| Site preparation | 0 |
| Contractor | $397,148 |
| Engineering/contractor | $211,046 |
| Start-up training | 0 |
| Contingency | 0 |
| Permitting | 0 |
| Initial catalysts/chemicals | 0 |
| Depreciable capital | $1,329,001 |
| Working capital | 0 |
| Subtotal | $1,329,001 |
| Interest on debt | 0 |
| Total capital requirement | $1,329,001 |
| Salvage value | 0 |
| Equity | 100% |
| Debt | 0% |
| Interest rate on debt (%) | 12.0% |
| *Debt repayment (years)* | 5 |
| *Equity investment* | $1,329,001 |
| *Debt principal* | 0 |
| *Interest on debt* | 0 |
| *Total financing* | $1,329,001 |
| *Depreciation period (years)* | 15 |
| *Income tax rate (%)* | 40% |
| *Escalation rate (compound value CVIF)* | 5% |
| *Cost of capital for net present value (%)* | 15% |

Note: The EPA's example has a value of 16%.

The IRRC directory, designed to help "green investors" select companies on the basis of their environmental performance, could also benefit registrars conducting ISO 14001 environmental audits. Auditors will undoubtedly find the directory of considerable value.

## Conclusion

The technique of total cost accounting (TCA) is a valuable tool that allows organizations to evaluate and rank their process improvement

**Table 6-8.** Comparative operating costs (TCA analysis).

| Operating Costs | Current Process | Alternative | Difference (Current − Alternative) |
|---|---|---|---|
| Raw materials/supplies | $536,700 | $382,700 | $154,000 |
| Waste management | 0 | 0 | 0 |
| Utilities | $1,217,480 | $709,945 | $507,535* |
| Labor | 0 | $3,120 | (3,120) |
| Other | 0 | 0 | 0 |
| Regulatory compliance | 0 | 0 | 0 |
| Insurance | 0 | 0 | 0 |
| Maintenance % of capital | | | |
| Labor | 0% | 0% | 0% |
| Materials | 0% | 0% | 0% |
| Overhead % of labor | 0% | 0% | 0% |
| Revenues | 0 | 0 | 0 |
| Marketable by-products | | | |
| Total | $1,754,180 | $1,095,765 | $658,415 |

*The TCA analysis revealed that the company's estimate for utilities cost of the current and alternative processes did not account for all costs; hence, the difference of $507,535 noted in the "Utilities" row. This difference will affect the profitability analysis (see Table 6-9).

strategy as it relates to pollution prevention and reduction. The overall benefits of quantifying and monitoring environmental performance go beyond accounting. Indeed, a 1995 study conducted by Dr. Mark Cohen of the Graduate School of Management at Vanderbilt University demonstrated that companies that are better environmental performers also tend to be as good as or better financial performers than firms that pollute more. Although Dr. Cohen wisely observes that "greener" enterprises pollute less because their superior financial position allows them to invest more in process improvements, the fact remains that firms that pollute less do so because their processes are more efficient. This, the study concludes, is likely to attract the attention of investors. As Cohen notes, "being a good environmental actor does *not* hurt the bottom line."[9]

One way to improve environmental performance that is likely to please investors is through the use of concepts such as Design for the Environment and Life-Cycle assessment, discussed in the next chapter.

*(Notes are on page 121)*

**Table 6-9.** Profitability analysis (TCA analysis) for ten years.

| Year | 0 | 1 | 2 | 3 | 4 | 5 | 6 | 7 | 8 | 9 | 10 |
|---|---|---|---|---|---|---|---|---|---|---|---|
| Escalating factor* | 1.0 | 1.050 | 1.102 | 1.158 | 1.216 | 1.276 | 1.341 | 1.407 | 1.477 | 1.551 | 1.629 |
| Revenues | | (1.050) | (1.103) | (1.158) | (1.216) | (1.277) | (1.341) | (1.408) | (1.477) | (1.552) | (1.630) |
| Operating (cost)/saving | | $0 | $0 | $0 | $0 | $0 | $0 | $0 | $0 | $0 | $0 |
| Raw materials/supplies | | $154,000 | $169,862 | $178,332 | $187,264 | $196,658 | $206,514 | $216,832 | $227,612 | $239,008 | $251,020 |
| Utilities | | 507,535 | 559,811 | 587,726 | 617,163 | 648,122 | 680,604 | 714,609 | 750,137 | 787,694 | 827,282 |
| Labor | | (3,120) | (3,441) | (3,613) | (3,794) | (3,984) | (4,184) | (4,393) | (4,611) | (4,848) | (5,086) |
| Total | | $658,415 | $726,232 | $762,445 | $800,633 | $840,796 | $882,934 | $927,048 | $973,138 | $1,021,860 | $1,073,216 |
| Capital costs $1,329,001 | | | | | | | | | | | |
| Double depreciation Investment cash flow | | $1,241,401 | $1,075,014 | $931,679 | $807,455 | $699,794 | $606,488 | $542,647 | $478,647 | $414,965 | $351,124 |
| Tax depreciation | | $88,600** | $88,600 | $88,600 | $88,660 | $88,660 | $88,600 | $88,600 | $88,600 | $88,660 | $88,660 |
| Double depreciation cash flow | | $88,600*** | $165,387 | $143,335 | $124,224 | $107,661 | $93,306 | $72,353 | $63,841 | $63,841 | $63,841 |
| Operating cash flow | | $658,415 | $726,232 | $762,445 | $800,633 | $840,796 | $882,934 | $927,048 | $973,138 | $1,021,860 | $1,073,216 |
| Depreciation | | $88,600 | $165,387 | $143,335 | $124,224 | $107,661 | $63,841 | $63,841 | $63,841 | $63,841 | $63,841 |
| Taxable income | | $569,815 | $560,845 | $619,110 | $679,409 | $733,135 | $789,628 | $863,207 | $909,297 | $958,019 | $1,009,375 |
| Income tax (40%) | | $227,926 | $224,338 | $247,644 | $270,564 | $293,254 | $315,851 | $345,283 | $363,719 | $383,208 | $403,750 |
| Net income | | $341,889 | $336,507 | $371,466 | $405,845 | $439,881 | $473,777 | $517,924 | $545,578 | $574,811 | $605,625 |
| Depreciation | | $88,600 | $165,387 | $143,335 | $124,224 | $107,661 | $93,306, | $63,841 | $63,841 | $63,841 | $63,841 |
| After-tax cash flow | | $430,489 | $501,894 | $514,801 | $530,069 | $547,542 | $567,083 | $581,765 | $609,419 | $638,652 | $669,466 |

*The escalating factor is equivalent to the compound value interest factor (CVIF). For a definition of CVIF and a listing of coefficients, see Appendix B, Table B-1. Figures in parentheses are figures reported in the original study and used for computations. Except for the last digit, the numbers match the numbers reproduced in Table B-1. The $169,862 found in the Raw Materials/Supplies row is $154,000 × 1.103, which equals $169,862.

**$88,600 is obtained by dividing (i.e., depreciating) the original investment of $1,329,001 over the life of the project, which is defined to be 15 years (this is known as straight-line depreciation). This averages to a depreciation rate of 6.66 percent per year (see Appendix B for definition of straight line method; also for years 11–15).

***The double depreciation method simply doubles the depreciation rate of 6.66% × 2 = 13.3%. The technique shown here is a modified double depreciation method that switches to straight-line; see Appendix B for further clarification.

**Table 6-10.** Financial calculations for NPV of project.

| Year | Net Cash Flow (from Table 6-9) | Net Present Value Interest Factor for 15% Interest Rate* | Present Value of Cash Flow |
|------|-------------------------------|--------------------------------------------------------|----------------------------|
| 1 | $430,489 | .870 | $374,525 |
| 2 | 501,894 | .756 | 379,432 |
| 3 | 514,801 | .658 | 338,739 |
| 4 | 530,069 | .572 | 303,199 |
| 5 | 547,542 | .497 | 272,128 |
| 6 | 567,083 | .432 | 244,980 |
| 7 | 581,765 | .376 | 218,735 |
| 8 | 609,419 | .327 | 199,280 |
| 9 | 638,652 | .284 | 181,377 |
| 10 | 669,466 | .247 | 165,358 |
| | | | Total $2,677,753 |
| | | | Less 1,329,001 |
| | | | **NPV $1,348,753** |

*PVIF is defined in Appendix B and a table of PVIF coefficients provided. Appendix B also estimates the internal rate of return.

**Table 6-11.** Partial summary of information contained within the IRRC directory.

| *Environmental Management* | *1993 Form 10-K Environmental* |
|---|---|
| | **Disclosure** |
| Senior Officer: | Env. Capital expenditures: Actual: |
| | Projected: |
| Title: | Env. Legal proceedings: |
| Levels to CEO: | |
| Reports to: | |
| Env. staff: | Secondary industries |
| | |
| Bd. Committee: | |
| Directors: | |
| Outside codes: | |
| | |
| ☐ Env. policy | ☐ Suppliers |
| ☐ Env. factor in pay | ☐ Partners |
| ☐ U.S. stds. overseas | ☐ Clients |
| ☐ Uniform corp. std. | ☐ Insurance |
| ☐ TQEM | ☐ Reserve fund of $200M |
| *Environmental Auditing & Reporting* | *Sustainability Indicators* |
| | Raw Indexed Change |
| Auditing Program: | Energy use: |
| Audited in last 2 yrs. (US/non-US): | Water use: |
| Avg. time between audits: | Material use: |
| Conducted by: | Recycled used: |
| Audit results (Yes/No): | Haz. waste: |
| Environmental report (frequency): | Latest: |
| | |
| *Environmental Achievements & Projects* | |
| EPA Voluntary programs: | Emission Reductions: Reduction Base |
| ☐ 33/50 Program: | Year Goal Target |
| ☐ Waste Wi$e: | All SARA 313: |
| ☐ GreenLights: | Air: |
| ☐ Energy Star: | Water: |
| Recycling: | Haz. waste disp.: |
| Hazardous waste: | Nonhaz. waste disp: |
| Nonhazardous waste: | VOCs: |
| Recycled material purchased: | ODs: |
| Underground storage tank removed | Other: |
|    or replaced: | Toxic use reduction: |

SOURCE: IRRC sample report.

**Table 6-12.** Sample compliance data published by IRRC.

| Statute | Penalties | Total Value ($) | Penalty Indices Company | Industry |
|---------|-----------|-----------------|-------------------------|----------|
| RCRA | 3 | 5,550 | 0.40 | 20.63 |
| CAA | 7 | 179,230 | 12.97 | 338.64 |
| CWA | 0 | 0 | 0 | 83.82 |
| SDWA | 0 | 0 | 0.00 | 0.00 |
| TSCA | 1 | 1,000 | 0.07 | 1.89 |
| FIFRA | 0 | 0 | 0.00 | 0.00 |
| OSHA | 0 | 0 | 0.00 | 0.67 |
| MSHA | 0 | 0 | 0.00 | 0.05 |
| AEA | 0 | 0 | 0.00 | 0.00 |
| ESA | 0 | 0 | 0.00 | 0.00 |
| Year | | | IRRC Compliance Index | |
| 1991 | 6 | 14,230 | 3.21 | 60.06 |
| 1992 | 3 | 146,750 | 31.04 | 224.59 |
| 1993 | 2 | 24,800 | 5.33 | 1,455.13 |
| Total, 1991–1993 | 11 | 185,780 | 13.44 | 445.70 |
| % change, 1988–93: | | | +8% | +2,258% |

SOURCE: IRRC sample report.

# Notes

1. Stephan Schimdheiney, *Changing Course* (Cambridge, Mass.: The MIT Press, 1992), pp. 15, 16.
2. EPA, *Total Cost Assessment: Accelerating Industrial Pollution Prevention through Innovative Project Financial Analysis. With Applications to the Pulp and Paper Industry* (Washington, D.C.: Office of Pollution Prevention and Toxics. EPA/741/R-92/002, May 1992), p. 57. Material information is defined as any information that a reasonable investor would likely deem important in determining whether to buy or sell a company's securities. Ever since the early to mid-1990s, major corporations have begun to publish environmental reports. General Motors and other corporations that endorse the CERES Principles have published environmental reports since the early 1990s. The CERES Principles are described in Chapter 3.
3. *Business Ethics*, July/August 1995, p. 39.
4. EPA, *Total Cost Assessment*, p. 9.
5. For case studies, see Daryl Ditz et al. (eds.), *Green Ledgers: Case Studies in Corporate Environmental Accounting* (Baltimore: World Resources Institute, 1995).
6. Allen L. White, "Accounting for Pollution Prevention," *EPA Journal*, July–September 1993, pp. 23–25.
7. The following section is based on *Total Cost Assessment: Accelerating Industrial Pollution Prevention through Innovation Project Financial Analysis. EPA/741/R-92/002, May 1992.*

8. *Other TCA methods include the EPA's Waste Minimization Opportunity Assessment Manual,* EPA/625/7-88/003 (Cincinnati, Ohio, 1988), and Waste Advantage, Inc., *Industrial Waste Prevention: Guide to Developing an Effective Waste Minimization Program* (Southfield, Mich., 1988).

9. Mark A. Cohen, Scott A. Fenn, and Jonathan Naimon, "Environmental and Financial Performance: Are They Related?" (Nashville, Tenn.: Owen Graduate School of Management, Vanderbilt University, April 1995), p. 10.

# 7

# Design for the Environment and Life-Cycle Analysis

After some twenty years of end-of-the-pipe regulations, an increasing number of companies have come to realize that the best way to clean up the environment and avoid confrontation with local, state, or national regulatory agencies is to prevent environmental deterioration in the first place. In order to eliminate or at least significantly reduce pollution *before* it is generated, companies have come to recognize that the best environmental solutions often involve innovative or, in some cases, simple "environmentally friendly" changes in the production process, the feedstocks, or the design itself.[1]

## Design for the Environment

The concept of Design for the Environment (DfE) is not new. Victor Papanek had realized as early as 1971 or even earlier that when it comes to pollution, "the designer is more heavily implicated than most people." Papanek therefore concluded that

> design, if it is to be ecologically responsible and socially responsive, must be revolutionary and radical (going back to the roots) in the truest sense. It must dedicate itself to nature's "principle of least effort," in other words, minimum inventory for maximum diversity . . . or, doing the most with the least. That means consuming less, using things longer, recycling materials, and probably not wasting paper printing books such as this.[2]

In an attempt to help business incorporate pollution prevention considerations in the design and redesign of products and services, researchers and consultants alike have, during the 1980s and early 1990s, rediscovered most of Papanek's ideas. Examples of recent projects would include: (1) *accounting and capital budgeting* that incorporate environmental costs and benefits into managerial accounting and capital budgeting practices (see Chapter 6); (2) *chemical design* to minimize or eliminate hazardous substances (see Chapter 9); (3) *curriculum development*, as with, for example, the University of Michigan National Pollution Prevention Center; (4) *risk management/insurance* in which the EPA works with the American Institute of Chartered Property and Casualty Underwriters to incorporate pollution prevention in the curriculum of the institute's certification program; (5) a *dry cleaning project* to reduce "perc," or perchloroethylene, a chemical solvent used by most dry cleaners; (6) a *printing (green) project* that explores different technologies such as waterless printing; and (7) *cleaning projects* that will develop standards for cleaning products, perform integrated risk assessments, and evaluate product performance (see Chapter 9 for several examples).

A 1994 EPA brochure entitled "Why Design for the Environment?" suggests that there are several ways for a business to "design for the environment." A business can implement pollution prevention, energy efficiency, and other resources conservation measures; produce and use less toxic materials; market products that can be refurbished, disassembled, or recycled; or keep careful track of the environmental costs associated with each product or process (see Chapter 6).[3] Examples of DfE have already demonstrated the cost-effectiveness of such projects. Within the printing industry, for example, the waterless process reduces make-ready time by 30 percent and cuts paper waste by 10 percent.[4] The EPA Energy Star Program has encouraged some computer manufacturers to redesign their products so that they will automatically power down to save energy. At Xerox, the design for the environment approach led engineers to reevaluate the life cycle of cartridges and devise ways to use returnable cartridges. The task was not without difficulties. Indeed, only a certain type of plastic could be used, and, moreover, since plastics are not always identified in the form of finished products, they are not easily recyclable. To solve the many difficulties and simplify the process of material separation, Xerox had to develop an international system for plastic identification. After months of perseverance, Xerox was able to reduce the number of thermoplastic resins from over 500 to fifty, and ten of these may satisfy 80 percent of the applications.[5]

Although the purpose of DfE is to consider, during the design phases, all factors associated with environmental safety and health over the entire product life cycle, one of the ultimate objectives of DfE is to prevent pollution of any kind. It is therefore not uncommon to see pollution prevention analyses (also known as $P^2$) associated with many DfEs. For example, most, if not all, of the case studies reported by the EPA in its *Design for the Environment* pamphlets and brochures describe examples of process improvements that led to a reduction in pollution for the dry cleaning industry and the printing industry.[6] Numerous other examples of pollution prevention/DfE projects have been reported by several industries (see box and Chapter 9).

---

**Solvent use reduction at GM's Fabrication Plant 3:** It now uses an adhesive that reduces toluene emission. Worked with supplier and developed a new nonsolvent adhesive for hood assemblies and other applications (trunk lid and doors). Results: Elimination of 300 tons per year of toluene released to air. Since adhesive residues and/or containers are nonflammable, they can be handled and disposed as nonhazardous materials at a lower cost. Hazardous waste was reduced at Plant 3 from 300,000 gallons to 400 gallons.

**Delco Remy recovery and recyling of lead from its battery-making operations at its Muncie, Indiana, plant:** Plant personnel developed a new method to recover the lead from the process water in a manner that makes it suitable for recycling. A chemical mixture developed in cooperation with an outside supplier is added to the tank containing the wastewater. After the lead has settled, 90 percent of the wastewater is removed, and the remaining lead is sent to a secondary smelter for reclaiming. 125,000 pounds of lead are reclaimed and recycled.

**Sun energy reduction:** Sun is reducing energy consumption at its refineries at a rate of about 1 percent per year, reducing its toxic releases, and had a 30 percent decrease in number of spills (483).

*Source: The Green Business Letter, March 1994.*

---

An important and related technique, which will be called for by the ISO 14000 series of guidelines (ISO 14040–14043) within the next two to three years, is life-cycle assessments.

# Life-Cycle Assessment

Life-cycle assessment (LCA) is one of several techniques available to environmental managers. It complements other techniques such as environmental impact assessment, hazard identification, risk assessment, technology assessment, waste audits and waste minimization assessment of processes, design for the environment (also known as life-cycle thinking), product stewardship, and management systems standards. The first study that came to be known as a life-cycle inventory analysis was conducted in 1963 by Harold Smith. In 1969 researchers initiated a study for the Coca-Cola Company that laid the foundations for the current life-cycle inventory analysis methodology. Encouraged by the success of these early studies, various industries began to expand on the concept of life-cycle inventory to include so-called cradle-to-grave analysis. During the early 1960s, the process of quantifying the resource use and environmental releases during the manufacturing of products came to be known in the United States as Resource and Environmental Profile Analysis (REPA) or cradle-to-grave analysis and in Europe as Ecobalance. By 1975 some fifteen REPAs were performed. Unfortunately, the interest in REPAs began to wane in the United States after 1975. This was not so in Europe, where interest grew with the establishment of an Environmental Directorate (DG X1) by the European Commission. The EPA's Life-Cycle Assessment explains its focus:

> European life-cycle assessment practitioners developed approaches parallel to those being used in the USA. Besides working to standardize pollution regulations throughout Europe, DG X1 issued the Liquid Food Container Directive in 1985, which charged member companies with monitoring the energy and raw materials consumption and solid waste generation of liquid food containers.[7]

Contrary to what some authors would have us believe, LCA studies are not easy to conduct and, despite the availability of software, still require considerable effort. Although the basic principles are relatively simple to grasp, conducting a proper LCA may not be within the reach of all organizations. Indeed, LCA requires a significant amount of time and resources as well as the need to follow a rigorous, but not yet standardized, methodology.

## An Outline of LCA Methodology

The Society for Environmental Toxiocology and Chemistry (SETAC) defines LCA as the

> process to evaluate the environmental burdens associated with a product, process, or activity by identifying and quantifying energy and materials used and wastes released to the environment; to assess the impact of those energy and material uses and releases to the environment; and to identify and evaluate opportunities to effect environmental improvements. The assessment includes the entire life-cycle of the product, process, or activity, encompassing extracting and processing raw materials; manufacturing; transportation and distribution; use, reuse, maintenance; recycling; and final disposal.[8]

The main focus of LCA is to determine the environmental impacts of the system under study in the areas of ecological well-being, human health, and resource depletion (see Figure 7-1).

SETAC recommends that a properly conducted life-cycle assessment should consist of four components: (1) goal definition and scoping; (2) inventory analysis; (3) impact assessment; and (4) improvement assessment (see Table 7-1 and Figure 7-2).

LCA may be used in a wide range of applications. A company can use LCA internally for strategic planning, product or process design or redesign, environmental auditing and waste minimization, and development of purchasing procedures and specifications to monitor suppliers and/or subcontractors. Externally, LCA can be used as a marketing tool to support marketing (environmental) claims, in public education and communication, for policy making, and perhaps in setting criteria for ecolabeling. Although LCA and life-cycle improvements (LCIs) are sufficiently developed to serve as a basis for applications such as ecolabeling, product certification programs, or environmental claims, in SETAC's opinion, "views concerning the degree to which such applications can or should rely on LCA or LCI information vary considerably."[9]

When conducting LCAs it is important to define the geographical scope of the study as well as the system's boundaries. For a cradle-to-grave study, the system's boundaries will likely extend backward as far as the mining of the raw materials and forward to the eventual termination and disposal of the product (see Figure 7-3). Figures 7-4–7-7 are

**Figure 7-1.** The product life-cycle system.

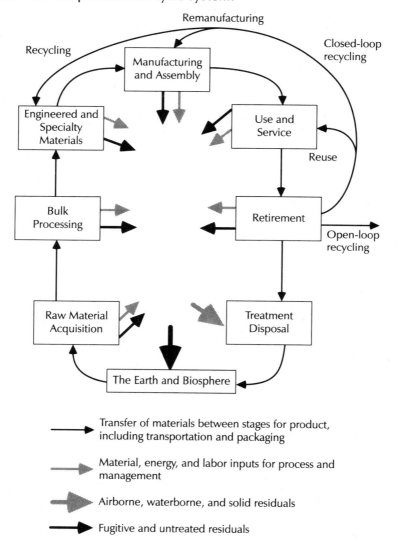

Transfer of materials between stages for product, including transportation and packaging

Material, energy, and labor inputs for process and management

Airborne, waterborne, and solid residuals

Fugitive and untreated residuals

SOURCE: EPA Risk Reduction Engineering Laboratory, Cincinnati, Ohio, Life-Cycle Design Manual: Environmental Requirements and the Product System. EPA/600/SR-92/226 (April 1993), p. 3. See definitions for open- and closed-loop recycling.

**Table 7-1.** The state of development of life-cycle assessment (LCA) methodology.

| LCA Components | Current State of the Art |
|---|---|
| **Goal definition and scoping:**<br>Purpose: To define the purpose and *scope* of the study as well as the *functional unit* for the study. The scope defines the system's boundaries, data requirements, assumptions, and limitations (see Figure 7-2). The functional unit is the measure of performance of the various input and output data (e.g., lbs. of chemical A/ton of output, kg wood pallets/kg product moved, 100 lbs. of emission/100 lbs. of product). Finally, the degree of confidence in the data (data quality) must also be defined. | Defined. |
| **Inventory analysis:**<br>Purpose: To define the system and system boundary, flowchart the processes (production sequence, production of ancillary materials), data collection (inventory tables), treatment of energy. | Defined and understood, but needs some further work. |
| **Impact assessment:**<br>Purpose: To characterize and assess the effects of the environmental burdens identified in the inventory component. | Defined, but needs further work. |
| **Classification**<br>Purpose: To group data from the inventory analysis into a number of impact categories (e.g., $NO_x$ has both an acidifying and eutrophication effect). | Conceptually defined and partly developed. |
| **Characterization:**<br>Purpose: To generate an impact profile such as Global Warming Potential and Ozone Depletion Potential. | |
| **Valuation:**<br>Purpose: To weigh and compare the various impact categories. | Conceptually defined, but needs to formalize how the technique can be applied. |
| **Improvement assessment:**<br>Purpose: To identify and evaluate options for reducing the environmental impact of the system under study. | Not yet documented, but relatively easy to implement, particularly if one relies on pollution-prevention methodology. |

**Figure 7-2.** The LCA framework.

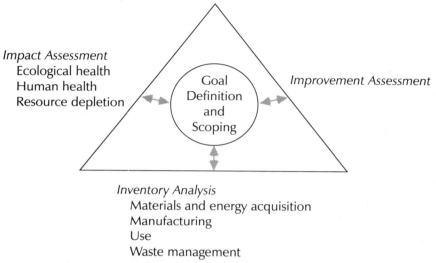

*Impact Assessment*
  Ecological health
  Human health
  Resource depletion

*Improvement Assessment*

*Inventory Analysis*
  Materials and energy acquisition
  Manufacturing
  Use
  Waste management

examples of system boundary definitions for the production of soap bars. Readers wishing to know a little more about life-cycle analysis outputs are referred to Appendix G.

Numerous life-cycle analyses have been conducted in the United States by several industries. In many cases, consulting firms such as Arthur D. Little, Franklin Associates, or the Tellus Institute have participated in the preparation of these studies. The Tellus Institute, for example, released a major packaging study that analyzed the life-cycle impacts of a full range of packaging materials (paper, recycled paper, and paperboard, aluminum, glass, steel, and several plastics).[10] Other studies have been conducted in Germany, Denmark, Canada, France, Australia, and elsewhere. But undoubtedly the leadership in life-cycle analysis comes from the Netherlands. The Dutch IVAM Environmental Research database on building materials consists of more than 250 processes and more than 100 materials that can be analyzed with one of the most popular LCA software packages, SimaPro3, developed in 1990 by the Dutch environmental consultant group Pré Consultancy.[11]

## Life-Cycle Assessment and National Policies

Ever since the mid-1990s, several European countries have attempted to incorporate in their national environmental plans guidelines to help

**Figure 7-3.** Defining system boundaries for life-cycle inventory.

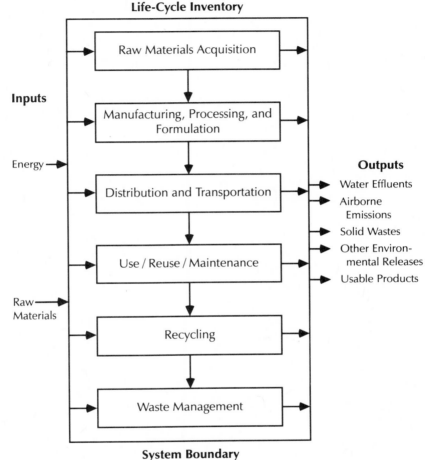

**Life-Cycle Inventory**

Raw Materials Acquisition

**Inputs**

Manufacturing, Processing, and Formulation

Energy →

Distribution and Transportation

Use / Reuse / Maintenance

Raw → Materials

Recycling

Waste Management

**System Boundary**

**Outputs**

Water Effluents

Airborne Emissions

Solid Wastes

Other Environmental Releases

Usable Products

SOURCE: *A Technical Framework for Life-Cycle Assessment* (Pensacola, Fla.: Foundation for Environmental Education, 1991), p. xix.

industries calculate ecoindicators that will help them choose the most environmentally friendly packaging. These ecoindicators attempt to capture in one index the health impact assessment of a product's complete life cycle. In Switzerland, the Swiss Environmental Protection Agency (Bundessamt für Umwelsschutz)—later renamed the Bundessamt für Umwelt, Wald und Landschaft (BUWAL)—has developed a

**Figure 7-4.** Flow diagram for bar soap manufacturing.

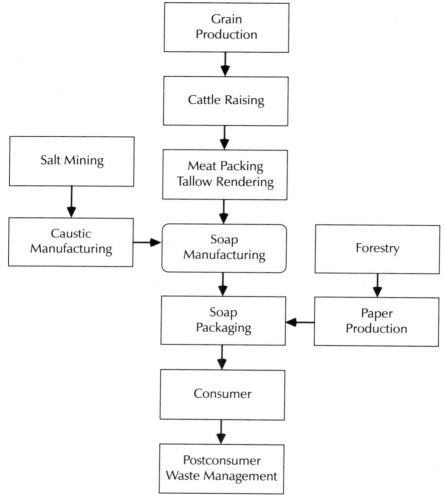

SOURCE: *Life-Cycle Assessment: Inventory Guidelines and Principles* (EPA/600/R-92/245, February 1993), p. 42.

method to compute ecofactors and ecopoints based on maximal emission concentration targets set by national policies. The higher the ecopoints, the worse the emission and hence the worse the product. In the Netherlands, a similar program has been developed by the NOH program. The Department of Environmental Technology at the Danish

**Figure 7-5.** Life-cycle inventory template with example.

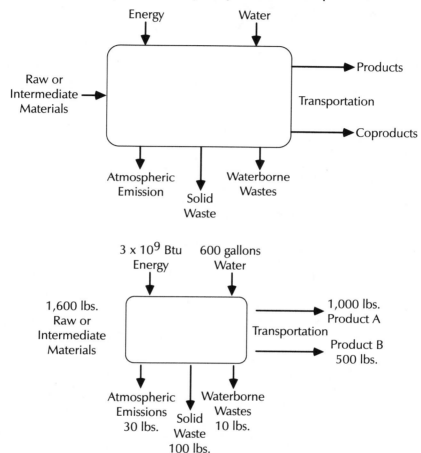

SOURCE: *Life-Cycle Assessment: Inventory Guidelines and Principles* (EPA/600/R-92/245, February 1993), p. 42.

Technological Institute has performed an environmental assessment of polyvinyl chloride (PVC). In Sweden, the Swedish Environmental Research Institute developed its Environmental Priority Strategies in Product Design (the EPS-system) to allow designers and constructors the possibility of assessing the total impacts of a product from cradle to grave.[12]

**Figure 7-6.** Product's life cycle.

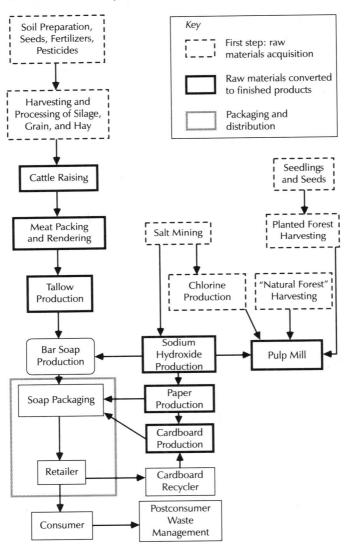

SOURCE: *Life-Cycle Assessment: Inventory Guidelines and Principles* (EPA/600/R-92/245, February 1993), p. 42.
Note: See Figure 7-7 for details of bar soap production.

**Figure 7-7.** Bar soap production.

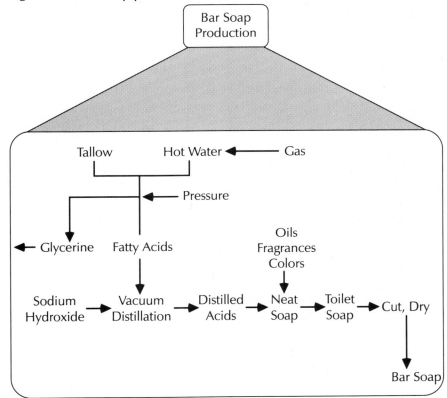

Source: *Life-Cycle Assessment: Inventory Guidelines and Principles* (EPA/600/R-92/245, February 1993), p. 42.

## Ecolabeling and Life Cycle

Environmental labeling, or eco-labeling, is a voluntary program designed to help customers select products that are less harmful to the environment (foods, drinks, and pharmaceutical products are excluded from the ecolabeling scheme). The ecolabel program is based on the "Blue Angel" scheme developed in Germany in 1978. The European Union ecolabeling program was adopted on March 23, 1992, for eventual adoption, sometime within the next few years, by all fifteen members of the Union. Although the intent of the ecolabel scheme is certainly noble, the implementation of ecolabeling is likely to be a complex process. Indeed, one of the difficulties with ecolabeling is that several countries have already implemented or will soon implement their own national ecolabeling program. Examples of ecolabeling programs already in place include: Green Seal (United States), Nordic Swan Label (Norway, Sweden, Finland, and Iceland), Eco Mark Program (Japan), Environmental Choice Program (Canada), AENOR Medio Ambiente (Spain), AFNOR (France), Ecolabel (United Kingdom and Italy), and Green Dot (Germany). Several other countries (Brazil, Greece, and Portugal, to name but a few) will soon have similar programs. Although there are some common features in all these labels, there is nonetheless just enough variation between countries to confuse and perhaps discourage the most devoted and environmentally conscious industrialist. Although it is true that the Scandinavian countries of Iceland, Norway, Sweden, and Finland have attempted to normalize the ecolabel process by recognizing each other's ecolabeling program, a company wishing to have its products marked with the ecolabel of all four Scandinavian countries must still apply for multiple certification.

The fundamental problem with the various national schemes of ecolabeling is that they vary across countries. Not only do the products considered to be important differ from country to country, but the application process, evaluation methodology, and fee structure vary from country to country. Generally speaking, the annual fee (as opposed to the application fee) is set at a percentage of the value of annual production of the product sold within the region. The Nordic Coordinating Body has set the annual fee at 0.4 percent of the approximate annual turnover of the product in its respective market. The maximum cannot exceed approximately $60,000. Canada has a different fee structure, which ranges from $300 Canadian for less than $100,000 of gross annual sales to a maximum of $5,000 for gross revenues of $1 million or more. It is not yet known what the percentage rate will be for the EU ecolabel scheme, but it will probably not exceed 0.4 percent. To add to the confusion, it is still too early to know whether or not the ISO 14020–14024 guidelines for ecolabeling will have any influence on the various national ecolabeling programs (particularly well-established programs). Nor is it known whether member countries will resist the temptation to include additional environmental requirements and/or criteria. The situation is actually much more complicated because cities or states within nations can also develop their own sets of environmental requirements!

As of 1995, the Regulatory Committee established by representatives of the member states of the EU had set, or were about to set, ecological criteria for the following products: washing machines (1994), dishwashers (1994), kitchen rolls (1994), toilet paper (1994), soil improvers (1994), writing paper (1995), textiles (1995), detergents (1995), paints (1995), varnishes (1995), batteries (1995), shampoos (1995), shoes (1995), cat litter (1995), deodorants (1995), and hairstyling products (1995).

### Some Potential Difficulties Associated With the Ecolabel Process

In order to support claims of "environmental friendliness," a manufacturer wishing to have a product or products registered under the ecolabel scheme must apply to a designated body, for example, AENOR in Spain, AFNOR in France, the Japan Environment Association (JEA), and so on. The manufacturer must then submit test results, which must comply with the ecological criteria set by the national committee or the EU Commission (confusion still exists as to mutual recognition). The test results will have to be verified by a government-approved laboratory (this is currently the case in most European countries), and an audit of the facility to verify the manufacturer's claims will eventually follow.

Perhaps the most challenging aspect of the ecolabel set of criteria, at least those set by European schemes, is that the ecolabel can be granted only after the manufacturer demonstrates that it has conducted an environmental impact assessment using life-cycle analysis (the ISO 14024 guidelines also favor life-cycle analysis). Such costly requirements will probably mean that companies will think twice before applying for an ecolabel. Moreover, since no standards for life-cycle analysis have yet been issued, it will be interesting to see if or how life-cycle studies conducted in one country will be accepted by other member states. Given these difficulties, it is not surprising to learn that some countries perceive the ecolabel scheme as a form of nontariff trade barrier. Packaging standards may indeed be unfavorable to the timber and associated industries. Canada's pulp and paper industry, for example, sees ecolabeling as a form of nontariff barrier against Canadian paper products. Similar objections have been raised by Latin American countries.

## Conclusion

Since international standards for LCA are currently being written and will probably not be released until 1997-98, it is difficult to predict what impact, if any, LCA will have on firms throughout the world. The brief review presented in this chapter will probably convince most readers that LCAs, particularly cradle-to-grave LCAs, will not be accessible to the majority of organizations. Indeed, even the most enthusiastic devotee will require much determination to successfully complete a realistic LCA. Some observers, such as Paul Hawken, have already suggested that companies will have to go beyond the life-cycle analysis methodology and apply "the concept of an ecosystem to the whole of an industrial operation, linking the 'metabolism' of one company with that of others."[13] One thing is certain: LCA is already important in Europe and if the ISO 14000 series experiences the same success the ISO 9000 series has had over the past eight years, organizations should begin to investigate the benefits and difficulties associated with LCA.

The last set of techniques to be reviewed relates to the evaluation of hazard. This vast field of knowledge, which has been developed over the past twenty-five years, is a logical extension of DfE and LCA analyses.

## Notes

1. See, for example, Carol M. Browner, "EPA's Technology Innovation Strategy." *EPA Journal*, Fall 1994, pp. 9–12.
2. Victor Papanek, *Design for the Real World: Human Ecology and Social Change* (New York: Pantheon Books, 1971), pp. 213 and 309.
3. EPA, "Why Design for the Environment" (brochure), EPA 774-F-94-003.
4. Jack Palmer, "Mastering Waterless," *American Printer*, October 1994, pp. 48–50.
5. Jack Azar, "Asset Recycling at Xerox," *EPA Journal*, July–September 1993, pp. 14–16. In order to make parts easier to sort and recycle, GM, Ford, and Chrysler use the same code for labeling plastic parts weighing more than 100 grams.
6. See, for example, EPA 744-F-93-015, EPA 744-K-93-001, EPA 744-F-93-003, and EPA 744-F-093-004.
7. EPA, *Life-Cycle Assessment: Inventory Guidelines and Principles*. EPA/600/R-92/245 (February 1993), p. 6.
8. *Guidelines for Life-Cycle Assessment: A "Code of Practice"* (Pensacola, Fla.: Society for Environmental Toxicology and Chemistry (SETAC), 1993), p. 5.
9. Ibid., p. 38. Other SETAC documents include *A Conceptual Framework for Life-Cycle Impact Assessment*, March 1993, and *Life-Cycle Assessment Data Quality: A Conceptual Framework*, October 1992.
10. The study was funded by the New Jersey Department of Environmental Protection and Energy, the U.S. EPA, and the Council of State Governments.
11. SimaPro 3 is a sophisticated third-generation LCA software package that allows for the modeling and study of interaction between a product and the environment. Similar software packages have been developed in Sweden (PIA), the United Kingdom (PEMS), and the United States (by the Tellus Institute and Franklin Associates).
12. Anders Schmidt et al. (Danish Technological Institute/Department of Environmental Technology), "Health Impacts and Life Cycle Assessment," in *Design for the Environment: Workshop on Identifying a Framework for the Future of Human Health and Environmental Risk Ranking*. EPA 744-S-93-001 (June 1994), pp. K1–K29.
13. Paul Hawken, *The Ecology of Commerce* (New York: HarperBusiness, 1993), p. 62. Hawken is referring to the type of industrial ecology already practiced in Kalundborg, Denmark.

# 8

# Hazard Evaluation Procedures

A hazard is defined as a physical or chemical characteristic of a material, system, process, or plant that has the potential to cause harm to human beings, the community, or the environment in general (see Figure 8-1). Hazard evaluation (HE) studies are designed to provide organizations with information to help them improve safety and better manage hazards so as to reduce or eliminate the risks associated with their various operations and processes. As such, HEs are "organized efforts to identify and analyze the significance of hazardous situations associated with process activities."[1] Specifically, HE studies are used to highlight weaknesses in the design and operation of facilities that

**Figure 8-1.** Adverse consequences resulting from process hazards.

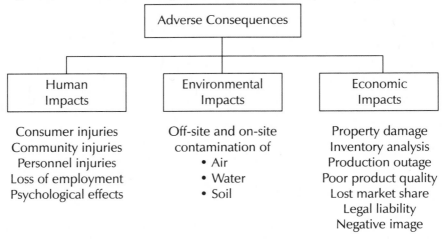

139

could lead to accidental chemical releases, fires, or explosions. Hazard evaluation studies are implied by paragraph 4.4.7, *Emergency preparedness and response,* of the ISO 14001 standard.

The basic process for hazard evaluation consists of the following four steps:

1. *Analyze material properties and process conditions.* This data-collecting phase consists of identifying all relevant information relating to the chemicals used in or produced by each process. Examples of relevant information would include flammability or combustibility, explosivity, toxicity, reactivity, odor threshold, and so on (see Table 8-1 for some

**Table 8-1.** Useful material property data for hazard identification.

| | |
|---|---|
| *Acute toxicity* | *Physical properties* |
|    Inhalation |    Freezing point |
|    Oral |    Coefficient of expansion |
|    Dermal |    Boiling point |
| |    Solubility |
| *Chronic toxicity* |    Vapor pressure |
|    Inhalation |    Density of specific volume |
|    Oral |    Corrosivity/erosivity |
|    Dermal |    Heat capacity |
| *Carcinogenicity* |    Specific heat |
| *Mutagenicity* | *Reactivity* |
| |    Process materials |
| *Teratogenicity* |    Material of construction |
| *Exposure limits* |    Incompatible chemicals |
| |    Pyrophoric materials |
| *Biodegradability* |    Kinetics |
| *Aquatic toxicity* | *Stability* |
| *Persistence in the environment* |    Shock |
| |    Temperature |
| *Odor threshold* |    Light |
| |    Polymerization |
| | *Flammability/explosivity* |
| |    Dust explosion parameters |
| |    Minimum ignition energy |
| |    Flash point |

examples). In the United States, one of the best sources of information is the material safety data sheets (MSDSs) provided by the chemical manufacturer. Databases are also available from the Chemical Abstracts Service and the American Institute of Chemical Engineers Design Institute for Physical Property Data (DIPPR), among other agencies.

2. *Use experience.* This advice, which should be obvious, is worth repeating. Whenever possible, a company must use the internal knowledge, experience, and expertise of its employees to complement information obtained from external sources.

3. *Develop an interaction matrix (or matrices).* The interaction matrix helps identify interactions among specific parameters such as chemicals, process conditions (temperature, pressure, static charge), environmental conditions (humidity, dust, temperature, odor threshold), human health effects, legal limits for spills or waste disposal, and so on. The matrix can be two-dimensional or higher. Three-dimensional matrices may be used if higher-order interactions among three or more chemicals need to be considered (see Figure 8-2). The use of several interaction matrices may be required to account for abnormal process conditions.

**Figure 8-2.** Basic interaction matrix.

| | Chemical A | Chemical B | Chemical Z | Mixture 1 | Mixture 2 | Notes | References |
|---|---|---|---|---|---|---|---|
| Chemical A | | X | | | | Mixture 1 = 10% A + 5% B | MSDS |
| Chemical B | | | | | | | |
| Chemical Z | | | X | | | | MSDS |
| Temp. 1 | X | | | | | | MSDS |
| Humidity 1 | | | | | | | |
| Pipe material | | | | | | | |
| Exposure limit | X | X | X | | | A = 50 mg/m$^3$<br>B = 100 ppm<br>C = 0.1 mg/m$^3$ | OSHA |
| Release limit | | | | | | A = 5,000 lbs.<br>B = 0.013 microgram/L | EPA |

Once the matrices are constructed, the consequence(s) for each interaction should be evaluated or, preferably, rated by using some rating scale (1 = high risk, 3 = low risk) or similar scheme.

4. *Use appropriate evaluation technique to identify hazard.* Several hazard evaluation techniques such as checklist analysis, what-if analysis, and HAZOP, as well as software packages, are available. The following section gives a brief description of these techniques.

## Hazard Evaluation Techniques

The type of hazard evaluation technique available for use depends on the type of results that are needed. Hazard analyses are conducted for three purposes: (1) conducting a general hazard analysis; (2) obtaining a list of safety improvement alternatives; or (3) obtaining a list of specific accident situations plus safety improvement alternatives. Each of these objectives requires a specific type of hazard analysis. Since the amount of time required for each technique can vary anywhere from fourteen to sixteen hours for the simplest technique applied to a simple process to as many as nine to fifteen days for a HAZOP analysis applied to a complex process, the selection of the appropriate technique is most important.

### General Hazard Analysis or Safety Improvement Alternatives

To conduct general hazard analyses or to obtain a list of safety improvement alternatives, the following techniques are most appropriate: safety review, checklist analysis, relative ranking, preliminary hazard analysis, what-if analysis, and what-if/checklist analysis.

1. *Safety review.* Also known as design review, process safety review, or loss prevention review, safety review generally consists of a walk-through inspection coupled with a series of interviews with staff and personnel. The purpose of the review is to assess risk and identify plant conditions and operating procedures that could lead to accidents, injuries, property damage, or environmental damage. During the walk-through, inspectors look for process or equipment changes that may have introduced new hazards, review the adequacy of maintenance and safety inspections, and may review operating procedures for necessary

revisions. Results of safety review consist of qualitative descriptions of potential problems and corrective actions that are required to correct nonconformance.

2. *Checklist analysis.* The checklist analysis is used to verify the status and conformance of a system. Checklists usually contain yes, no, and not applicable boxes. They are very similar to audit checklists, and unless the auditor appends some comments to his yeses and noes, the list may be of little value. Nonetheless, they provide a convenient summary that can be rapidly read by management.

3. *Relative ranking.* The various techniques of relative ranking (there are a few) aim at ranking fire, explosion, and toxicity hazards and their associated safety, health, environmental, or economic effects for a process or activity. The ranking is achieved by calculating a numerical score, or index, using a set of risk index equations and parameters that are obtained from a variety of relative ranking indices (see Table 8-2). Since the empirical formulation of these equations can be very time-consuming, organizations may prefer to select accepted standard techniques.[2]

**Table 8-2.** Summary of relative ranking indexes.

**Dow Fire and Explosion Index (F&EI):** Evaluates fire and explosion hazards associated with discrete process units.

**Mond Index:** Developed by ICI's Mond Division, it is an extension of the Dow F&EI.

**Substance Hazard Index (SHI):** This method was proposed by the Organization of Resources Counselors (ORC) in its advice to OSHA. This index is based on a ratio of the equilibrium vapor pressure (EVP) at 20 degrees C divided by the toxicity concentration.

**Material Hazard Index (MHI):** This index is used by the state of California to determine threshold quantities of acutely hazardous materials for which risk management and prevention programs must be developed.

**Chemical Exposure Index (CEI):** Also developed by Dow Chemical Company, it addresses five types of factors.

**SARA Title III Threshold Planning Quantity (TPQ) Index:** Developed by the Environmental Protection Agency to determine which extremely hazardous substances and threshold quantities should be covered under SARA Title III.

4. *Preliminary hazard analysis.* Because of the specialized nature of this technique, which is usually performed during a plant's conceptual design, it is not described here.

5. *What-if analysis.* As its name implies, the what-if technique consists of asking questions about processes and operating procedures or activities. For example, after reviewing the specification for incoming material (an acid, for example), someone may ask: "What if the acid delivered is of the wrong concentration?" The team of experts would then attempt to determine how the process would respond. What-if analyses are usually documented using the following format:

| Analyst: | | | |
|---|---|---|---|
| What-if | Consequence/ Hazard | Safeguards (Optional) | Recommendations |
| Temp > 110F | Flammability might increase | None | Install more fans |

6. *What-if/checklist analysis.* This technique combines two techniques described above. The advantage of adding the checklist method is that it increases the chance for thoroughness while at the same time compensating for the shortcoming already noted.

## List of Specific Accident Situations Plus Safety Improvement Alternatives

The techniques used in these cases are both more thorough and more labor-intensive. They are hazard and operability analysis (HAZOP), failure mode and effect analysis (FMEA), fault tree analysis, event tree analysis, cause-consequence analysis, and human reliability analysis. Only HAZOP and fault tree analyses are described here. All other techniques are detailed in the *Guidelines for Hazard Evaluation Procedures* cited above.

### HAZOP

HAZOP was developed in the early 1970s by Imperial Chemical Industries. The HAZOP study focuses on specific points (nodes) of a process or operation and examines each section for potentially hazardous *process deviations*. If available the study begins with an analysis of the Piping and Instrumentation Diagram (P&ID) available in most chemical plants. [*Note:* HAZOPs can be performed without a P&ID diagram.] The methodology relies on the use of certain key guide words used on certain parameters (see Tables 8-3 and 8-4). [*Note:* Software has been developed for most of these techniques.]

A HAZOP analysis consists of the following three steps: (1) preparing for the review, (2) performing the review, and (3) documenting the results.

The following list demonstrates how the guide words given in Table 8-3 are used to analyze a diammonium phosphate (DAP) process. A definition of some of the terms can be found in Table 8-4.

| | |
|---|---|
| *Process section:* | Phosphoric acid feed line to the DAP reactor. |
| *Design intention:* | Feed phosphoric acid at a controlled rate to the DAP reactor. |
| *Guide word:* | No |
| *Process parameter:* | Flow |
| *Deviation:* | No flow |
| *Consequences:* | (1) Excess ammonia in the reactor, leading to . . . |
| | (2) Unreacted ammonia in the DAP storage tank, with subsequent . . . |
| | (3) Release of unreacted ammonia from DAP storage tank to the enclosed work area |
| | (4) Loss of DAP production |
| *Causes:* | (1) No feed material in the phosphoric acid storage tank. |
| | (2) Flow indicator/controller too low. |
| | (3) Operator set the flow controller too low. |
| | (4) Phosphoric acid control valve B failed to close. |
| | (5) Plugging in the line. |
| | (6) Leak or rupture of the line. |
| *Safeguards:* | (1) Periodic maintenance of valve B |
| *Actions:* | (1) Consider adding an alarm/shutdown of the system for low phosphoric acid flow to the reactor. |
| | (2) Ensure that periodic maintenance and inspection for valve B are adequate. |
| | (3) Consider using a closed tank for DAP storage. |

This process is repeated with other combinations of guide words and process parameters for each section of the design. Every process section

**Table 8-3.** Some HAZOP guide words and process parameters.

| Guide Words | Meaning |
|---|---|
| no | Negation of the design intent |
| less/lower | Quantitative decrease |
| more/higher | Quantitative increase |
| part of | Qualitative decrease |
| as well as | Quantitative increase |
| reverse | Logical opposite of intent |
| other than | Complete substitution |
| sooner or later | When considering time |

*Process Parameters*

| | | | |
|---|---|---|---|
| flow | time | frequency | mixing |
| pressure | composition | viscosity | addition |
| temperature | pH | voltage | separation |
| level | speed | information reaction | |

SOURCE: Simplified from *Guidelines for Hazard Evaluation Procedures* (New York: American Institute of Chemical Engineers, 1992), p. 133. Copyright 1992 by the American Institute of Chemical Engineers; reproduced by permission of Center for Chemical Process Safety of AIChE.

is evaluated and the relevant information is recorded in a HAZOP study table (Table 8-5).

### Fault Tree Analysis

Fault tree analysis (FTA) is a deductive technique that uses Boolean AND OR logic to break down the causes of a specific hazardous situation, known as a *top event*, into basic equipment failures and human errors. Top events may be identified using previously defined hazard evaluation techniques such as what-if analysis or HAZOP. The fault tree is a graphic representation of the relationships between failures and a specific accident or undesired event. When defining a top event, it is important to define the problem as precisely as possible. A vaguely defined top event such as "explosion at the plant" will lead to frustration and inefficient analysis. When defining a top event, always try to specify *what* has happened or may happen, *where* it may happen or has happened, and *when* it is likely to happen or did happen. For example, "Forgetting to close valve 1020 to tank B may lead to a runaway reaction in tank B" would be an acceptable statement. If the causes of the top event can be easily determined, the problem should perhaps be evalu-

**Table 8-4.** Common HAZOP analysis terminology.

**Process sections (or study nodes):** Sections of equipment with definite boundaries within which process parameters are investigated for deviations; the locations on P&IDs at which the process parameters are investigated for deviations.

**Guide words:** Words used to qualify or quantify the design intention and to guide and stimulate the brainstorming process for identifying process hazards.

**Process parameters:** Physical or chemical properties associated with the process. Includes general items such as reactions, mixing, concentration, pH, and specific items such as temperature, pressure, phase, and flow.

**Deviations:** Departures from the design intention that are discovered by systematically applying guide words to process parameters, resulting in a list for the team to review for each process section.

**Causes:** Reasons why deviations might occur. Causes can be hardware failures, human errors, unanticipated process states such as change of composition, external disruption such as loss of power or rapid change in weather conditions, and so on.

**Consequences:** Results of deviations such as release of toxic materials, out-of-specification product, hazardous situation, etc.

**Safeguards:** Engineered systems or administrative controls designed to prevent the causes or mitigate the consequences of deviations.

**Actions (or recommendations):** Suggestions for design changes, procedural changes, or areas for further study.

SOURCE: Simplified from *Guidelines for Hazard Evaluation Procedures* (New York: American Institute of Chemical Engineers, 1992), p. 133. Copyright 1992 by the American Institute of Chemical Engineers; reproduced by permission of Center for Chemical Process Safety of AIChE.

ated using a simpler method such as failure mode and effect analysis (FEMA).

Before conducting an FTA, be sure to define the physical boundaries of the system, which encompass the initial equipment configuration, the equipment interfaces, and the initial operating conditions. Figure 8-3 defines some of the key symbols used in fault tree analysis. Other symbols include the hexagonal *inhibit gate,* the diamond-shaped *undeveloped event* (a fault event that is not examined because the information is unavailable), and the *external* or *house event,* a condition that is assumed to exist as a boundary condition for the fault tree.

**Table 8-5.** Example of a HAZOP analysis table.

**Team: HAZOP Team #3**

| Deviation | Causes | Consequences | Safeguards | Actions |
|-----------|--------|--------------|------------|---------|
| Leak | Corrosion | Small continuous leak of ammonia to the enclosed work area | Periodic maintenance of line | Ensure that adequate ventilation exists for enclosed work area |
| | Erosion | | | |
| | External impact | | | |
| | Gasket + packing failures | | | |
| | Maintenance errors | | | |

### Process Equipment Reliability Data

One of the important components of hazard evaluation is the estimation of process equipment failure rate. To evaluate the likelihood of occurrence of an incident that may have an impact on human health or the environment in general, one must be able to assess the failure rate of particular equipment. In most cases, however, the analyst does not have any data and must either guess or build an equipment failure database, a process that may well take several years for some equipment. Fortunately, data have been compiled by several organizations in the United States and abroad. The Center for Chemical Process Safety (CCPS) publishes *Guidelines for Process Equipment Reliability Data*, in which one can find numerous databases as well as time-related failure rates per $10^6$ hours and demand-related failure rates per $10^3$ demands, for components ranging from absorbers and accumulators to wire meshes and wires and wiring (see Table 8-6 for some examples).

## Conclusion

Hazard evaluations are valuable techniques that allow management to qualitatively and quantitatively assess risks associated with processes and procedures. Used in conjunction with the methodology of continu-

**Figure 8-3.** Examples of event symbols used in fault trees.

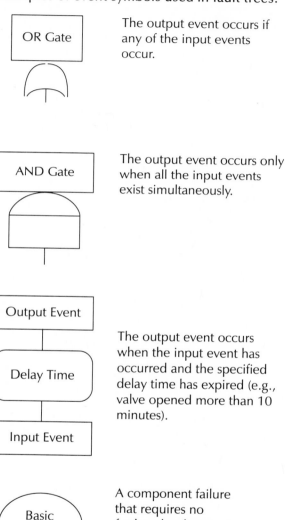

OR Gate

The output event occurs if any of the input events occur.

AND Gate

The output event occurs only when all the input events exist simultaneously.

Output Event

Delay Time

Input Event

The output event occurs when the input event has occurred and the specified delay time has expired (e.g., valve opened more than 10 minutes).

Basic Event

A component failure that requires no further development (e.g., pump breaks down).

**Table 8-6.** Examples of equipment failure rates.

**Taxonomy no.** 1.2.3.2       **Equipment Description:** Circuit Breakers-DC

| Failure Mode | Failures (per $10^6$ hrs) | | | Failures (per $10^3$ demand) | | |
|---|---|---|---|---|---|---|
| | Lower | Mean | Upper | Lower | Mean | Upper |
| *Catastrophic* | | | | | | |
| Spurious operation | 0.0348 | 3.80 | 14.4 | | | |
| Failure to open on demand | | | | 0.0927 | 0.883 | 2.85 |
| Failure to close on demand | | | | | | |

**Taxonomy no.** 2.1.4.1.4       **Equipment Description:** Switches Electric Temp.

| Failure Mode | Failures (per $10^6$ hrs) | | | Failures (per $10^3$ demand) | | |
|---|---|---|---|---|---|---|
| | Lower | Mean | Upper | Lower | Mean | Upper |
| *Catastrophic* | 0.102 | 2.28 | 10.1 | | | |
| Functional without signal | 0.107 | 1.16 | 4.69 | | | |
| Failed to function when signaled | 0.0971 | 3.40 | 13.4 | | | |

SOURCE: Center for Chemical Process Safety, *Guidelines for Process Equipment Reliability Data with Data Tables* (New York: American Institute of Chemical Engineers, 1989). Copyright 1989 by the American Institute of Chemical Engineers; reproduced by permission of Center for Chemical Process Safety of AIChE.

ous improvement and internal auditing, as stated in the ISO 9001 and ISO 14001 standards, hazard evaluation should help an organization improve its processes as well as simultaneously encourage health and safety amelioration. As a company's environmental liability is continually reduced, it is likely that these activities will be viewed favorably by the financial community and, perhaps even more importantly, by the insurance community.

# Notes

1. The following discussion and examples are based on the excellent book published by the Center for Chemical Process Safety, *Guidelines for Hazard Evaluation Procedures* (New York: American Institute of Chemical Engineers, 1992), p. 11 and passim.

2. These can be found in H. R. Greenberg and J. J. Cramer, eds., *Risk Assessment and Risk Management for the Chemical Process Industry* (New York: Van Nostrand Reinhold, 1991); J. Gillet, "Rapid Ranking of Process Hazards," *Process Engineering* 66, no. 219 (1985); *Technical Guidance for Hazards Analysis: Emergency Planning for Extremely Hazardous Substances* (U.S. Department of Transportation, December 1987); R. H. Ross and P. Lu, *Chemical Scoring Systems Development* (Oak Ridge, Tenn.: Oak Ridge National Laboratory, 1981).

# Part IV

# Economic Benefits of Pollution Prevention

This final part consists of several examples of pollution prevention techniques. These techniques, also known as P², are a logical extension of the principles presented in Part III. Chapter 9 includes several examples of flow process diagrams, which can be used to identify points of chemical input and output. Such diagrams can often be used as the first step toward process improvement. Examples for the following industries are covered: paint manufacturing, pharmaceuticals, metal casting and heat treatment, furniture manufacturing, chemical manufacturing, auto body restoration and painting, agricultural irrigation, and cement plants. Chapter 10 deals with the manageability of the environment.

Part IV concludes with eight appendixes.

# 9
# Preventive Action: Some Examples

The amount of toxic chemicals spewed into the biosphere by American industries is staggering. In 1990, the nation's 23,638 largest industrial users of chemicals released into the air, water, and land or transferred to treatment or disposal facilities some 4.8 billion pounds of about 320 specific toxic chemicals (a fraction of the 70,000 chemicals currently in commercial use). Every day, more than 200,000 companies ranging in size from very small businesses (such as dry-cleaning establishments) to major chemical plants expose millions of employees to thousands of chemicals[1] (see Tables 9-1 and 9-2).

In order to minimize health risks associated with chemical exposure, companies have, over the past ten years, relied on the pollution prevention methodology outlined in Figure 9-1. In 1986, a survey designed to analyze the pollution prevention practices of twenty-nine small and very large companies was conducted by the New York-based firm INFORM. The survey revealed that the forty-four preventive initiatives identified by all firms fell into the following four major categories:

1. Efficiency changes such as process refinements
2. Equipment modifications
3. Better on-site housekeeping
4. Basic actions such as product changes or chemical substitutions

When the same plants were revisited in 1992, 137 additional preventive initiatives were identified (see Table 9-3 for some examples).

Four major conclusions were reached:

**Table 9-1.** Commercial establishments and their potential discharges of concern.

---

**Automotive repair and service shops:** Chemical oxygen demand, heavy metals, solvents, paints, surfactants, oil and grease

**Car washes:** Chemical oxygen demand, zinc, lead, and copper

**Dry cleaners:** Total dissolved solids, chemical oxygen demand, phosphate, N-butyl benzene, suflonamide, perchloroethylene, iron, zinc, and copper

**Laundries:** Chemical oxygen demand, ethyl toluene, n-propyl alcohol, iso-propyl alcohol, toluene, m-xylene, p-xylene, ethylbenzene, bis(2-ethyl-hexyl)phthalate, iron, lead, zinc, copper, chromium, phosphate, and sulfide

**Hospitals:** Total dissolved solids, chemical oxygen demand, phosphate, surfactants, formaldehyde, phenol, fluoride, lead, iron, barium, copper, mercury, silver, and zinc

**Photoprocessors:** Chemical oxygen demand, ammonia, cyanide, sulfur, phosphates, silver, arsenic, chromium, phenol, and bromide

**Laboratories:** Chemical oxygen demand, mercury, silver, and toxic organics

**Dental offices:** Copper, zinc, silver, and mercury

---

Note: For a description of the toxicity of some of the chemicals listed, see Appendix D.

1. Half the source reduction initiatives reduced targeted waste streams by 90 percent or more.
2. Two-thirds of the initiatives were quick and easy to implement (taking six months or less with few technological changes).
3. One-fourth required no capital investment. Two-thirds resulted in payback in six months or less.
4. Total savings came to $21 million, the average savings per project being $351,000.

Yet, despite these encouraging findings, the study also showed that the majority of companies had not established programs that would make aggressive pollution prevention possible. Similar results were uncovered by Paul Ferraro in his study of small and medium-size businesses (up to 500 employees). Ferraro found that many business owners or managers believed that prevention would save them money only "in the long run." Most businessmen also wanted to be sure that before investing in an expensive pollution prevention program, "pollution prevention

**Table 9-2.** Consumer products and their potential toxic or hazardous constituents.

| Product | Toxic or Hazardous Constituents |
| --- | --- |
| Antifreeze (gasoline or coolant systems) | Methanol, ethylene glycol |
| Automatic transmission fluid | Petroleum distillates, xylene |
| Battery acid (electrolyte) | Sulfuric acid |
| Degreasers for driveways or garages | Petroleum solvents, alcohols, glycol ether |
| Degreasers for engines and metal | Chlorinated hydrocarbons, toluene, phenols, dichloroperchloroethylene |
| Engine and radiator flushes | Petroleum solvents, ketones, butanol, glycol ether |
| Hydraulic fluid (brake fluid) | Hydrocarbons, fluorocarbons |
| Motor oils and waste oils | Hydrocarbons |
| Gasoline and jet fuel | Hydrocarbons |
| Diesel fuel, kerosene heating oil | Hydrocarbons |
| Grease, lubricants | Hydrocarbons |
| Rustproofers | Phenols, heavy metals |
| Car wash detergents | Alkyl benzene sulfonates |
| Car waxes and polishes | Petroleum distillates, hydrocarbons, heavy metals |
| Asphalt and roofing tar | Hydrocarbons · |
| Paints, varnishes, stains, dyes | Heavy metals, toluene |
| Paint and lacquer thinner | Heavy metals |
| Paint and varnish removers, deglosser | Methylene chloride, toluene, acetone, xylene, ethanol, benzene, methanol |
| Paintbrush cleaner | Hydrocarbon, toluene, acetone, methanol, glycol ethers, methyl ethyl ketones |
| Floor and furniture strippers, polishes, and waxes | Xylene, heavy metals |
| Metal polishes | Petroleum distillates, isopropanol, petroleum naphtha |
| Laundry stain removers | Petroleum distillates, tetrachloroethylene |
| Spot removers and dry-cleaning fluid | Hydrocarbons, benzene, trichloroethylene, 1,1,1-trichloroethane |
| Other solvents | Acetone, benzene |
| Pesticides | Naphthalene, phosphorus, xylene, chloroform, heavy metals, chlorinated hydrocarbons |
| Photochemicals | Phenols, sodium sulfite, silver halide, potassium bromide, thiocyanate, ferricyanide, dichromate bleaches, phosphate, ammonium compounds |
| Printing ink | Heavy metals, phenol-formaldehyde |
| Jewelry cleaners | Sodium cyanide |

SOURCE: *Guides to Pollution Prevention: Municipal Pretreatment Programs* (EPA/625/R-93/006, October 1993), p. 15.

**Figure 9-1.** Pollution prevention.

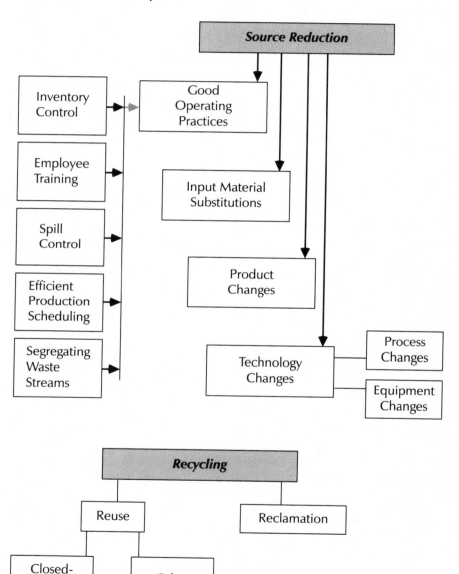

**Table 9-3.** Examples of pollution prevention initiatives.

* Exxon Chemical Company used "floating roofs" on 16 of its 200 chemical storage tanks that contained the most volatile chemicals, thereby reducing evaporation emissions by 90 percent and saving $200,000 per year.

* A medium-size Borden resin and adhesives facility in California implemented one-stage, instead of two-stage, rinsing of its chemical vats. This simple operational change reduced by 93 percent its phenol-laden waste stream and saved $150,000 a year in waste disposal costs.

* Fischer Scientific Company computerized its material-tracking system and cut 600,000 pounds of waste.

would pay for itself, have a demonstrable effect on the environment, or improve employee health."[2]

Trying to explain the phenomenon, Joanna Underwood suggests that most companies

> *assumed* their processes were efficient. Making a product was their main job, and they measured their waste at the end of the pipe. Without knowing where—in process terms—the waste came from, they were not in a position to spot preventive opportunities. Further, the staffs of their pollution control departments were neither responsible for, nor knowledgeable about, the plant processes that produced the waste they had to handle.[3]

To avoid or minimize similar difficulties with pollution prevention problems, Underwood recommends the following five steps:

1. Create top management leadership, including production and environmental skills, to implement the policy.
2. Motivate plant officials to find prevention opportunities.
3. Conduct audits to identify all waste sources within the plants in process and nonprocess areas.
4. Establish full-cost accounting systems to account for the cost of waste management and material losses to the parts of the plants generating waste.
5. Establish corporate policies making source reduction the top environmental priority. [Note the similarity with some of the ISO 14001 requirements.]

# Case Studies of Pollution Prevention

Most pollution prevention studies[4] start with flow diagrams identifying all chemical and/or waste inputs and outputs. Some of these flow diagrams could be generated during a hazard analysis. Figures 9-2 and 9-3 illustrate how block diagrams can be used to describe a process and all of the associated pollutants coming into or leaving the various subcomponents. Once a process has been broken down into a series of block diagrams, and all of the pollution inputs and outputs have been identified, it is easier to begin analyzing how processes can be improved using either DfE or LCA analyses.

## Paint Manufacturing Industry

The primary raw material used by paint manufacturers consists of:

‣ Resins (alkyd, acrylic, vinyl, and others)
‣ Aromatic solvents (aliphatics, aromatics, ketones [ethyl ketone], alcohols [methanol], others)

**Figure 9-2.** Example of a process flow diagram identifying hazardous inputs and outputs.

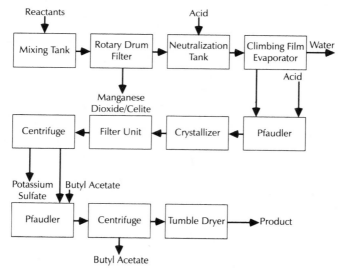

**Figure 9-3.** Example of a flow diagram for spray molding.

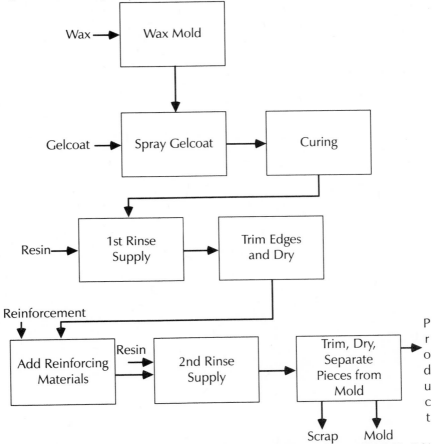

SOURCE: The Fiberglass Reinforced and Composite Plastics Industry (EPA/6-25, 7-91/014), p. 8.

- ▸ Pigments (titanium and yellow dioxide, inorganic and organic)
- ▸ Extenders (calcium carbonate, talc, clay, others)
- ▸ Miscellaneous (drying oil, plasticizers, others)

Examples of source reduction measures are summarized in Table 9-4. Table 9-5 illustrates how a company can phase in various process improvements as well as new waste disposal methods.

**Table 9-4.** Examples of source reduction measures and
better operating practices.

**Source reduction measures**

- Replacement of caustic cleaning solution used for cleaning tanks with an alkaline solution. Cleanup residuals cut in half.

- Use of high-pressure spraying systems, leading to a reduction of 25% in waste volume

- Dedication to let-down tanks. Dedicated white paint tanks led to a reduction of 5–10% in associated cleanup waste volume.

- Proper batch scheduling. Batches are now sequenced in the order of light to dark paint, which often leads to the elimination of intermediate cleanup steps.

- Pigment substitution such as lead and chromium pigments

**Recycling and resource recovery measures**

- Segregation of water- and solvent-based wastes
- Segregation of alkaline cleanup wastes from rinsewater wastes
- Reuse of water-based equipment cleanup wastes
- Reuse of alkaline cleaning wastes
- Reuse of solvent-bearing cleanup wastes
- Rework of wastes
- Recycling of equipment-cleaning wastes

**Change in operating procedures**

- Counter-current rinsing sequence using recycled "dirty" solution to initially clean the tank

- Use of alternative cleaning agent

SOURCE: EPA Risk Reduction Laboratory.

## Pharmaceutical and Hospital Industries

The pharmaceutical industry, which is characterized by highly automated processes, uses a broad range of solvents such as acetone, methylene chloride, ethyl acetate, butyl acetate, methanol, ethanol, isopropanol, butanol, pyridine, methyl ethyl ketone, methyl isobutyl ketone, tetrahydrofuran, and more. Guided by the principles of Continuous Good Manufacturing Practices (CGMP), the industry learned long ago to recycle most of its solvents. As a regulated industry, the pharma-

**Table 9-5.** Waste description and process origin for a
typical paint manufacturer.

| No. | Waste Description | Process Origin | Treatment/Disposal Method | | | |
|---|---|---|---|---|---|---|
| | | | 1994 | 1995 | 1996 | 1997 |
| 1 | Equipment-cleaning waste | Solvent and water cleaning of process equipment | D | E | A | A |
| | | Alkaline cleaning of process equipment | F | G, H | B | B |
| | | Mechanical cleaning of process equipment | C | C | C | C |
| 2 | Obsolete stock | Paint that is no longer marketed or outdated raw materials | | | | B |
| 3 | Returns from customers | Unused or spoiled paints returned by customers | | | | B |
| 4 | Off-spec products | Spoiled batches | | | | B |
| 5 | Spills | Accidental discharge | | B | B | B |
| 6 | Filter bags | Filtration of paint | I | I | I | I |
| 7 | Empty bags and packages | Unloading of pigments and other additives into mixing tanks | I | I | I | I |

SOURCE: *Guides to Pollution Prevention: The Paint Manufacturing Industry* (EPA/625/7-90/005), p. 57.

Key:  A =  Reuse to extent possible, distillation on-site to recover solvent, rework of still bottoms
    B =  Blend to make a marketable product
    C =  Landfill disposal
    D =  Off-site recycling
    E =  Same as A except that still bottoms are land-disposed
    F =  Overflow discharge to sewer and landfill disposal of solids settled in weirs
    G =  Flocculation followed by discharge of decanted water to sewer and landfill disposal of settled solids
    H =  Vacuum filtration
    I =  Sanitary landfill after washing

ceutical industry has had to closely monitor its hazardous material handling and generation.

Hospitals handle thousands of drugs produced by the pharmaceutical industry. Since hospitals are required by law to dispose of drugs when their potency decreases to less than 95 percent, hospitals must dispose of very large quantities of drugs. Rather than destroy drugs/medicines that have exceeded their shelf life, hospitals could explore the possibility of exporting these products to other countries where shelf life for medicine may not be defined or may be different. Besides the thousands of products that must be disposed of daily, hospitals do generate many hazardous wastes. Table 9-6 lists some typical hazardous wastes generated by hospitals and suggests means of reducing them.

**Table 9-6.** Typical hazardous wastes from hospitals and suggested ways to reduce them.

---

**Chemotherapy and antineoplastics:** Reduce volumes, return outdated drugs, centralize chemotherapy compounding location, provide spill cleanup kits, segregate wastes.

**Formaldehyde reduction:** Minimize strength of solution, capture waste, use reverse osmosis water treatment to reduce dialysis cleaning demands.

**Photographic chemicals:** Return off-spec developer to manufacturer, cover developer and fixer tanks to reduce evaporation and oxidation, recover silver efficiently, recycle waste film and paper, use counter-current washing.

**Radionuclides:** Use less hazardous isotopes whenever possible, segregate and properly label radioactive wastes.

**Solvents:** Substitute less hazardous cleaning agents, reduce volume requirements, use premixed kits for tests involving solvent fixation, use calibrated solvent dispensers for routine tests, segregate solvent wastes, recover/reuse solvents through distillation.

**Mercury:** Substitute electronic sensing devices for mercury-containing devices, recycle uncontaminated mercury waste.

**Waste anesthetic gases:** Purchase low-leakage equipment, maintain equipment to avoid leaks.

**Toxics, corrosives, and miscellaneous chemicals:** Reduce volumes used in experiments, neutralize acid wastes, use physical instead of chemical cleaning methods, substitute less toxic compounds.

---

## Metal-Casting and Heat-Treating Industry

Typical chemicals used by the metal-casting industry include sodium cyanide, barium chloride, potassium chloride, sodium cyanate, sodium carbonate, and plain salt (sodium chloride). The types of wastes generated by the metal-casting and heat-treating industry are listed in Tables 9-7 and 9-8; Table 9-9 lists some waste minimization options.[5]

Additional tables listing typical waste materials by process and type of industry can be found in Appendix H.

The following success stories, documented by the Washington Department of Ecology, demonstrate that waste reduction or elimination programs need not be expensive and do bring rapid, sometimes instant, economic returns.

**Table 9-7.** Metal-casting wastes.

| Process | Waste |
|---|---|
| Molding and core making | Spent system sand, sweepings, core butts, dust, and sludge |
| Melting | Dust and fumes slag |
| Casting | Investment casting, shells, and waxes |
| Cleaning | Cleaning room waste |

**Table 9-8.** Heat-treating wastes.

| Process | Wastes |
|---|---|
| Heat treating | Refractory material |
| Case hardening | Spent salt baths (sludge from baths and corroded bath pots) |
| Quenching | Spent quenchants (cyanide salts, liquid nitrided parts, liquid carburized parts) |
| Descaling | Spent abrasive media |
| Cleaning and masking | Solvents, abrasives, copper-plating wastes |

**Table 9-9.** Waste minimization options.

| Metal Casting | Heat Treating |
|---|---|
| Controlling the quality of scrap metal | Controlling input material |
| Installing induction-melting furnaces | Removing chemicals from cyanide-bearing baths and quenching media |
| Recycling slag or furnace dust | Drying workpieces to prevent spattering from high-temperature baths |
| Implementing state-of-the-art process control | Extending bath life by removing impurities |
| Maximizing sand-to-metal ratios[1] | Using alternative technologies |
| Segregating foundry sand from shot blasting and grinding dust | Recycling spent bath solutions |
| Avoiding excessive metal-pouring temperatures | Rinsing, filtering, evaporating, desludging, and other separation techniques |
| Reclaiming metals from waste streams | |
| Using sand waste as a feed stock to a primary smelter for metal extraction | |

[1]For this option, see Gary E. Mosher, *Modern Casting* (October 1994), pp. 28–31.

## Wooden Furniture Manufacturing: Increased Productivity for Less

This small manufacturer of modular components that can easily be replaced or repaired employs thirty to seventy employees. Computerized processes such as boring machines maximize the use of raw materials and help reduce rework.

*Types of Wastes:* Various solvents, stains and lacquers (which produce volatile organic compounds, or VOCs), solid wastes.

*Process improvements:* Manufacturing methods were redesigned to increase productivity while simultaneously lowering the amount of solid waste and the use of toxic chemicals. These included:

‣ Use of launderable cloth rags to apply stain instead of disposable paper wipers. This improvement helped the manufacturer to reduce refuse by 25 percent.

‣ Switch to seven-ply veneered plywood from particleboard or chipboard. This helped reduce formaldehyde and other volatile compounds by 35 percent over a period of two years.

‣ Use of dry-joint construction techniques to eliminate the need for adhesives during assembly.

‣ Conversion to waterborne stains and lacquers to help reduce volatile organic compounds. The conversion also improved the work environment because the new water-based coatings helped clean up the atmosphere and significantly reduced workers' eye irritation.

## Chemical Manufacturing: Innovation and Ingenuity

This chlor/alkali and inorganic chemical production facility employs 125 people. Its products include chlorine, hydrogen, sodium hydroxide, sodium chlorate, and hydrochloric acid.

*Types of wastes:* Halogenated solvents, chrome waste from the chromium catalyst system, acidic effluents, hazardous air emissions.

*Process improvements:* The following process improvements and preventive actions were implemented:

‣ Replacement and eventual elimination, in 1990, of halogenated solvents (used for degreasing) with biodegradable citrus-based solvents. This led to a substantial reduction in disposal cost, permit cost, and overall management costs.

‣ Waste recycling program initiated throughout the plant.

‣ Process improvement in the chrome recovery system that led to a 90 percent reduction of filter waste. This led to savings of $100,000 in dangerous-waste disposal costs. In addition, the chrome content of the product was reduced from 10,000 ppm to 5 ppm.

‣ Investment of $1.7 million in a waste management treatment system to more effectively control the pH of effluents. As a result, the pH has not exceeded the permitted range of 6.0 to 9.0 since 1989. The risk of being cited by the Department of Ecology (the local enforcement agency) has been reduced to zero.

‣ Solid waste generated reduced by 82 percent.

## Auto Body Restoration and Painting: Small but Effective

This family-owned auto body repair shop employs seventeen people.

*Types of wastes:* Paint filters used to filter overspray from primer paints contain dangerous heavy metals (such as cadmium, lead, and chrome), lacquer thinners, oil, and other chemicals.

*Process improvements:* Several process changes were implemented, including:

> ‣ Replacement of yellow-based sealers with gray-based sealers that contain lower concentrations of lead and chromium.
> ‣ Reclamation of 80 percent of spent solvent (lacquer thinner) instead of sending it off-site as dangerous waste, giving an estimated annual savings of about $5,000 per year.
> ‣ Replacement of the use of paint cans with the use of freezer jars that can be rinsed and reused, leading to annual savings in excess of $1,000.
> ‣ Use of continuous vacuum systems to reduce VOCs and dust. In the sanding area, dust was reduced by 80 percent. High-volume, low-pressure spray guns are also used to reduce VOCs.
> ‣ Reduction of solid waste by recycling cardboard, metal and auto body parts, and plastic bumpers and by replacing masking paper with liquid spray mask, which can be washed off with water.[6]

## Agricultural Irrigation Products: Working With Vendors

This medium-size company of 140 people manufactures a wide range of agricultural irrigation products. Because of the well-known health and safety hazard caused by chlorinated solvents, the company decided to eliminate its vapor degreaser and the use of 1,1,1-trichloroethane used for cleaning aluminum, brass, and steel parts.

Although detergents could be used to replace chlorinated solvents, the problem with detergent cleaning systems is that they tend to lubricate parts slightly. If the part needs to be assembled to exact torque specifications, the torque setting must be readjusted to avoid stripping the part. The company worked with a detergent vendor who was willing to experiment with various detergents. The engineering department helped alleviate the problem by reducing torque specifications.

*Process improvements:* Two were implemented:

▶ Installation ($55,000) of a new cleaning system that uses "off-the-shelf" detergent ($3,800 per year). The residue and sludge from the system, which amounts to only half a drum per year, is nonhazardous. Savings in disposal costs were estimated at $16,500. Regulatory requirements have also been substantially reduced since the company no longer has to report toxic air emissions.

▶ Reduction of wastewater by using water from the rinse tank as makeup for the detergent bath.

---

The Environmental Award was issued to a foundry for introducing a pelletized dry-ice cleaning system that removes resin from process equipment. The dry ice replaces methyl alcohol and methylene chloride (a potential carcinogen), thus reducing volatile organic compound (VOC). $185,000 to install the system, and $69,000 annual savings through reduced cleaning time, labor, and material costs. Elimination of trichloroethane saves the foundry $11,000 per year in solvent usage and disposal costs.

SOURCE: *Foundry Management and Technology*, June 1995, p. 12.

---

## Cement: Waste Synergism

This Seattle plant produces 460,000 tons of finished cement per year and 30,000 tons of kiln dust per year.

*Type of waste:* The dust's high pH makes it a dangerous waste in the state of Washington.

*Process Improvements:*

▶ The kiln dust is pressed into briquettes and reused to supply minerals in the kiln.

▶ The alkaline kiln dust is used as an agricultural soil amendment. The minerals found in the kiln dust make it a valuable soil conditioner and fertilizer.

▶ The alkaline properties of kiln dust also allow it to be used as a wet scrubber lime solution for controlling air emissions from waste incinerators and coal power plants. Since kiln dust hardens after it is moistened, it can be used to stabilize and solidify liquid wastes headed for land disposal.

▸ Sandblast grit is reused as a source of iron and silica essential to cement production. The sandblast grit is obtained from a nearby shipbuilding operation. Savings are $6.50 per ton, or (at 20,000 tons per year) $130,000 per year.

▸ A local wood pulp waste processor now provides the cement plant with its lignin-containing waste (known as vanillin black liquor solids and used to thin slurries). This allows the cement plant to reduce its water consumption by as much as 30 percent without thickening its feed slurries.

Table 9-10 lists additional examples of pollution prevention savings by industry.

## Conclusion

The case studies presented in this chapter help demonstrate that pollution prevention pays, which will, with luck, convince skeptics. As we have seen, pollution prevention does not necessarily imply the use of sophisticated and costly technological improvements. Moreover, and of particular interest to upper management, the initial investment can in most cases be repaid within a few months. There is little doubt that when used in conjunction with total cost accounting, the application of pollution prevention and/or reduction becomes not only an ethical necessity but also a financially rewarding investment.

**Table 9-10.** Pollution prevention savings by industry.

| Manufacturer | Process Improvements | Savings |
|---|---|---|
| Paints and specialty coating systems | • Reducing and reusing rinses<br>• Reuse of wash water in formulating water-based paints<br>• Solvents purified in a still and reused | $25,000 to $35,000 per year in adjusted disposal fees |
| Wooden sections for overhead garage doors | • New infrared ovens that provide fast, energy-efficient drying | • $1,000 per year on permit fees |
| | • Recycling waste coupled with flow reduction techniques | • $3,600 per year in sewer fees |
| | • Collaboration with a glue manufacturer to find ways to reuse wash-down water when mixing up glue | • $10,000 a year in pretreatment costs |
| | • Recycling of wastewater, water-based cleaning, and antirust and grinding solutions | • Reduction of wastewater flows by 250,000 gallons a month |
| | • Use of paper-lined filter trays to remove dirt and metal particles | • Reclamation of 70 gallons of solvents per day should help repay the cost of the unit within a year. |
| | • Converting from a "wet" to a "dry" engine-degreasing process | • Reduction of solvents from 1,700 gallons to 400 gallons per month |
| | • Use of a vacuum distillation unit to recycle solvent | |
| | • Roofing the engine receiving and storage areas to prevent storm water from being contaminated. Storm water can now be discharged in the storm water system | |
| | • Training of employees in waste reduction programs | |
| Distributor of beverages | • Purchase of can crusher<br>• Recycling of computer paper | • Reduction of disposal costs ($34,000 saved)<br>• $62,000 in revenues generated from recycled materials |

*(continues)*

**Table 9-10.** (Continued)

| Manufacturer | Process Improvements | Savings |
|---|---|---|
| Kitchen and bath cabinets | • Raw material reformulation that eliminated the generation of hazardous waste (filters)<br>• Purchase of two wood-grinding machines to process scrap wood used by a plywood plant | • Elimination of land disposal cost estimated at $3,200 per month<br><br>• $1,500-a-month reduction in landfill fees |
| Printed circuits | • Metal recovery (copper) system that uses less water in the plating process, achieved by counter-current rinsing. Sequential rinsing baths now use effluent from cleaner baths as makeup from more contaminated rinse stages.<br>• Lead precipitated through the addition of sodium borohydride. The recovered lead is sold to recyclers.<br>• Conductivity bridges monitor bath cleanliness to maximize use of the plating solution.<br>• Use of carbon filters in the ion-exchange treatment to remove organics | • Instead of being changed every four to five months, baths can now be used indefinitely.<br>• Water consumption reduced from 5,000 gallons per week to 100 gallons per week |
| Transportation maintenance shop | • The shop built its own filtration unit for $1,200 to filter and reuse antifreeze fluid.<br><br>• Replacement of ethylene glycol antifreeze (a hazardous waste in the state of Washington) with the less toxic propylene glycol<br>• Used motor oil now filtered and blended with diesel fuel to power trucks<br>• Oil filters now drained for 24 hours before being crushed | • Antifreeze now recycled at a cost of $0.19 a gallon compared to $4.35 a gallon for virgin antifreeze (1991 prices)<br>• Reduction in solvent disposal cost |

| Manufacturer | Process Improvements | Savings |
|---|---|---|
| | • A distillation unit installed to recover solvents<br>• Use of dedicated paint guns allowing for the gun nozzle to be cleaned every third or fourth day. This led to a solvent reduction of 75 percent. | |

## Notes

1. Joanna D. Underwood, "Going Green for Profit," *EPA Journal,* July–September 1993, pp. 9–13.
2. Paul Ferraro, "Colorado's Pollution-Prevention Partnership," *EPA Journal,* July–September 1993, pp. 30–31. The sample consisted of businesses engaged in furniture manufacturing, printing and publishing, rubber and plastic manufacturing, fabricated metal manufacturing, electrical machinery manufacturing, instrument manufacturing, dry cleaning, pulp and paper manufacturing, chemical manufacturing, primary metal manufacturing, machinery manufacturing, transportation equipment manufacturing, photo finishing, and auto maintenance and repair.
3. Joanna D. Underwood, "Going Green for Profit," p. 12. Peter Cebon, in his "Corporate Obstacles to Pollution Prevention," raises the same point when he writes,

   [T]o determine whether a particular solution is feasible, people need a really intimate understanding of the way the plant works. This kind of understanding doesn't come from design drawings but from the uses and working idiosyncrasies of the individual pieces of equipment. Emission control devices, on the other hand, are physically quite separate from the rest of the production process. Pollution prevention presents a difficult information processing problem because it requires people to understand more than the intimate details of the production process; they must also understand the technical possibilities. . . . Pollution prevention solutions, then, require a nexus between two very dissimilar types of information: contextual and technical. (*EPA Journal,* July–September 1993, pp. 20 and 21.)

4. The following case studies are summarized from a series of documents published by the EPA between 1990 and 1993. All the waste minimization studies published within these EPA reports were sponsored in 1986 by the California Department of Health Services (DHS). The twelve reports were published by the EPA Risk Reduction Engineering Laboratory, Center for Environmental Research Information, Cincinnati, Ohio 45268.
5. In the United States, foundries are subject to the following emission controls by the EPA—on CO, Pb, $NO_x$, particulate, PM10, $SO_x$, and VOCs. Foundries must keep records of their annual purchases of binders to get the information needed to fill out the annual SARA 313 Form R Toxic Release Inventory Report.
6. There exist in the United States several waste exchanges known as Industrial Materials Exchanges. These exchanges list services that match up companies having unneeded commodities such as surplus materials, off-spec products, or manufacturing by-products with companies that can make use of those materials. See Joel Makower, *The E-Factor* (New York: A Plume Book, 1995), pp. 218–21. See Glossary of Some Key Terms for additional information.

# 10

# Can the Environment Be Managed?

The title of this final chapter was inspired by Morton and Marsha Gorden's book on environmental management. To some, including this author, the notion that the environment can be managed is not only potentially confusing but also borders on the arrogant. Indeed, there are at least two diametrically opposed points of view to consider when one speaks of environmental management. The first approach, favored by man ever since he learned to cultivate the earth, looks upon the environment as a set of infinite resources placed at his disposal to be used or disposed of as he sees fit. This philosophy was certainly favored by one of America's early conservationists, Gifford Pinchot, when he wrote, "[T]he first principle of conservation is the use of the natural resources now existing on this continent for the benefit of the people *who live here now.*"[1] This philosophy contradicted the views of yet another famous conservationist (or deep ecologist), John Muir, for whom the management of nature meant that it had to be protected from the continued assault brought about by mechanization and technology. To this day, the schism between those who favor developing natural resources now and those who favor protecting them for future generations still exists, but the debate covers a broader spectrum of ideas. Those who view nature as an infinite resource to be used and abused by man are now opposed by those who favor a sustainable approach to economic growth. Both are challenged by deep ecologists.

The deep ecology movement originated nearly thirty years ago with the Norwegian Arne Naess, who in turn based his ideas on those developed by the Norwegian writer Wessel Zapffe. Naess's ecophilosophy proposes that technologies and management must be integrated within the natural process and redefined in a more ecological manner so as to respect the landscape. To most deep ecologists (there are several philosophies), including Naess, the only way to preserve nature is to establish, as Muir proposed nearly ninety years ago, large areas, or parks, free from human development.[2]

Given these differences in opinion, one should not be surprised to learn that environmental management means very different things to different people. Back in 1972, when the Gordens published one of the first books on environmental management, they noted:

> [W]e are managing the environment today, albeit in ignorance of consequences and without the skills we concede are necessary to manage a business or household . . . our present culture does not provide us with anything near an adequate ethical base to deal with problems of environmental management.[3]

A change in ethical base is precisely what members of the Elmwood Institute in Berkeley, California, are proposing. Reviewing the concept of environmental auditing, members of the Elmwood Institute "believe that there is a difference between *environmental* auditing, which they consider a comparatively shallow perspective, and *ecological* auditing, which they see as having more profound implications." An ecological audit is defined as

> an examination and review of a company's operations from the perspective of deep ecology, or the new paradigm. It is motivated by a shift of values in the corporate culture from domination to partnership, from the ideology of economic growth to that of ecological sustainability. It involves a corresponding shift from mechanistic to systematic thinking and, accordingly, a new style of management known as systematic management. The result of the eco-audit is an action plan for minimizing the company's environmental impact and making all its operations more ecologically sound.[4]

Although the ISO 14001 standard does not address issues proposed by the deep ecology movement, the fundamental principles outlined within its few pages are an important first step toward achieving those goals and, perhaps more important, are within the reach of all companies large or small currently operating throughout the globe. Naturally, the ISO 14001 standard will be challenged by many. To some, the globalization of environmentalism brought about by ISO 14001 will mean that "environmental priorities will be set by the shrill rather than the serious." Referring specifically to the limited success of international agencies such as the World Bank, the International Monetary Fund, and the United Nations, Fred Lee Smith remarks that "unfortunately, the track record of these agencies in the economic area provides little justification for optimism in the ecological sphere. . . . Economic central planning has failed. Why should we expect ecological central planning to do any better?"[5] Smith's observations, written in 1990, have certainly proved to be true, but, fortunately, the ISO 14001 standard is not about central planning. Even if governments were to integrate the standard within their national policies, the standard recognizes industrial variability and allows for flexibility in implementation. Events over the past two to three years suggest that world political and public opinion is closer to the views expressed by Jessica Mathews when she stated:

> Thus for both economic and environmental reasons, the notion of collective security is slowly replacing that of individually defined national security. Nation states are not going to disappear, nor is world government in the offing. But nations are seeing irrefutable evidence that their future well-being rests increasingly on actions taken far from their shores, an insight that is putting an unprecedented premium on international cooperation.[6]

Let us hope that the primary motivation for companies throughout the world seeking to achieve ISO 14001 certification will be a real concern for the environment, not merely a hope to increase sales. I am not suggesting that the ISO 14001 standard will necessarily solve all our global environmental problems. Indeed, as Paul Hawken suggests, in a style somewhat reminiscent of the nineteenth-century American essayist and naturalist Henry David Thoreau, "[I]t is difficult, if not perilous to propose solutions to global problems."[7] Yet, with the proper intent and focus on environmental preservation and sustainability, the ISO 14001 system for environmental management could become an important stepping-stone toward environmental protection at the global level.

## Notes

1. Quoted in Bill Devall and George Sessions, *Deep Ecology: Living As If Nature Mattered* (Salt Lake City: Gibbs Smith Publisher, 1985), p. 133.
2. Arne Naess, *Ecology, Community and Lifestyle* (Cambridge: Cambridge University Press,

1989), pp. 15, 17, 115, 123, and 212. Naess recognizes, as others have, the limitations of the use of the GNP, which he refers to as the Gross National Pollution. He proposes that negative impacts on the environment be deducted from the GNP. Some observers have labeled deep ecologists as radical environmentalists. Obviously, such critics are not aware of the ancient (1300 A.D.) Hawaiian system of law known as "Kapu." The Kapu was meant to protect certain species of fish that were known to protect fishermen. Anyone who broke the Kapu was subject to death by strangulation. Respect for the environment in ancient Hawaii was certainly a serious affair. Source monet@aloha.net.

3. Morton Gorden and Marsha Gorden, *Environmental Management Science and Politics* (Boston: Allyn and Bacon, 1972), p. 538.
4. Joel Makower, *The E-Factor* (New York: A Plume Book, 1995), p. 247.
5. Fred Lee Smith, Jr., "National Sovereignty and Environmental Imperatives: Two Views," *EPA Journal*, July/August 1990, p. 26.
6. Jessica Tuchman Mathews, "National Sovereignty and Environmental Imperatives: Two Views," *EPA Journal*, July/August 1990, p. 28.
7. Paul Hawken, *The Ecology of Commerce* (New York: HarperBusiness, 1993), p. 201.

# Appendixes

# A

# Guidance to Pollution Prevention Planning

## Washington State's *Environment 2010*

The state of Washington first launched its long-range environmental planning *(Environment 2010)* in December 1988. A year later, then-Governor Booth Gardner noted in his introductory statement to the first *Environment 2010* report that "preserving Washington's environment for future generations will require fundamental changes in the way we live our lives, personally, publicly and corporately."[1] Recognizing that environmental management was often synonymous with crisis management, the report readily acknowledged that the "state did not have a systematic approach for identifying and assessing existing and environmental and natural resource management issues, for anticipating emerging ones, and for setting priorities among them."[2] Realizing that environmental information in the state was still limited in a number of ways, Governor Gardner wisely recognized that before acting he required an environmental status report. To achieve that objective, he appointed a Public Advisory Committee consisting of citizens, educators, farmers, businesspeople, legislators, environmental advocates, and others. Influenced by earlier research conducted by the EPA, the authors of the report emphasized the use of risk analysis for setting priorities among environmental issues. The committee also emphasized in its concluding remarks that economic growth and environmental preservation are interdependent, not mutually exclusive, interests.

By 1990, Governor Gardner, perhaps influenced by international reports published in the late 1980s, began to edge closer to the need for economic sustainability: "If we do no more that maintain the status quo in our environmental programs," he observed, "our children will not enjoy the same quality of life that we do. . . . we can change our lifestyles for the benefit of our environment and future generations without affecting the overall quality of our lives."[3]

In barely three years, the state of Washington had accumulated a vast array of data and statistics, which it now published in its *Environment 2010* reports for all to review. As vast amounts of information began to be collected in various databases and eventually processed, state officials soon recognized the importance of regulating hazardous waste. Recognizing that the disposal of hazardous waste can be harmful and costly to dispose of, the state legislature in 1990 passed the Hazardous Waste Reduction Act. This act required "certain hazardous waste generators and hazardous waste substance users to prepare plans for voluntarily reducing hazardous substance use and hazardous waste generation."[4] The Pollution Prevention Plan called for by Chapter 173-307 WAC, summarized below,[5] anticipates many of the requirements called for by environmental management international standards.

## Summary of the "Guidance to Pollution Prevention Planning"

### Definitions

*chemical abstract service (CAS) number*    A number that uniquely identifies regulated chemicals. Some examples are acetone (67-64-1), benzene (71-43-2), chromium (7440-47-3), copper (7440-50-8), ethylene (74-84-1), mercury (7439-96-5), methyl isobutyl ketone (108-10-1), peracetic acid (79-21-0), styrene (100-42-5), toluene (108-88-3), vinyl bromide (593-60-2), and zinc (7440-66-6). Section 313, Toxic Chemical List for Reporting Year 1992, includes approximately 345 toxic chemicals along with their associated minimum allowable concentrations.

*hazardous or toxic substances*    In the United States, a hazardous or toxic substance (the terms are used interchangeably) is anything listed as a hazardous substance pursuant to Section 313 of Title III of the Superfund Amendments and Re Authorization Act (SARA) and any further updates, and all ozone-depleting compounds as defined by the Montreal Protocol of October 1987 and any further updates.

*hazardous waste*  This can be a solid, liquid, or gas. When managed improperly, hazardous waste can pose a substantial threat (including death) to human health or the environment. Hazardous waste does not include radioactive wastes.

## The Process

With the exception of facilities that distribute or use fertilizers or pesticides (which are regulated by other federal agencies), any facility that uses hazardous substances and/or generates a minimum of 2,640 lbs./year (1,200 kg) of hazardous waste(s) is required to prepare a pollution prevention plan.

An executive summary containing key information from the plan must also be prepared and submitted to the Washington Department of Ecology by certain dates. Upon review and approval of the executive summary, which is subject to public inspection (ISO 14001 §4.2 f), the applicant will receive a letter certifying that the executive summary is complete and adequate. Penalties can be levied if plans are either not prepared or deficiencies not corrected within an allocated time.

# ISO 14001 and the Washington Pollution Prevention Plan

The following pages summarize the format and contents of a typical Pollution Prevention Plan as required by the Washington Department of Ecology and Chapter 173-307 of the Washington Administrative Code (WAC). To demonstrate how the ISO 14001 standard fits within the local environmental regulation of the state (other regulations, such as the Storm Water Pollution Prevention Plan, or SWPP, exist), I have included, in parentheses, references to the ISO 14001 international standard. The ISO 14001 references do not necessarily duplicate Chapter 173-307, nor do they or could they repeat verbatim the local law. Nevertheless, in many cases, one can demonstrate that the text found in ISO 14001 aligns rather well with state requirements. Naturally, since the ISO 14001 is intended for use throughout the world, its contents cannot be as specific as regional and/or national laws and regulations. State laws are necessarily written to satisfy local requirements and reflect the consensus of the general public and business community.

# Structure of a Pollution Prevention Plan as Required by the Washington Department of Ecology as per Chapter 173-307 WAC (ISO 14001 §4.2 c, *Environmental policy*, and §4.3.2, *Legal and other requirements*)

## 1. Policy Scope and Objectives

Name of Facility: _____

**Scope and Objective.** Identify the facilities and buildings to be covered by the plan. State the objectives to be achieved through planning and implementation (ISO 14001 §4.3.1, *Environmental aspects,* and 4.3.3, *Objectives and targets*).

**Management Policy.** The management policy must express support for planning and a commitment to implementation (ISO 14001 §4.2 c, *Environmental policy*). The policy should also state that when implementing improvements or opportunities, risks will not be shifted from one part of a process, environmental medium, or product to another *unless a reduction in risk occurs.*

**Management Signature.** The owner, chief executive officer, or other person with the authority to commit management to the plan must sign the plan or the executive summary (implied in ISO 14001 but not specifically stated).

[*Name of Facility*] _____
is committed to the purpose of this plan and hereby submits it to the State of Washington Department of Ecology. This Pollution Prevention Plan has been prepared in compliance with Chapter 173-307 WAC.

_____

Type or Print Name

_____

Signature                                              Date

_____

Title

## 2. Description of How Employees Are Involved in the Planning Process

The plan must describe how employees were involved in the preparation of this plan (ISO 14001 §4.4.2, *Training, awareness and competence*). Members of the planning team may be identified. Records of team meetings and activities must be kept (ISO 14001 §4.5.3, *Records*).

## 3. Facility Description (not specified by ISO 14001)

Facility and industry type: _____

Primary Standard Industrial Code (SIC): _____

Facility's EPA identification number: _____

**Description of Products and/or Services** (not specifically required by ISO 14001)

**Production Levels** (ISO 14001 §§4.3.3, *Objectives and targets,* and 4.5.1, *Monitoring and measurement*) State the production or service level(s) at your facility for the previous calendar year. This information can be used to monitor the effectiveness of your hazardous waste and/or substances reduction/elimination program.

## 4. Processes, Wastes, and Toxic Releases

**Overview of Processes** (ISO 14001 §§4.3.1, *Environmental aspects,* and 4.4.6, *Operational Control*) Provide an overview of the process(es) used in the production of goods and/or services, particularly process(es) that either use or generate hazardous substances/wastes.

**Hazardous Wastes and Toxic Releases** (addressed in a modified form by ISO 14001 §4.3.1) If applicable, provide the following data for the past calendar year:

Total pounds of extremely hazardous waste: _____

Total pounds of dangerous waste: _____

Total pounds of remedial or one-time waste: _____

## 5. Current and Past Practices

Describe any reduction, recycling, and treatment activities currently under way at your facility. If possible, estimate the reductions in pounds

and percentages, the year implemented, and any cost savings you hope
to achieve (ISO 14001 §4.3.3, *Objectives and targets*).

## 6. Hazardous Substances Identification, Pounds Approach (ISO 14001 §4.5.1, *Monitoring and measurement*)

List each product that contains 50 percent or more of any combination
of hazardous substances (HS) if more than 1,000 pounds of the product
were used.

| Product (> 1,000 lbs. or 454 kgs) | Amount Used (lbs.) | Total Concentration (HS%) | Processes Where Used |
|---|---|---|---|
| | | | |
| | | | |
| | | | |
| Subtotal | | | |

Repeat above table for product that contains between 25 and 49 percent
hazardous substances if more than 4,000 pounds of the product were
used.

| Product (> 4,000 lbs. or 1,818 kgs) | Amount Used (lbs.) | Total Concentration (HS%) | Processes Where used |
|---|---|---|---|
| | | | |
| | | | |
| Subtotal | | | |

Repeat above table for product that contains between 10 and 24 percent
hazardous substances if more than 10,000 pounds of the product were
used.

| Product (> 10,000 lbs. or 4,540 kgs) | Amount Used (lbs.) | Total Concentration (HS%) | Processes Where Used |
|---|---|---|---|
| | | | |
| | | | |
| Subtotal | | | |

The Washington State law also requires a facility to identify hazardous products that would account for 90 percent of the total amount (in pounds) of hazardous substances. Calculate 90 percent of the total amount of hazardous products and rank products by quantity used until 90 percent of total weight is accounted for.

| Product | Amount Used (lbs.) | Total Concentration (HS%) | Process Where Used |
|---------|--------------------|---------------------------|---------------------|
| | | | |
| | | | |
| | | | |
| Subtotal | | | |

The law also requires a facility to identify 90 percent of all wastes. You must first identify all waste generated, multiply by 0.90, and rank all wastes in decreasing order until 90 percent of the total weight is accounted for.

| Waste Name | Amount (lbs.) | Percent of Total | Generating Process |
|------------|---------------|------------------|--------------------|
| | | | |
| | | | |
| Subtotal | | | |

ISO 14001 does not specify the need for such computations; however, the answers to questions asked in the above tables could certainly be helpful in satisfying several of the ISO 14001 paragraphs already mentioned. *Also, an ISO 14001 auditor would need to know about these requirements in order to ensure that a facility operating in the state of Washington complies with the intent of 173-307-030 WAC.*

## 7. Waste Identification, Pounds Approach (ISO 14001 §4.4.6, Operational control)

This is similar to paragraph 6, above, except that the focus is now on extremely hazardous and dangerous wastes generated in excess of 500 pounds by processes.

| Waste Name | Amount (lbs.) | Percent of Total | Generating Process(es) |
|---|---|---|---|
|  |  |  |  |
|  |  |  |  |
| Subtotals |  |  |  |

## 8. Processes to Cover in Planning (ISO 14001 §4.3.6, *Operational control*)

List processes referenced in paragraphs 6 and 7 in which hazardous substances are used and/or hazardous wastes are generated. These are the production processes that must be described in paragraph 9 below and for which reduction opportunities must be identified.

| Process Name | Hazardous Substance Used | Waste Generated |
|---|---|---|
|  |  |  |
|  |  |  |
|  |  |  |

## 9. Process Description (ISO 14001 §4.4.6, *Operational control*)

Describe each process listed in paragraph 8. You may use flow diagrams or process flow sheets. Include sufficient detail to identify all the steps in which hazardous substances are used and/or in which hazardous wastes are generated. You may want to consider identifying, for each process, the disposal method for each waste.

## 10. Opportunities, by Priority Category (ISO 14001 §4.3.3, *Objectives and targets*)

There are many sources of information about pollution prevention opportunities for most processes. Vendors of hazardous substances are a good source of information. Don't hesitate to talk to vendors to explore if or how hazardous substances can be reformulated (by reduced concentration, for example) or if less hazardous but equally effective products can be substituted. Local universities or technical colleges may also be helpful.

Process name: _____

Identify via brainstorming or other team-facilitating techniques opportunities to reduce or eliminate process pollution. To ensure thoroughness, you will need to investigate various sources, review the literature available in trade journals, contact vendors and employees, and possibly even conduct statistical experiments.

Categorize the opportunities using the following headings:

1. Hazardous substance use reduction
2. Hazardous waste reduction
3. Recycling
4. Treatment

## 11. Opportunity Evaluation (vaguely alluded to in ISO 14001 §4.3.3, where financial and business requirements are stated)

The pollution prevention opportunities identified in paragraph 10 must be financially and technically evaluated as to their feasibility.

### Part A: Technical Analysis

Will risks be reduced and not shifted by implementing this opportunity? (See appendix on risk analysis.) Yes _____ No _____

You may want to consider listing all impediments to implementing this opportunity.

Is opportunity technically feasible? If yes, continue with Part A Economic analysis. If no, stop analysis and proceed to Part B.

**Economic analysis.** The economic analysis tries to establish the total cost (full accounting) of the current practice compared to implementing this alternative.

Five-year estimated implementation costs: $ _____

Five-year estimated savings from implementation: $ _____

Five-year net costs or savings: $ _____

Intangible costs and benefits: _____

Changes in risks and/or potential liabilities: _____

Part B: Decision (check one)

Opportunity selected: _____

Opportunity rejected: _____

State reason(s): _____

Further study needed: _____

Anticipated date of completion: _____

## 12. Selected Opportunities and Performance Goals (implied to some extent by paragraph 4.4.6, *Operational control of ISO 14001*)

For each opportunity identified in paragraph 10, you must identify the affected process(es). You must next estimate by weight or percentage reduction how much of the hazardous substances and hazardous wastes will be reduced, recycled, or treated by each opportunity by the fifth year of implementation.

| Opportunity Name | Process(es) Affected | HS Reduced (lbs.) by 5th Year | Haz. Wastes Reduced by 5th Year | Recycling (lbs.) by 5th Year | Treatments (lbs.) by 5th Year |
|---|---|---|---|---|---|
| _____ | _____ | _____ | _____ | _____ | _____ |
| _____ | _____ | _____ | _____ | _____ | _____ |
| _____ | _____ | _____ | _____ | _____ | _____ |
| | Opportunity Total | | | | |

## 13. Five-Year Implementation Plan

You will need to develop a schedule for implementing the reduction opportunities identified in step 12.

| Opportunity | Estimated Implementation Data | | | | |
|---|---|---|---|---|---|
| Name | Year 1 | Year 2 | Year 3 | Year 4 | Year 5 |
| _____ | _____ | _____ | _____ | _____ | _____ |
| _____ | _____ | _____ | _____ | _____ | _____ |
| _____ | _____ | _____ | _____ | _____ | _____ |

## 14. Cost-Accounting Procedures

The intent of the law is to encourage the development of accounting systems that cover the hidden costs associated with the use of hazardous substances and with hazardous waste management. The so-called concept of the hidden factory, where nonconforming parts are reworked, is well known to quality engineers.

You will need to describe and account for the total costs of current practices, including compliance and auditing/monitoring costs of pollution prevention alternatives (see total cost accounting).

## 15. Financial Description (no ISO 14001 equivalent)

This section focuses on the cost/benefit analysis of the plan.

Estimate costs of implementing the selected opportunities over the past five-year planning period (including operating and depreciation costs): $ _____

Estimate savings from implementation of selected opportunities over the five-year planning period: $ _____

Estimate net savings or costs: $ _____

Describe any intangible costs that may result from implementing the selected opportunities: _____

Describe any intangible benefits that may result from implementing the selected opportunities: _____

## 16. Personnel Training Program (ISO 14001 §4.4.2)

The pollution prevention plan must describe how employees are trained in various pollution prevention training programs. Since some federal agencies (and the ISO 14001 standard) require that training records be maintained, it is recommended that you document and record your pollution prevention and other related programs (see Chapter 3 for guidelines on record retention).

## 17. Documentation of Research (no ISO 14001 equivalent)

This is an interesting requirement of 173-307 WAC. In effect, the Washington State law requires that a facility document and keep records of any research activity conducted for the purpose of evaluating opportunities for pollution reduction. Research projects or implementation programs such as pollution prevention studies, life-cycle analyses, or design for the environment projects could be documented here.

## 18. Research Labs, Policies, and Procedures (ISO 14001 §4.4.6, Operational control)

This is not limited to laboratory practices but applies to *all* processes. If a facility has a research laboratory, the Washington law requires that policies and procedures be developed for personnel using hazardous substances or generating hazardous wastes through laboratory research.

## 19. Executive Summary Addenda (no ISO 14001 equivalent)

When submitting an executive summary, the following points must be considered.

### A. Reasons for Rejecting Opportunities

Provide a summary of the reasons for rejecting opportunities from further consideration.

| Opportunity Name | Reason for Rejecting |
|---|---|
| 1. _____ | _____ |
| 2. _____ | _____ |
| 3. _____ | _____ |
| 4. _____ | _____ |

## B. Impediments

Provide a summary of all identified impediments to implementing opportunities.

## C. Production Levels

Describe the assumptions of changing production levels or service activity levels during the five-year period covered by the plan.

## Notes

1. Governor Booth Gardner letter, *The State of the Environment Report* (Olympia, Wash.: Department of Ecology, November 2, 1989), p. i.
2. *The State of the Environment Report*, p. 2.
3. Governor Booth Gardner letter, *A Citizen's Guide to Washington's Environment* (Olympia, Wash.: Department of Ecology, October 1990). The transition to sustainability was completed in 1990; see Chapter II, "Creating a Sustainable Future: A Vision of Washington in 2010," in *Towards 2010: An Environmental Action Agenda* (Department of Ecology, July 1990). The well-known definition of sustainability published in 1987 by the World Commission on Environment and Development is reproduced in the Introduction to *The 1991 State of the Environment Report*: "[Sustainability means] meeting the needs of the present without compromising the ability of future generations to meet their own needs."
4. *Pollution Prevention Planning Guidance Manual for Chapter 173-307 WAC*, Publication #91-2 (Olympia: Washington State Department of Ecology, September 1993), p. 1.
5. Abstracted from the Washington Department of Ecology *Guidance Manual for Chapter 173-307 WAC*, September 1993.

# B

# Financial Indicators: Definitions and Financial Coefficients Used in Chapter 6

## Definitions

***compound value interest factor (CVIF)*** CVIFs are used to compute compound value, for example, when a person deposits $1,000 for five years in a savings account. Suppose the account has an interest rate ($i$) of 5 percent. How much will the person have in the savings account at the end of the fifth year? The amount can be calculated using the following formula:

$$P_n = P_0 (1 + i)_n$$

Where:

$P_n$ = principal value at the end of $n$ period.
$i$ = interest rate.
$P_0$ = principal, or beginning amount, at time 0.

The answer to the above question is easily obtained by referring to Table B-1. For a $P_0$ of $1,000, Table B-1 reveals that $P_5$ = $1,000 × 1.276 = $1,276.

Note that the values down the 5% column were used in Chapter 6 (Table 6-9).

Table B-1. CVIF.

| Period | 3% | 5% | 8% | 10% |
|--------|------|------|------|------|
| 1 | 1.030 | 1.050 | 1.080 | 1.100 |
| 2 | 1.061 | 1.102 | 1.166 | 1.210 |
| 3 | 1.093 | 1.158 | 1.260 | 1.331 |
| 4 | 1.126 | 1.216 | 1.360 | 1.464 |
| 5 | 1.159 | *1.276* | 1.469 | 1.611 |
| 6 | 1.194 | 1.340 | 1.587 | 1.772 |
| 7 | 1.230 | 1.407 | 1.714 | 1.949 |
| 8 | 1.267 | 1.477 | 1.851 | 2.144 |
| 9 | 1.305 | 1.551 | 1.999 | 2.358 |
| 10 | 1.344 | 1.629 | 2.159 | 2.594 |
| 11 | 1.384 | 1.710 | 2.332 | 2.853 |
| 12 | 1.426 | 1.796 | 2.518 | 3.138 |
| 13 | 1.469 | 1.886 | 2.720 | 3.452 |
| 14 | 1.513 | 1.980 | 2.937 | 3.797 |
| 15 | 1.558 | 2.079 | 3.172 | 4.177 |

*double declining balance (DDB)*   A method of accelerated depreciation that requires the application of a constant rate of depreciation each year to the *undepreciated* value of the asset at the close of the previous year. Thus, if the straight line rate (see definition) is 10 percent a year, the double declining rate would be 20 percent. This rate is applied to the full purchase price, not the cost less salvage value. For example, suppose a machine costing $1,000 has an estimated useful life of ten years, after which time it will be scrapped for $100. The depreciation under the DDB method is 20 percent of $1,100, or $220. The second year the depreciation would be $176, or

$$20\% \times (1{,}100 - \$220) = \$176$$

and so on (see Table B-2).

The method shown in Chapter 6 is a combination of the DDB switching to straight line after the fifth year. [*Note:* Rather than discounting the first year at $176,757, or 13.3 percent of 1,329,000, the first year is discounted at half the rate; this is known as the ½-year method.] Adding all of the depreciation up to the sixth year ($722,513), we find that the balance due is: $1,329,000 − $722,513 = $606,487. For the remaining nine years (years 7 through 15), the

**Table B-2.** Comparison of depreciation methods for a ten-year $1,000 asset with a $100 salvage value.

| Year | Depreciation Method | |
| --- | --- | --- |
| | Straight Line | Double Declining Balance |
| 1 | $ 100 | $220 |
| 2 | 100 | 176 |
| 3 | 100 | 141 |
| 4 | 100 | 113 |
| 5 | 100 | 90 |
| 6 | 100 | 72 |
| 7 | 100 | 58 |
| 8 | 100 | 46 |
| 9 | 100 | 37 |
| 10 | 100 | 29 |
| Total | $1,000 | $982 |

$606,487 is discounted using the straight line method. Therefore, $606,487 divided by 9 = $67,387. This figure is slightly different from the $63,481 reported in the study. I have no explanation for the discrepancy.

*present value:* The reverse of compound value. Present value is defined as follows:

$$\text{Present value} = P_0 = P_n/(1 + i)^n$$

Suppose the year is 1996 and the interest rate for a savings account is 5 percent. We would like to know the present (1996) value (also known as *discounted* value) of $1,000 in the year 2001. The answer to this question is obtained by looking up the present value interest factors (PVIF), which are nothing more than 1/CVIF (see Table B-3). The PVIF for 5 percent for $n = 5$ years is .784. Therefore, $1,000 (in the year 2001) is worth only $784 today.

The coefficients listed under the 15% column were used to compute the projected net present value found in Table 6-10.

## Ranking Investment Proposals: Definitions

*payback method* Number of years/weeks/months required to return the original investment from net cash flows. (See Appendix C for an example.)

**Table B-3.** PVIF.

| Period | Interest Rate | | |
|---|---|---|---|
| | 5% | 10% | 15% |
| 1 | .952 | .909 | .870 |
| 2 | .905 | .826 | .756 |
| 3 | .864 | .751 | .658 |
| 4 | .823 | .683 | .572 |
| 5 | **.784** | .621 | .497 |
| 6 | .746 | .564 | .432 |
| 7 | .711 | .513 | .376 |
| 8 | .677 | .467 | .327 |
| 9 | .645 | .424 | .284 |
| 10 | .614 | .386 | .247 |

Factors were computed by using the formula $1/(1+i)^n$, where $i$ is set at .05, .10, and .15 respectively.

**net present value (NPV) method**  Present value of future returns discounted at the appropriate cost of capital, minus the cost of the investment. The equation for the net present value (NPV) is

$$NPV = \sum_{t=1}^{N} \frac{R_t}{(1 + k)^t} - C$$

Where $R_1$, $R_2$, and so on represent the net cash flows (the operating cash flow in Table 6-9); $k$ is the marginal cost of capital (15 percent for the case study found in Chapter 6); $C$ is the initial cost of the project ($1,329,000 in the case study presented in Chapter 6); and $N$ is the project's expected life (fifteen years in the case study presented in Chapter 6).

**internal rate of return (IRR) method:**  An interest rate that equates the present value of future returns (cash flows or receipts) with the initial investment outlay. The formula for the IRR is

$$\sum_{t=1}^{N} \frac{R_t}{(1 + r)^t} - C = 0$$

The internal rate of return is the value $r$ for which the equation is equal to 0. This IRR is found via an iterative process. First compute the present value of the cash flows from an investment using an arbitrary rate (e.g., 15 percent). Compare the present value so obtained with the investment's cost. If the present value is higher than the cost figure, try a higher interest rate and go through the procedure again. The calculations shown in Table B-4 indicate that the IRR must be higher than 30 percent (it is in fact approximately 35 percent).

*straight line rate:*   Rate arrived at by simply dividing the economic life into the total cost of the machine (or project), minus the estimated salvage value, if any. For example, in Chapter 6 the initial investment of $1,329,000 is depreciated over a period of fifteen years. Therefore, the straight line depreciation rate is: 1,329,000 ÷ 15 = $88,600, or 6.66 percent annually. The double declining rate would simply be: 2 × 6.66 = 13.3 percent.

**Table B-4.** IRR calculations.

| Year | Net Cash Flow (from Table 6-10) | PVIF for 30% | Present Value |
|------|--------------------------------|--------------|---------------|
| 1 | $430,489 | .769 | $331,046 |
| 2 | 501,894 | .590 | 296,117 |
| 3 | 514,801 | .455 | 234,234 |
| 4 | 530,069 | .350 | 185,524 |
| 5 | 547,542 | .269 | 147,288 |
| 6 | 567,083 | .207 | 117,386 |
| 7 | 581,765 | .159 | 92,500 |
| 8 | 609,419 | .122 | Total = $1,404,095* |
| 9 | 638,652 | .094 | |
| 10 | 669,466 | .072 | |

*Since the subtotal exceeds the initial investment of $1,329,000 by the seventh year, a new set of present values must be computed with a higher PVIF. Recompute with a PVIF for 35% using the formula for present value.

# C

# Economic Evaluation Case Study

### Solvent Rinse Use Reduction

In this example, current total solvent use per month is determined from a knowledge of the quantity of nonepoxy solvent (NES) disposed of each month. This plant produces 70 percent epoxy resin-based products and 30 percent nonepoxy resin-based products.

Current solvent use per month = 8,400 gal./month.

Volume of solvent saved at 25% use reduction = 2,100 gal./month.

### Raw Material Savings (RMS)

| | | |
|---|---|---|
| RMS = | 2,100 gal. × 0.45 (acetone) × 0.792 (8.32 lbs./gal.) ($0.23/lb.) = | $1,400/mo |
| RMS = | 2,100 gal. × 0.45 (MEK)* × 0.792 (8.32 lbs./gal.) (0.365/lb.) = | 2,300 |
| RMS = | 2,100 gal. × 0.10 (methanol) × 0.792 (8.32 lbs./gal.) (0.96/lb.) = | 1,300 |
| | Total | $5,000/mo |

*MEK = methyl ethyl ketone

### Disposal Cost Savings (DCS)

DCS = $590 month.

## Labor Cost Increase (LCI)

LCI = 15 additional minutes/cleanout × 339 cleanouts/
mo. × $22/60 minutes of labor = $1,865/month.

## Monthly Cost Savings (MCS)

MCS = $5,000 + $590 − $1,865 = $3,725.

## Operator Training Cost (OTC)

OTC = 15 operators × 8 hr. × $22/hr. = $2,640.

## Payback Period (PP)

PP = $2,700/$3,725 = 0.724 × 4 wks./mo. = 3 wks.

# D

# Partial List of Toxic or Hazardous Chemicals With OSHA and FDA Maximum Recommended Exposures

| Chemical | OSHA Limit in Workplace | FDA Limit |
|---|---|---|
| Acetone | 750 ppm | 30 ppm residue. Concentrations of 20,000 ppm are considered dangerous. |
| Aluminum | Metal dust: 10 mg/m$^3$ Welding fumes: 5 mg/m$^3$ | No data (ND) |
| Ammonial | 17.5 mg/m$^3$ or 25 ppm | ND |
| Benzene | 5-minumte limits: 16.5 mg/m$^3$ | Maximum contamination level in drinking water: 5 micrograms/L |
| Carbon tetrachloride | 10 ppm | Drinking water standard: 5 ppb |
| Chlorine, hydrogen chloride, hydrochloric acid, hypochlorite | Chlorine: 3 mg/m$^3$ (1 ppm) Hydrogen chloride: 7 mg/m$^3$ or 5 ppm | ND |
| Chromium | Chromium VI: 50 micrograms/m$^3$ Chromium III: 0.5 mg/m$^3$ | ND |
| Ethylene glycol | 50 ppm | May be used only in some cosmetics and in packaging adhesives. |
| Formaldehyde | 3 ppm | 42.4 micrograms/L |
| Methylene chloride | 100 ppm | 30–220 ppm |
| Mercury | 0.1 mg/m$^3$ | |
| Styrene | 430 mg/m$^3$ (50 ppm) | 0.14 mg/L |
| Tetrachloroethylene | 50 ppm | 0.001 ppm |
| Toluene | 375 mg/m$^3$ | 2 mg/m$^3$ |
| Trichloroethane | 350 ppm | 350 ppm |
| Trichloroethylene | 50 ppm | 10–30 ppm |
| Xylene | 100 ppm | ND |
| Zinc | zinc chloride fume: 1 mg/m$^3$ zinc oxide fume: 5mg/m$^3$ | ND |

# E

# Some Examples of Environmental Policies

The following environmental policies are published in *Life Cycle Design Framework and Demonstration Projects: Profiles of AT&T and AlliedSignal,* published by the United States Environmental Protection Agency, Office of Research and Development, EPA/600/R-95/107, July 1995, pp. 22, 23, 70, and 98. The ISO 14001 requirements contained in paragraph 4.2 are included to allow the reader to determine which one (if any) of the environmental policies listed below best satisfies the intent of paragraph 4.2 (a–f).

## Environmental Policy (ISO 14001 Draft International Standard, September 1995)

Top management shall define the organization's environmental policy and ensure that it:

a) is appropriate to the nature, scale and environmental impacts of its activities, products or services;

b) includes a commitment to continual improvement and prevention of pollution;

c) includes a commitment to comply with relevant environmental legislation and regulations and with other requirements to which the organization subscribes;

d) provides the framework for setting and reviewing environmental objectives and targets;

e) is documented, implemented and maintained and communicated to all employees; and

f) is available to the public.

## Xerox Environmental Policy

Xerox Corporation is committed to the protection of the environment and the health and safety of its employees, customers, and neighbors. This commitment is applied worldwide in developing new products and processes.

 ‣ Environmental health and safety concerns take priority over economic considerations.
 ‣ All Xerox operations must conduct themselves in a manner that safeguards health, protects the environment, and conserves valuable materials and resources.
 ‣ Xerox is committed to the continual improvement of its performance in environmental protection and resource conservation.
 ‣ Xerox is committed to designing products for optimal recyclability and reusability. We are equally committed to exploring every opportunity to recycle or reuse waste materials generated by our operations.

*Author's comment:* Although the policy's implied reference to Design for the Environment and other references go well beyond the ISO 14001 requirements, the policy does not mention the framework for setting and reviewing environmental objectives and targets.

## General Motors Environmental Principles

As a responsible corporate citizen, General Motors is dedicated to protecting human health, natural resources, and the global environment. This dedication reaches further than compliance with the law to encompass the integration of sound environmental practices into our business decisions.

The following environmental principles provide guidance to General Motors personnel worldwide in the conduct of their daily business practices.

1. We are committed to actions to restore and preserve the environment.
2. We are committed to reducing waste and pollutants, conserving resources, and recycling materials at every stage of the product life cycle.

3. We will continue to participate actively in educating the public regarding environmental conservation.
4. We will continue to pursue vigorously the development and implementation of technologies for minimizing pollutant emissions.
5. We will continue to work with all governmental entities for the development of technically sound and financially responsible environmental laws and regulations.
6. We will continually assess the impact of our plants and products on the environment and the communities in which we live and operate with a goal of continuous improvement.

## AT&T (Proposed Environmental Policy)

AT&T is committed to fully integrating life-cycle environmental consequences into our design, development, manufacturing, marketing, and sales activities worldwide. Implementation of this policy is a primary management objective and the responsibility of every AT&T employee.

*Guidelines*

‣ Utilize Design for Environment principles to design, develop, manufacture, and market products and services worldwide with environmentally preferable life-cycle properties.
‣ Promote achievement of environmental excellence by designing every new generation of product, process, and service to be environmentally preferable to the one it replaces.
‣ Determine the environmental impacts of products, processes, and services on an individual basis to prioritize the order in which they can be effectively addressed within technological and economic constraints.
‣ To the extent that proven and efficient technology allows, eliminate or reduce production of waste; seek economic uses of materials which would otherwise become wastes; where it is produced, eliminate or reduce discharge of waste.

▶ Design, develop, and market products and services worldwide which support our customers in their efforts to reduce or eliminate harmful environmental impact of their activities.

▶ Integrate applicable life-cycle environmental considerations into each of our business decisions and planning activities, including acquisition/divestiture activity, and into the measurement standards applied to management performance.

▶ Work with suppliers, customers, governments, the scientific community, educational institutions, public interest groups, and the general public worldwide to develop and promote environmental management policies and environmental standards based on life-cycle, system-based principles.

*Corporate Environmental Goals*

▶ Phase out CFC (100% reduction by 1994).
▶ Reduce total toxic air emissions (95% reduction by 1995, 100% by 2000).
▶ Decrease total manufacturing process waste disposal by 25% by 1994.
▶ *Paper use and recycling:*
   —Increase recycling by 35% by 1994.
   —Decrease paper use 15% by 1994.

## AlliedSignal Environmental Policy and Goals

AlliedSignal addresses environmental protection through both a vision statement and an environmental policy. A section of the AlliedSignal mission statement entitled "Our Values" includes six areas: customer integrity, people, teamwork, speed, innovations, and performance. Environmental protection is addressed under "integrity" in the following statement:

We are committed to the highest level of ethical conduct wherever we operate. We obey all laws, produce safe products, protect the environment, practice equal employment, and are socially responsible.

AlliedSignal's health, safety, and environmental policy, effective April 1992, states:

> It is the worldwide policy of AlliedSignal Inc. to design, manufacture, and distribute all its products and to handle and dispose of all materials without creating unacceptable health, safety, or environmental risks.
>
> The corporation will:
>
> ▸ Establish and maintain programs to assure that laws and regulations applicable to its products and operations are known and obeyed;
> ▸ Adopt its own standards where laws or regulations may not exist or be adequately protective;
> ▸ Conserve resources and energy, minimize the use of hazardous materials, and reduce wastes;
> ▸ Stop the manufacture or distribution of any product or cease any operation if the health, safety, or environmental risks or costs are unacceptable.
>
> To carry out this policy, the corporation will:
> 1. Identify and control health, safety, or environmental hazards related to its operations and products;
> 2. Safeguard employees, customers, and the public from injuries or health hazards, protect the corporation's assets and continuity of operations, and protect the environment by conducting programs for safety and loss prevention, product safety and integrity, occupational health, and pollution prevention and control, and by formally reviewing the effectiveness of such programs;
> 3. Conduct and support scientific research on the health, safety, and environmental effects of materials and products handled and sold by the corporation; and
> 4. Share promptly with employees, the public, suppliers, customers, government agencies, the scientific community, and others significant health, safety, or environmental hazards of its products and operations.
>
> Every employee is expected to adhere to the spirit as well as the letter of this policy. Managers have a special obligation to keep informed about health, safety, and environmental risks

and standards so that they can operate safe and environmentally sound facilities, produce quality products, and advise higher management promptly of any adverse situation which comes to their attention.

## Bahia Sul (Brazil) Environmental Policy

The following environmental policy is from Bahia Sul. This Brazilian pulp and paper company is located in the state of Bahia. The company registered its environmental management system in April 1995 to the British environmental standard BS 7750, from which the ISO 14001 is partly derived. The 1994 annual report of Bahia Sul states that, "[B]eing the first company in the world to obtain this certification (BS 7750) is another demonstration of Bahia Sul's concern with the environment." In 1993, 18.7 percent of the company's pulp and paper was exported to Europe. Although the figures do not show how much is exported to the Netherlands, it would be interesting to find out if Bahia Sul's opening statement on its environmental policy is somehow connected to the Netherlands' green plan objectives (see, for example, the insert following Table 2-5 for comments regarding the Netherlands' policy vis-à-vis sustainable development).

The following is Bahia Sul's environmental policy statement:

Our commitment is to operate our business based on the guideline of sustainable development and supported by the following principles:

▸ Recognition that environmental management is one of our priorities
▸ Contributing so that mankind may act in an environmentally responsible fashion
▸ Continuous improvement of processes, products, and service for constant environmental enhancement; and
▸ Compliance with environmental legislation

The System of Environmental Management encompasses industrial production including all stages of manufacturing pulp and paper, as well as the area of natural resources, including their operational nuclei.

The objectives and goals of the organization are updated annually and published in an official publication of the company,
available for consultation by interested parties in the areas of
Communication and Guaranteed Quality.

*Comments:* This is a noble and ambitious environmental policy. I would
like to know more about how the company implements its policy to
follow the "guideline of sustainable development" referred to in the
policy (see discussion in Chapters 2 and 6, particularly Tables 6-11
and 6-12). Notice how the last paragraph of the policy addresses the
requirements of 4.2.d and of 4.2.f of the standard. The annual report
does mention a 10 percent reduction in industrial water consumption
and an unspecified decrease in atmospheric emissions (referred to as
Total Reduced Sulfur).

# F

# Generic Environmental Management System for the Shades of Green Company

The following manual is by design a generic manual. It is intended only to give a general idea of how to address each of the requirements. Naturally, the details of how some of the statements, policies, or procedures are to be implemented are left to the reader. Using ISO 9000 parlance, the following sample document is a first-tier document. The reader will note the references to other lower-tier documents in which details of how a policy or procedure is (supposed to be) implemented, or how data are to be collected, can be found. Because there are many ways to address these implementation issues, lower-tier documents are not included here. Finally, as will be obvious to readers from the chemical or pulp industries, the fictitious Shades of Green Company is not intended to represent their industries. Rather than transforming this manual into a technical document littered with specific and incomprehensible jargon, I have deliberately tried to focus my attention on a "typical" company that is not likely to have had much experience with environmental management. Frequency of reports such as quarterly reports or annual reviews are only the author's suggestion. No such frequencies are specifically mentioned in the ISO 14001 standard. The reader will recognize type 2 implementation, which blends some elements of both the quality assurance system and the environmental management system.

The following manual was written by Luis Tryne: _____

Approved by Frank Pizzaro (President): _____

Release date: January 14, 1996 (first ISO 14001 edition)

Revision history:  First edition: March 8, 1989
                 Second edition: August 23, 1993
                 Third edition: October 18, 1995

## Manual Sections as Related to ISO 14001 Paragraphs

**Company background (optional):** *Include here a brief outline of your company. Include history, type of products made, and other information of interest. Try to limit this to one page.*
    The following document is available to the public.

### 1.0, Environmental policy (required)

The Shades of Green Company is committed to complying with and keeping itself up-to-date as to all city, county, state, and national environmental legislation and regulations relevant to its industry. In addition, Shades of Green Company continually seeks to reduce, prevent, and/or eliminate various types of pollution to the best of its ability.
    Corporate environmental objectives and targets for pollution prevention and reduction are set and approved yearly by the environmental executive board. These objectives, which are monitored during the company's environmental management audit, are reviewed during the last quarter of each fiscal year.

References:   Environmental executive board minutes
               Environmental audits

### 2.0, Planning
### 2.1, Environmental aspects

The Shades of Green Company handles some materials that have been classified by various government agencies as potentially hazardous to the environment (for a list of products, see the Material Safety Data Sheets maintained by the environmental engineer). These materials are either used throughout out processes or are by-products of our processes (wastewater for example). Chemicals and/or materials are handled, disposed of, or stored according to manufacturer specification or government regulations.

## 2.2, Legal and other requirements

The person in charge of environmental compliance is in regular and direct contact with the local, state, or other regulatory agencies to ensure compliance with all related regulation. Pertinent regulations and/or legislation relating to environmental issues affecting our industry are maintained by [*state the department or individual*].

## 2.3, Objectives and targets

Quantitative environmental objectives and targets for hazardous chemicals are reviewed yearly by the environmental executive board. Our primary objective is to focus on reduction, substitution, and eventual elimination. Target reductions are set as a percentage of the previous year's consumption. Objectives are reviewed yearly to assess their effectiveness. The efficacy of the process is monitored by way of our corrective and preventive action program.

In addition to the above objectives and targets, the Shades of Green Company has, with the help of its employees, also implemented a variety of environmental programs such as recycling, share-a-ride, paper reduction, and office energy efficiency.

Reference:  Environmental executive board minutes
            Corrective and preventive actions file

## 2.4, Environmental management programs

The director and/or manager of a process or processes in which hazardous chemicals are either used or generated is responsible for implementing the necessary steps and/or procedures necessary to ensure that the objectives and targets specified by the environmental executive board are met to the best of his/her ability. Unless otherwise specified, the standard time frame for satisfying stated objectives and targets is the fiscal year.

Reference:  Departmental environmental objectives

*Note: One way to record the necessary information would be to define a simple matrix identifying the process(es), process owner(s), type of chemicals, action to be taken, and method. See Appendix A for some suggestions.*

## 3.0, Implementation and operation
## 3.1, Structure and responsibility

The environmental director, who reports directly to the president, is responsible for ensuring that the environmental management system described in this manual is implemented and maintained in accordance with this standard. The performance of the environmental system is reported on a quarterly basis (or more frequently if required) by the environmental director to the environmental executive board. Measures of performance include, among things, the number of environmental nonconformities.

Reference: Quarterly environmental reports

*Note: By simply referring to the environmental director, I have taken the easy way out. Obviously, many companies will not have an environmental director or manager. In the United States and probably most other countries, it is not unusual to find that in small companies (50 or less employees), the so-called position of environmental manager is a part-time one. I have seen human resource managers, process engineers, and others act in this capacity. The same could be said for many larger companies.*

## 3.2, Training, awareness, and competence

All personnel at the Shades of Green Company receive general training in health, safety, and hazard procedures as well as more specialized training relating to their specific areas and/or processes. In addition, all employees receive training in the principles defined in this environmental management system. The training is renewed every year or more frequently if needed. Records of said training are maintained by the manager in charge of the department. (Another option is to have records maintained by human resources.)

Reference: Human resources department (or other departmental records)

## 3.3, Communication

All external correspondence relating to environmental issues, such as community requests or governmental requests, will be handled by [*state function*]. In case of an emergency that might affect the community, local authorities and public emergency services are immediately notified as specified in the emergency preparedness procedure.

Reference:  Emergency preparedness procedure

*Note: In the United States and other countries, companies are required by law to notify local authorities and emergency services in case of disasters that might lead to health hazards or life-threatening situations for the surrounding population. In some countries, these requirements are clearly spelled out in specific regulations. Your procedure must ensure that these local or national regulations are addressed.*

### 3.5, Document control

The document control procedure is identical to the quality assurance system procedure.

Reference: Document control procedure QS 9001-20

*Note: Once again, I have taken the easy way out. If you already have a quality assurance system that is registered to one of the ISO 9000 standards (9001, 9002, or 9003), there really is no need to reinvent the wheel. Procedure QS 9001-20 would describe how documents relating to the quality and environmental systems are controlled (dated, approved, retained, etc.). If you do not have such a procedure in place, it is relatively easy to write a one-page, or shorter, procedure that will address the requirements of this paragraph. See discussion in Chapter 4.*

### 3.6, Operational control

All processes that either use or produce hazardous materials, that is, materials that are subject to local, state, or federal regulations, are diagrammed to indicate hazardous material inputs, outputs, and a reference to the proper disposal procedure. Critical process parameters identifying settings and safe operational ranges are also specified on the process diagram. These process diagrams are maintained by the process manager.

Reference:  Process diagrams
            Preventive maintenance equipment matrix
            Material safety data sheets

*Note: This paragraph will require that someone (probably a process engineer or the nearest equivalent) spend some time preparing flow diagrams or other*

*documented procedures to define operational parameters. The reference to a
preventive maintenance matrix is one of the most convenient ways I know of to
identify equipment and maintenance schedules.*

### 3.7, Emergency preparedness and response

The Shades of Green Company conducts yearly general hazard analysis
and safety improvement reviews as specified by the Center for Chemical
Process Safety. These analyses and reviews are documented and maintained by the [*state title; for example, environmental director, safety manager,
environmental and safety manager*].

Reference: Hazard analysis reports

### 4.0, Checking and corrective action
### 4.1, Monitoring and measurement

The monitoring of all hazardous materials is maintained [*you may want
to state by whom*] in a database that keeps track of the quantity [*pounds,
number of drums, bags, etc.*] of hazardous chemicals processed through
the plant. The information collected in the database is used to establish,
whenever feasible, new objectives and targets.

Although the Shades of Green Company is not legally required to
measure any effluents, wastewater is automatically sampled every hour
for pH (4.0–9.0). The pH meter is calibrated twice a year.

Reference: Environmental database and pH record sheets

*Note: This is a very simple example. However, to my surprise, most small to
medium-size companies (up to about 400 employees) do not even do as much as
specified here.*

### 4.2, Nonconformance, corrective and preventive action

Nonconformities such as out-of-range process parameters, excess effluents, or other environmentally related violations are recorded (by the
person discovering the nonconformity) on corrective action forms. It is
the responsibility of the manager or supervisor in charge of the (nonconforming) process, area, or department to address the nonconformity
within a mutually agreed upon time period.

Preventive actions follow the procedure described in the quality assurance manual.

Reference:  Corrective action forms
            Preventive action procedure (quality manual)

*Note: Another easy way out. If your company is ISO 9000-registered, this requirement must already be implemented. Simply follow the same procedures.*

## 4.3, Records

The need to record information is specified in each process diagram or procedure. The following table identifies records, their location, and their retention time.

*Note: You could include a table here. The need for retention time is borrowed from the ISO 9000. Do not set very long retention dates unless you are legally required to do so or unless you think you will need these records for a very long period. Also, do not simply say that you will keep all records for seven or ten years or even "forever." Some records such as pH readings, for example, may have to be kept for only six months. You may want to transfer the records to a disk or other electronic medium and retain them for the life of the diskette (which should last three to five years or more). I must confess to never having really understood why the ISO 9000 series of standards and the ISO 14001 standard require the establishment and maintenance of procedures for record keeping! Whatever you do, keep your procedure short and simple.*

## 4.4, Environmental management audit

The environmental management system defined and referenced in this manual is completely audited every eighteen months. The date and selection of paragraph(s) and function(s) or department(s) to be audited is left to the discretion of the environmental manager, who will inform, in writing, the appropriate manager no less than five working days prior to the scheduled audit. As required, the environmental manager will select additional auditors with the appropriate technical expertise to assist during the audit.

All audits are results, and nonconformities are forwarded to the responsible manager for corrective action.

Reference:  Audit reports
Corrective action forms

*Note: Paragraph 4.4 could be considered a procedure. This example illustrates that some procedures can be included in the environmental system manual.*

## 5.0, Management review

Results of environmental audits are reviewed by the executive board twice a year, or more frequently if called for by the environmental director. The purpose of these reviews is to assess the effectiveness of the environmental system and to recommend improvements or request further studies or data collection to guide potential policy or procedure changes.

Reference: Minutes from environmental audit reviews

# G

# Case Study of a Life-Cycle Analysis

The following example is a condensed version of a life-cycle analysis conducted by Franklin Associates, Ltd., for Union Carbide Corporation.[1] The complete report consists of approximately 140 pages and thirty-six tables. This example is solely intended to illustrate the type of calculations, analyses, and peer reviews that are required in any LCA. In the majority of cases the text that follows is directly quoted from the original report. Pagination from the original text is referenced in parentheses at the end of each sentence. The author's comments appear in italics.

## Purpose

The purpose of the study is to assess the energy requirements and environmental emissions for the manufacture and disposal of two different kinds of antifreeze used in automobiles: ethylene glycol-based antifreeze and propylene glycol-based antifreeze (2-1).

## Geographical Scope

*The study is limited to operations within the United States (2-10).*

## Systems Examined

The systems examined in this study encompass the antifreeze solution and primary and tertiary packaging. Filling, packaging, and disposition are also included in the life-cycle results. The results represent U.S. conditions (3-1).

## Data Sources

*Franklin Associates relied on its extensive database as a starting point for this assessment. Franklin Associates also relied on confidential industry data, government publications, technical literature, industry statistics, and interviews with industry representatives (2-4).*

Tables G-1 and G-2 are abbreviated versions of the complete tables found in the report. Table G-2 reproduces only a few of the values found in the original table, which contains two and a half pages of data. The type and nature of the data reproduced here illustrate the quantitative nature of LCA studies.

As can be seen from Table G-2, the analysis includes a substantial amount of information. For each of the items left blank in Table G-2, as many as ten chemicals can be identified. For example, "Eutrophication/ Plant Life" is assessed by measuring the contribution for ethylene and propylene glycol production for each of the following variables: nitrogen oxides, sulfur oxides, metal ion, ammonia, phosphates, nitrogen (nitrate), herbicides, pesticides, and acid. In addition, industrial environ-

**Table G-1.** Industrial environmental emissions for 1,000 gallons of antifreeze solution (in pounds).

| Atmospheric Emissions | Ethylene Glycol | Propylene Glycol |
| --- | --- | --- |
| Acid | — | 0.20 |
| Ammonia | 0.050 | 0.30 |
| Carbon dioxide | 11,499 | 18,348 |
| Hydrocarbons | 112 | 159 |
| Methane | 2.19 | 0.19 |
| Particulates | 13.0 | 26.8 |
| Sulfur oxides | 34.8 | 71.3 |
| | | |
| *Waterborne Wastes* | | |
| Acid | 2.40 | 48.7 |
| BOD | 0.60 | 0.66 |
| COD | 0.73 | 0.85 |
| Dissolved solids | 23.5 | 44.6 |
| Iron | 1.60 | 3.30 |
| Sulfides | 0.18 | 0.19 |
| Suspended solids | 2.31 | 0.85 |

Source: Franklin Associates, *Life-Cycle Assessment of Ethylene Glycol and Propylene Glycol-Based Antifreeze*, Table 1.

**Table G-2.** Industrial environmental emissions by classification for ecosystem health (pounds per 1,000 gallons of antifreeze solution).

| | Ethylene Glycol | Propylene Glycol | % Difference |
|---|---|---|---|
| *Acid rain* | | | |
| Nitrogen oxides | 41 | 73 | 69 |
| Sulfur oxides | 35 | 71 | 69 |
| Particulates | 13 | 27 | 69 |
| *Air Dispersion* | | | |
| Sulfur oxides | 35 | 71 | 69 |
| *Aquatic life* | | | |
| Dissolved solids | 24 | 45 | 62 |
| Suspended solids | 2.3 | 0.85 | −92 |
| Aldehydes | 0.29 | 0.39 | 29 |
| Herbicides | 0.000017 | 0.000018 | 6 |
| Pesticides | 0.0000086 | 0.0000091 | 6 |
| Mercury | 0.0000037 | 0.0014 | 199 |
| Sodium hydroxide | — | 6.3 | — |
| *Aquifer Contamination* | | | |
| Nickel | 0.00000001 | 0.0000021 | 199 |
| *Chemical/biological Content alteration* | | | |
| COD | 0.73 | 0.85 | 15 |
| Oil | 0.25 | 0.27 | 8 |
| *Eutrophication* | | | |
| Plant life | | | |
| *Phosphates* | 0.0019 | 0.020 | 5 |
| Acid | — | 0.20 | — |
| *Greenhouse gas* | | | |
| Carbon monoxide | 19 | 28 | 41 |
| Methane | 2.2 | 0.19 | −168 |
| *Oxygen depletion* | — | — | — |
| pH alterations | — | — | — |
| Smog precursors | — | — | — |
| Thermal changes | — | — | — |
| Visibility alterations | — | — | — |
| Weather alterations | — | — | — |

SOURCE: Franklin Associates, *Life-Cycle Assessment of Ethylene Glycol and Propylene Glycol-Based Antifreeze,* Table 1.

mental emissions by classification for human health (not reproduced here) are also estimated and include the following classes: allergenicity, behavioral effects, cardiovascular system effects, central nervous system effects, human carcinogens, irritants/corrosives, blood diseases, odors, renal effects, reproductive effects, and respiratory system effects.

The energy requirement analysis for the two processes reveals that the ethylene glycol process requires as much as 67 percent less energy than the propylene glycol process. Most of this difference is attributed to the manufacture of ethylene oxide versus propylene oxide and the manufacture of the raw materials required for each process (1-3).

The report concludes with a detailed peer review, which consists of comments, observations, and criticism offered by four experts. Each comment is in turn addressed by Franklin Associates. Fifty-four comments, in all, were made by a four-member panel of experts. A sample of some of the comments and the associated replies from Franklin Associates (in italics) are given in the accompanying box.

---

### Comments on Table G-1 From the Peer Review and Associated Replies

6. Page 1-7, para 5. "Improper disposal" methods should be defined or listed. It would help the reader to briefly explain current EPA requirements.

*Improper disposal is now defined in Chapter 1 of the report as it is in the more detailed discussion in Chapter 3. Improper disposal is considered to be antifreeze that is dumped to a storm sewer or to the ground or antifreeze that is lost to the environment due to leaks. This antifreeze is not treated before it enters the environment.*

31. Page B-7. Data should be presented per 1,000 lb ethane/propane. For both natural gas and crude oil, the reader cannot translate from crude oil and natural gas to ethylene feedstocks.

*The processing of natural gas, as described in the discussion, produces ethane/propane feedstocks for olefins. The text and the title for Table B-4 have now been changed to clarify this.*

---

## Note

1. *Life-Cycle Assessment of Ethylene Glycol and Propylene Glycol Based Antifreeze. Final Report and Peer Review* (Prairie Village, Kan.: Franklin Associates, Ltd., August 1994).

# H

# Waste Material by Industry and Processes

The following table (H-1) includes a list of processes and their associated waste materials and composition for several industries: automotive-related, commercial printing, paint manufacturing, pesticide formulation, industrial and commercial laundries, pharmaceutical manufacturing, photo processing, hospitals, fabricated metal products, electroplating and other surface treatment processes, and printed circuit board manufacturing. The table is intended to help organizations not familiar with waste prevention measures to identify potential sources of waste material generation.

**Table H-1.** Waste material by industry and process.

| Type of Industry | Process | Waste Material | Composition |
|---|---|---|---|
| Automotive-related | • Auto maintenance | Motor oil | Oil and grease and heavy metal |
| | | Transmission fluid | Oil and grease and heavy metal |
| | | Engine coolant | Ethylene glycol, lead, copper, zinc |
| | | Batteries | Sulfuric acid and heavy metals |
| | | Brake fluid | Chlorinated compounds, metals |

222

| Type of Industry | Process | Waste Material | Composition |
|---|---|---|---|
| | • Shop cleanup | Outdated supplies | Solvents, caustic cleaners, automotive fluids |
| | | Acid floor cleaners | Acid, heavy metals |
| | | Alkaline floor cleaners | Caustics, oil and grease, heavy metals |
| | | Clarifier sludge | Oil and grease, heavy metals |
| | • Parts cleaning | Solvents | Petroleum distillates, mineral spirits, naphtha, chlorinated compounds, oil and grease, heavy metals |
| | | Aqueous cleaners | Acid and alkali, oil and grease, heavy metals, blended heavy oils, heavy metals |
| | • Auto refinishing | Paint waste | Petroleum distillates, heavy metals |
| Commercial printing | • Image processing | | Photographic chemicals, silver |
| | • Platemaking | | Acids, alkalis, solvents, plate coatings (dyes, photopolymers, binders, resins, pigments, |

*(continues)*

**Table H-1.** (*continued*)

| Type of Industry | Process | Waste Material | Composition |
|---|---|---|---|
| Commercial printing (*continued*) | | | organic acids), developers (isopropanol, gum arabic, lacquers, caustics) |
| | • Printing | | Spent fountain solutions (may contain chromium) |
| Paint manufacturing | • Equipment cleaning (water or caustic solutions) | Waste rinsewater | Low pH, solvent residue, heavy metals (lead, chromium) |
| | • Equipment cleaning using solvent | Waste solvent | Solvents (methanol, methyl ethyl ketone, toluene, lacquer thinner, mineral spirits, isobutyl isobutyrate) |
| | • Accidental discharge | Spills | Paint (lead, chromium), solvents |
| | • Color-matching production, poor process control | Off-specifications products | Wastewater contaminated with paint pigments, solvents, caustic solutions |
| | • Equipment cleaning, sludge removed from cleaning solution, | Paint sludge | If metal mesh filters are used, contaminated wastewater will be created by cleaning and reuse. |

| Type of Industry | Process | Waste Material | Composition |
|---|---|---|---|
| | • Undispersed pigment | Filter cartridges | |
| Pesticide formulation | • Equipment cleaning, area wash-down, hot water bath for leak checking | Waste rinsewater | Pesticide- and solvent-contaminated wastewater |
| | • Washing of protective clothing | Laundry wastewater | Pesticide-contaminated wastewater |
| | • Unloading of dry pesticides into blending tank | Scrubber water from air pollution equipment | Pesticide-contaminated wastewater and solvents |
| | • Pesticide spillage and fallout of pesticide dust in open process areas | Storm-water runoff | Pesticide-contaminated wastewater |
| | • Equipment cleaning | Waste solvent | Pesticide-contaminated wastewater |
| | • Accidental discharge | Spills | Waste pesticide formulations, waste solvents (xylene, toluene, chloroform, tetrachloride, benzene, ethyl alcohol, methyl alcohol, isopropyl |

*(continues)*

**Table H-1.** (continued)

| Type of Industry | Process | Waste Material | Composition |
|---|---|---|---|
| Pesticide formulation (continued) | | | alcohol, tetrachloroethylene, amyl acetate, MEK) |
| | • Formulation and testing | Off-specification products and laboratory analysis wastes | Waste pesticide formulations |
| Pharmaceutical manufacturing | • Equipment cleaning, extraction residues | Waste rinsewater | Contaminated water |
| | • Dust or hazardous waste generating processes | Scrubber water from air pollution equipment | Contaminated water |
| | • Solvent extraction processes | Spent aqueous solution | Contaminated water |
| | • Fermentation processes | Spent fermentation broth | Oxygen-demand suspended solids |
| | • Organic synthesis | Process liquors | Solvents, suspended solids, high/low pH |
| | • Solvent extraction or wash practices | Spent solvent | Solvents, oxygen demands |
| | • Accidental discharge from manufacturing and | Spills | Miscellaneous chemicals of environmental concern |

| Type of Industry | Process | Waste Material | Composition |
|---|---|---|---|
| | laboratory operations | | |
| | • Manufacturing operations | Off-specification or outdated products | Miscellaneous products and nonhalogenated solvents |
| | • Research and development operations | Used chemical reagents | |
| Photo processing | | Solutions: prehardeners, hardeners, developers, stop baths, ferricyanide bleaches, clearing baths, fixing baths, neutralizers, stabilizers, soundtrack fixer, or redeveloper, monobaths | Organic chemicals, chromium compounds, ferricyanide, phosphates, ammonium compounds |
| Fabricated metal products | Metal parts cleaning and stripping subprocesses: | | |
| | • Equipment cleaning using water and/or caustic solutions | Waste rinsewater | Water contaminated with solvent residue, additives, heavy metals |

*(continues)*

**Table H-1.** (*continued*)

| Type of Industry | Process | Waste Material | Composition |
|---|---|---|---|
| Fabricated metal products (*continued*) | | | from paint removal (chromium, lead) |
| | • Removal of rust, scale, polishing of metal | Abrasives | Grease-contaminated water |
| | • Descaling, removal of organic coatings | Spent alkaline solutions or spent acid solutions | Water contaminated with alkaline salts, additives, organic material such as ammonium hydroxide, potassium hydroxide, and sodium hydroxide, dissolved metal, additives such as hydrobromic acid, hydrochloric acid, hydrofluoric acid, nitric acid, phosphoric and sulfuric acids, perchloric and acetic acids. |
| | • Cleaning of oily surfaces | Waste solvent | Halogenated and non-halogenated solvents, oil- |

| Type of Industry | Process | Waste Material | Composition |
|---|---|---|---|
| | | | based contaminants such as 1,1,1-1 trichloroethane, carbon tetrachloride, trichlorofluroethane, toluene, methyl ethyl ketone, benzene, o and p-dichlorobenzene, acetone, xylene, kerosene, butyl alcohol |
| Electroplating and other surface treatment processes | Electroplating bath composition<br>• Brass and bronze<br>• Cadmium cyanide<br>• Cadmium fluroborate<br>• Copper cyanide<br>• Copper fluoroborate<br>• Acid copper sulfate<br>• Fluoride-modified copper cyanide<br>• Chromium | Spent bath solutions | Sample of chemicals: copper cyanide, zinc cyanide, sodium cyanide, carbonate cyanide, ammonia, Rochelle salt cadmium cyanide, cadmium oxide, sodium hydroxyde, copper fluoroborate, boric acid, potassium cyanide, sulfuric acid, fluoride |

*(continues)*

**Table H-1.** (continued)

| Type of Industry | Process | Waste Material | Composition |
|---|---|---|---|
| Electroplating and other surface treatment processes (continued) | • Chromium with fluoride catalyst Other metal-plating and treatment wastes | | |
| | • Case hardening | Quench oils and quench oil tank cleanup wastes | Water contaminated with oils, metal fines, combustion products |
| | • Vent scrubbing | Vent scrubber wastes | Sodium or potassium cyanide and cyanate |
| | • Demineral-ization of process water | Ion exchange reagents | Brine, hydrochloric acid, sodium hydroxide |
| | • Plating and chemical conversion | Filter sludges | Silica, silicides, carbides, ash |
| | • Wastewater treatment | Sludge | Metal hydroxides, sulfides, carbonates |
| | • Accidental discharge | Spills and leaks | Water contaminated with process/rinse solution |
| Printed circuit board manufacturing | • Cleaning/ surface preparation | Airborne particulate, acid fumes, organic vapors, spent acid and alkaline solutions, spent | Board materials, sanding materials, metals, fluoride, acids, halogenated solvents, alkali |

| Type of Industry | Process | Waste Material | Composition |
|---|---|---|---|
| | | halogenated solvents, waste risewater | |
| | • Catalyst application/ electrolysis plating | Spent copper bath, spent catalyst solution, spent acid solution, waste rinsewater | Acids, stannic oxide, palladium, complex metals, alkali |
| | • Pattern printing/ masking | Spent developing solution, spent removal solution, spent acid solution, waste rinsewater | Vinyl polymers, chlorinated hydrocarbons, organic solvents, alkali |
| | • Etching | Spent etchent, waste rinsewater | Ammonia, chromium, copper, iron, acids |

# Glossary of Key Terms

*biochemical oxygen demand (BOD)*   The use of (or demand for) oxygen dissolved in water during the decomposition or metabolism of biodegradable organic compounds by microbes. As the amount of waste materials added to water increases, the requirement for dissolved oxygen needed to convert the organic material to the mineral state increases.

*chemical oxygen demand (COD)*   A measure of the amount of organic substances in water or wastewater.

*closed-loop recycling*   A recycling system in which a particular mass of material is remanufactured into the same product (e.g., glass bottle into glass bottle, plastic into plastic, paper into paper).

*coproduct*   A marketable by-product from a process. This includes materials that may traditionally be defined as wastes, such as industrial scrap that is subsequently used as a raw material in a different manufacturing process.

*hydrocarbon*   A substance that contains a preponderance of hydrogen and carbon atoms, usually of biological origin.

*inorganic*   Not of biological origin; generally a substance without significant carbon content.

*industrial waste exchanges*   Waste exchanges were established to facilitate recycling and reuse of industrial and commercial waste. The earliest known waste exchange (the National Industrial Materials Recovery Association) was established in England in 1942. In 1972 the concept of promoting transfers of industrial wastes was reborn in Europe with the formation of two exchanges: the Federation of Belgian Chemical Industries and the Association of Netherlands Chemical Industries. Most European countries had waste exchanges by 1978. The first North American waste exchanges were established in 1973 in California (Zero Waste Management Systems) and Ontario, Canada (ORTECH). Today, ten exchanges operate in

Canada and approximately forty in the United States. In 1991 the waste exchange program was computerized with the National Materials Exchange Network (NMEN). For further information, see "Solid Waste and Emergency Response," EPA-530-K-94-003, September 1994.

*Material Safety Data Sheet (MSDS)* A reference form required by OSHA listing certain types of hazardous chemicals found in the workplace and describing precautionary measures.

*Occupational Safety and Health Administration (OSHA)* A U.S. agency responsible for health and safety conditions in the workplace.

*open-loop recycling* A recycling system in which a product made from one type of material is recycled into a different type of product. The product receiving recycled material may or may not be recycled.

*process emission* Waste materials generated or produced from the raw materials, reactions, processes, or related equipment inherent to the process.

*REPA* Resource and Environmental Profile Analysis; also commonly called cradle-to-grave analysis or life-cycle analysis.

*risk assessment* An evaluation of potential consequences to humans, wildlife, or the environment caused by a process, product, or activity and including both the likelihood and the effects of the event.

*risk* A complex evaluation of both the amount of potential damage and the probability of the damage actually occurring.

*sustainability* The following definition, provided by Paul Hawken, is helpful: "Sustainability means that your service or product does not compete in the marketplace in terms of its superior image, power, speed, packaging, etc. Instead, your business must deliver clothing, objects, food, or services to the customer in a way that reduces consumption, energy use, distribution costs, economic concentration, soil erosion, atmospheric pollution, and other forms of environmental damage." *The Ecology of Commerce* (New York, HarperBusiness, 1993), p. 139.

*volatile organic compounds* Carbon-containing substances released by natural processes and human activities that readily produce fumes; their reaction with nitrogen oxides in the presence of sunlight produces photochemical smog; sometimes called reactive organic compounds (ROC).

# Index

[Numbers in *italics* refer to illustrations. Numbers followed by an n. refer to notes at the end of the chapter.]

[Numbers in *italics* refer to illustrations. Numbers followed by an n. refer to notes at the end of the chapter.]

[Numbers in *italics* refer to illustrations. Numbers followed by an n. refer to notes at the end of the chapter.]

[Numbers in *italics* refer to illustrations. Numbers followed by an n. refer to notes at the end of the chapter.]